Richard Thomas was a career diplomat. Early postings included Ghana, NATO HQ, India and Czechoslovakia, before he became ambassador to Iceland and to Bulgaria, and high commissioner in the Eastern Caribbean. His time in Bulgaria coincided with the collapse of communism. After retirement, he headed the international arm of a disability charity, and helped run a couple of arts festivals. He is married to Catherine, an Australian, and they have three children and numerous grandchildren. He was appointed CMG in 1990.

To Catherine.

Richard Thomas

LUCKY DIP

AUSTIN MACAULEY PUBLISHERS™

LONDON * CAMBRIDGE * NEW YORK * SHARJAH

A CIP catalogue record for this title is available from the British Library.

ISBN 9781528984911 (Paperback)
ISBN 9781528984928 (ePub e-book)

www.austinmacauley.com

First Published (2021)
Austin Macauley Publishers Ltd
25 Canada Square
Canary Wharf
London
E14 5LQ

Table of Contents

Foreword

The city where I live and have lived for nearly fifty years is one of the world's major diplomatic hubs. There are, at the latest count, 182 embassies or high commissions in Delhi. Richard and his wife Catherine became friends of mine and of my family when they were posted to the British High Commission in Delhi. That is how I have come to be writing the foreword for his memoir, *Lucky Dip*. From many friendships with diplomats I have come to marvel at the variety of the tasks they undertake. They have to be generalists and acquire the skills of specialists too in order to promote their countries' interests, and protect their countries' people. During his long career of just over 36 years Richard had to deal with problems as varied as the drugs war in the Eastern Caribbean, keeping the notoriously bibulous foreign secretary, George Brown out of the bars during a crucial meeting of the North Atlantic Council in Paris, and persuading the communist government of Bulgaria not to expel him when he was ambassador in Sofia. He became an expert on trade and on aid.

A British diplomat currently serving in the high commission in Delhi told me one of the most fruitful ways of promoting a country's interests was getting to know people who matter, and in particular young people who will matter in the future. Getting to know people requires self-confidence, and Richard was lucky in his education, which must have laid the foundation of his self-confidence. In *Lucky Dip* he makes a point of saying that, unlike many, he was happy at his schools. He attributes his skill in drafting and marshalling of arguments to the headmaster of Leighton Park. He also had the enriching experience of singing in a choir which was good enough to take over temporarily from the resident choir in Westminster Abbey. I am very envious of that having been told by the director of music at my school that I couldn't sing. In later life I have been told that I or anyone else can sing with a little training. After Oxford and national service, which he did his best to avoid, but then greatly enjoyed, Richard sailed into the Commonwealth Relations Office (CRO) near the top of the entrance exam. He transferred to the Foreign and Commonwealth Office when the CRO and FO were merged.

With this background Richard might have fallen into the trap many clever people with good establishment credentials fall into – excessive self-confidence, or to put it more bluntly, arrogance. That is a failing which does not help in getting to know people. It erects barriers between them. Richard worked under one such high commissioner while he was in Delhi. He himself had the modesty to realise that he was not up to the job when he was short-listed as assistant private secretary to the secretary of state. The conclusions of his research during a sabbatical year were published as a Chatham House book, an outcome which he attributed to the opportunities provided by his FCO research fellowship there.

When Richard was ambassador in Sofia, the capital of Bulgaria, during the collapse of communism, his ability to get on with people who matter was witnessed by the recently retired head of the FCO. He was staying with Richard when the newly elected prime minister of Bulgaria came to consult him on the formation of the new cabinet. When Richard was ambassador in Iceland he found 'the judicious administration of alcohol' helped break down the Icelanders' reserve. Bottles of scotch were used as a currency during Richard's time in Prague in the days when Czechoslovakia was still behind the Iron Curtain. He didn't have much success in penetrating what he describes as 'the brutality and inhumanity' of that regime.

Diplomats are responsible for protecting their country's people. Richard saw looking after his staff as an important aspect of this. In Prague the regime used to harass his junior staff, particularly the young and single ones. Richard did what he could to stand up for them by holding the communist authorities to account. In Sofia he lived through the 'gradual and peaceful revolution' which accompanied the end of the Cold War and the lifting of the Iron Curtain. In neighbouring Romania however the revolution was anything but peaceful. The British ambassador's wife was holed up in the cellar of the residence in Bucharest while upstairs a sniper had taken up a position which enabled him to pick off his opponents. Richard had to receive the British and Canadian mission staff and families who were evacuated to Bulgaria, and arrange for them to be sent home.

Richard became a specialist in trade, gaining experience in the FCO's economic and trade departments and at Chatham House. While high commissioner to seven Commonwealth island states in the East Caribbean, all at the same time, he worked to prevent their banana exports from being swamped by the produce of the vast Latin American plantations. He spent his years in India steering the UK's aid programme through the complexities of the Indian government bureaucracy, and had the satisfaction of initiating the first aid agreement between Britain and the remote Himalayan kingdom of Bhutan.

Richard's memoir is a frank and fascinating record of a diplomatic career stretching from the days of Harold MacMillan's Wind of Change to the last days of the Iron Curtain and the beginning of the disappointments which followed that. The distinguished British diplomat Sir Ivor Roberts, giving advice to young people considering a diplomatic career said, "The core thing is are you prepared to get stuck in and really understand a country, what motivates the people of that country." Richard certainly got stuck in. In Bulgaria he seems to have fallen in love with the country but he did not commit the cardinal diplomatic sin of going native.

A more ambitious diplomat would have been disappointed that he never headed one of the most important missions. Richard 'never had the faintest idea how to network', and, as in any other bureaucracy, networking is essential if you want to climb to the very top in the Foreign Office. But he was satisfied with a remarkably varied and interesting career – communist Czechoslovakia, Iceland in the Arctic Ocean, the warm sunny islands of the Eastern Caribbean, Bulgaria in the eastern corner of Europe, India the world's largest democracy, and African postings in the days of the Commonwealth Relations Office.

Richard's diplomatic life was shared by his wife Catherine, who had to endure the frustration of guests who treated their homes as hotels, and her as the manageress, unpaid of course, but one who nevertheless kick-started a new, more humane approach to the care of severely disabled and unwanted children in Bulgaria. Richard's memoir ends with Catherine and him sharing a well-earned, fulfilling, retirement in a home where they choose their own guests.

Mark Tully

Sir Mark Tully was BBC Chief of Delhi Bureau and South Asia Correspondent 1972-94, and has presented BBC Radio 4's *Something Understood* since 1995.

Chapter 1
Prologue

One day in the summer of 1961 in the Scottish Highlands, on leave from the Army and staying in a rented cottage with my parents, I received a small brown envelope which contained news that I had gained entrance to the civil service by means of the Open Competition. I had been allocated to the department of my choice, the Commonwealth Relations Office. I had chosen the CRO because I had a friend in it, who when I had last seen him was living comfortably, with free housing, reasonable pay and not too much to do, in Dublin.

I told my parents the good news and in answer to their enquiries explained that the CRO, as its full name implied, looked after Commonwealth relations.

"Yes dear, but what does that mean?" asked my mother, herself the daughter of a civil servant and given to inconvenient bouts of intellectual rigour. I hadn't a clue, but so as not to let the side down I said that perhaps it meant that I would be showing visitors from the Commonwealth round London.

"That sounds very interesting, dear," replied my mother, in a tone that suggested less than total conviction. My father, who earned a precarious living on the fringes of the theatre and who was appalled at the prospect of having a son in anything as boring as the civil service, merely shrugged. It was a beautiful day and I was relieved to think that I would not have to look for a job when my national service ended that November. We carried on with our holiday.

The reality, when it materialised one dreary late autumn day, was not much less off-beam than my untutored expectations. Because of my national service, I had missed the induction course and was thrown straight into the CRO's west and general Africa department. There my duties were to fetch, twice a day, the telegrams on the current Congo crisis from the Foreign Office next door, sort them into date and time order and give them to my immediate superior, a retired colonial deputy governor. What he did with them I never discovered.

The room in which I was thus employed was an attic, housing half a dozen bureaucrats. My roommates seemed busy enough, scratching away at manuscript drafts and occasionally dictating into astonishing machines that resembled tea trolleys, recording on discs which were sent to Blackpool for transcription. (The results came back two or three weeks later after one had forgotten what they were about and in a form that did not encourage recall.) I did not have enough to do, but my colleagues advised me not to point this out. Instead, they directed me to a secret makeshift bed, hidden behind a row of steel presses at the end of the room, for the use of anyone in need of a little rest.

After a few months of this curious existence, so far from my expectations and, frankly, so boring, I told the head of Estabs that I was inclined to seek alternative employment if things did not look up. Without further ado, I was made private secretary to the CRO's parliamentary undersecretary, who fortunately had a forgiving nature, and from then on things did indeed look up. Not least of the improvements was the successful hostile takeover bid, three or four years later, mounted by the FO on the CRO. I had put the FO second on my preference list because I believed it to be staffed by toffs with triple-barrelled names who had been to Eton and thus a less suitable milieu for a keen young radical like me, whose sole previous contact with it had been as a Suez demonstrator outside in the street in 1956. But my forays into its Congo section had now disabused me of this view.

This extract from my valedictory despatch, mildly edited, explains how I became a career diplomat more or less by happenstance. In a tradition that has since been discontinued, ambassadors and high commissioners could at their career's end finally let their hair down and write more or less what they felt like in a farewell despatch, unfettered by considerations of policy or political correctness. I used mine to argue against the current structure, from which I had luckily though unfairly benefitted, whereby those who had managed at the outset to get into the 'A Stream', however ignorant (like me), were more or less guaranteed to rise smoothly up the promotion ladder, whereas those in the 'B Stream', however brilliant, were held back and rarely got to the top. The A Stream was composed largely of people like me who were Oxbridge graduates and had been to a public (i.e. private) school. I accepted that this didn't seem quite right, but had prudently kept this opinion to myself until I had completed my service and had thus managed to extract the maximum benefit from any injustice while it lasted.

I went to Oxford straight from school. There, most of my fellow students had already done their national service and had had longer not only to grow up a bit but also to develop some ideas about what they might want to do after graduation. I really had very few ideas of this sort. One day I wanted to 'go into management' (whatever that might mean), the next I reckoned that if I just managed to hang around I would in due course somehow morph into an academic. My degree, nominally in English but actually a mish-mash of Old and Middle English, Old Norse and Mediaeval Welsh, so far from any reasonable concept of practicality or vocational use, encouraged this line of thought. And then on other days, brought up short by the realisation that one didn't just 'become' a don without some indication of application, even if not of scholarship, an indication that I suspected would be unlikely to be apparent to my tutor, I wondered whether I should consider the civil service. This prospect sounded awfully dull and one which the functionary in the Careers Advisory Service with whom I shared it advised me to forget. Had I not realised, he asked, that I would first have to get a First, or at any rate an Upper Second and then pass another exam, one which he could see at a glance I would not have a snowball in hell's chance of passing?

Fortunately, national service intervened, though only just. By the time it caught up with me, in the November after I left Oxford, it was swallowing only 'deferees' and indeed it gave up the ghost altogether just weeks after I had begun my square-bashing. To my surprise, I rather enjoyed my time in the army, especially – perhaps not surprisingly – after I had managed to get commissioned. I had a platoon of ambulances, dotted around Northern Ireland, which I had to visit now and again to ensure that they were still in working order and properly equipped with a driver, bandages and so on. These trips entailed lunch in the officers' mess of whichever unit I had chosen to visit that day and so were a pleasant social break from the routine of garrison life at command headquarters in Lisburn. One of the messes was, in fact, a wardroom since one of the ambulances was stationed at an RN base at Londonderry. And Ulster was going through a quiet period, some years before all hell broke loose in 1969.

As well as keeping an eye on my ambulances, I somehow contrived to become the command HQ's 'adventure training officer' – quite a surprise since I had never been particularly adventurous – well, not in the tough, physical way that was expected of a military ATO. But I calculated – rightly as it turned out – that provided I could demonstrate at least a modicum of proficiency in mountain walking, kayaking etc., I should be in a position to mount adventure training 'exercises' (holidays with pay, well away from Lisburn) as often as I could drum up a few willing soldier volunteers to accompany me. And so it was that I enjoyed two or three very agreeable stints in Glenbrittle on Skye, where in due course the volunteers and I together became quite enthusiastic rock climbers. Skye's Cuillins are formidable mountains, not really suitable for tyro mountaineers, and it is a wonder that we managed not to injure or kill ourselves.

When I wasn't engaged in swanning around Northern Ireland 'inspecting' my ambulances and having lunch in other peoples' messes, or in holidaying in Glenbrittle, my thoughts began to turn again to the tiresome business of finding a job when my time in the army came to an end. Dublin was only a couple of hours away by train, where the friend mentioned earlier, recently married, had been posted to the embassy, and the two of them, Peter and Helen Heap, had me to stay for the odd weekend. They encouraged me to sit the civil service exam. "After all," said Peter, generously, "if I managed to pass it, there's no reason why you shouldn't." I wasn't quite sure. Peter had been one of the grownups at my Oxford college, Merton. He'd done his national service, as an officer in the glamorous Gloucesters and the British West African Frontier Force, not in something as mundane and decidedly unglamorous as the Royal Army Service Corps, which is where I had ended up. And he'd seemed so at ease with everything about Oxford, mixing with dons, Rhodes Scholars, girls (one of whom he'd married), you name it.

But still, I took Peter's advice and applied to sit the exam. The first bit was clearly designed as a means of sifting out the no-hopers and consisted of a series of written questions and essays. To my pleasant surprise, I got through and was selected to face the second stage, popularly but inaccurately known as the 'country house weekend'. One of the best things about this part of the exam was that the army was obliged to pay my fare to London, with subsistence, but disappointingly the country house proved to be merely a shabby government office in Regents Park, while the weekend turned out to be midweek, taken up with syndicate exercises, interviews and individual tests. My group's exercises centred on where London's third airport should be sited. We rejected the Thames Estuary (too many birds) and plumped for a disused airfield in Essex called Stansted. *Plus ça change* – and rather satisfactorily so in this case, given that the eventual real choice was indeed for Stansted.

Again, I passed and so was treated to another free trip to London, this time to be grilled by an alarming bunch of important looking people, seated at an enormous, highly polished round table in a far from shabby office at the top end of Whitehall. To my consternation, I was closely questioned about things I'd written in my essays, months earlier in Belfast, which I had quite forgotten. I somehow fluffed my way through – again successfully, as indicated by the contents of the small brown envelope that found its way to me later that summer in a village facing the Isle of Skye. Apparently, I had passed third in the Home Civil Service competition, third for the Foreign Service and top of the list of those who had, like me, applied for both, a surprising performance which I subsequently never came anywhere near repeating. I must have been carried forward on the crest of a wave of army-induced self-confidence.

Nevertheless, whatever my shortcomings as a working diplomat and the largely unremarkable progress of my career, I was present at or marginally involved in several events, some of them historic, others quirky or surprising and not all of them during my time as a diplomat. And of course, I encountered many interesting people. So I have jotted down accounts of those events and people and arranged them in roughly date order, linked together where necessary to form a narrative which, I hope, leaves out all the duller bits. I have also included the texts of a few articles and even an obituary where these seem to assist the general flow.

I am writing this in a house in Winchelsea, a *soi-disant* town with a village population of about four hundred in East Sussex, where my wife Catherine and I are happily frittering away the years of our retirement. The house backs on to the one where I tell people I was born eighty years ago, which suggests a degree of residential stasis that is, in fact, unwarranted, as I left Winchelsea when I was sixteen months old and did not return till seventy-two years later, and then only by chance of the local housing market. And for Catherine, there is even less of a connection, for she was born in Richmond New South Wales.

Strictly speaking, I was not born in Winchelsea, as my mother nipped up to NW3 to produce me there, in a nursing home, at her parents' expense, on 18 February 1938. But Winchelsea is where my parents were living. There they ran a small guesthouse called Petronilla's Plat, facing onto the splendid part-ruined church, sacked by the French in 1390 and never properly repaired. I moved in aged about a week and sixteen months later moved out again, as my father had been offered a job which entailed living within reach of the West Midlands. So we settled, rather tentatively, in Chipping Campden in the Gloucestershire Cotswolds, where my grandparents already had a foothold, conveniently near their Arts and Crafts architect friend Charles Wade, who was busy restoring Snowshill Manor, near Broadway, while filling it with all manner of eclectic bits and pieces, which is what you pay to go and see now that he is dead and Snowshill belongs to the National Trust. A few years later, when I was old enough to be able to join in, I spent the odd blissful afternoon there helping Charles and my grandfather sort out the model village and railway on the banks of the lily pond.

But back to 1939, when soon the country was at war with Germany and my father, now the National Association of Boys' Clubs drama adviser and simultaneously their West Midlands gofer, was beginning to do rather more in the way of checking on the clubs' preparedness for wartime conditions and rather less advising on drama. His patch stretched from Birmingham to Bristol and included the South Welsh Valleys, so the job brought with it a car and an enhanced petrol ration. In due course, the job was declared a 'reserved occupation', which meant that he would avoid conscription even if the age limit, which he exceeded by four or five years, were to be raised. Even so, like thousands of his unconscripted contemporaries, he joined the Home Guard and someone somewhere in a position of authority decreed that his position in the NABC required him to be an officer in the army Cadet Corps. So my father, that most unmilitary of men, became simultaneously a private in the Home Guard and a captain in the Cadet Corps. As he had only one uniform, my mother was kept busy sewing on and cutting off his captain's shoulder pips, or so she said, to enable him to turn up correctly accoutred for whatever activity he was attending. I sometimes wonder whether he ever got it wrong and paraded in the Campden Home Guard apparently masquerading as a captain and if so what the Campden version of Captain Mainwaring had to say about it.

By the time we had been in Campden a year and the 'phoney' war had become a very real one, my sister Elizabeth and I were caught up in events that are now half-forgotten. They are the subject of an excellent book, *Out of Harm's Way* by Jessica Mann, which helped me fill many of the gaps in my knowledge of those events and broaden my understanding of them, and thus how Elizabeth and I fitted into them.

Chapter 2
Canada

Early in the morning of 18 October 1944, just as it was getting light, Elizabeth, aged twelve, introduced me, now six, to my parents. They were on the dockside in Liverpool and it was quite difficult for her to be absolutely sure, in the semi-darkness, that she had picked the right couple. The war was still on, blackout regulations were strict and there were quite a number of grownups standing around to choose from. But in the next few seconds, as soon as they had spotted us and come rushing forward, all doubts were resolved.

I had only a vague idea of what my parents looked like, gleaned from studying a couple of photographs on Elizabeth's dressing table. True, I did just remember – and still do – being tucked up in a bed so high off the floor that I seemed to be at head level with the person who was doing the tucking and knowing that that person was my mother and realising that she was in considerable distress. But I could not remember her features. Which was hardly surprising, since that tucking-up had taken place over four years earlier when I was only two and a bit. We were in a cabin in a ship and I had been put on the top bunk as it had a board along its side forming a kind of protective fence and therefore seemed marginally safer than the bottom one, which was open to the floor eighteen inches below.

Exceptionally, our parents had been allowed on board to see us off, and when they put me to bed that evening in June 1940 they had no idea if they would ever see us again. They did not even know the identity of the ship we were on, as that was classified information. They did not learn till a few weeks later that it was, in fact, a Canadian Pacific liner called *Duchess of Richmond*, rechristened after the war as *Empress of Britain*. Now, in 1944, we had just disembarked from the New Zealand Line's *Rangitiki*, which had brought us safely back from New York, after a ten-day crossing. Our ship, packed with children returning from evacuation to Canada and the United States, had been at the centre of concentric rings of cargo ships and naval escorts, forming a huge convoy which had zig-zagged across the Atlantic as far south as the Azores before turning north. The U-Boat menace had largely abated, but it was still necessary to take evasive measures.

In the late summer of 1939 one and a half million children were evacuated to the country from the big cities in Operation Pied Piper. This colossal exercise had been accomplished over the course of just four days, three of which proved to be the last three days of peace, before the outbreak of war on 3 September. But then nothing much happened – just a 'phoney war' – and gradually many of those children drifted back home, only to be caught up and in far too many cases killed in the Blitz a year later, when many of the survivors were sent back to the country once again.

During those first months of the war some children were evacuated overseas, but only a few and all of them the privileged offspring of very well-heeled parents. But as the German army advanced and more and more countries were invaded, what had started as a trickle had by midsummer 1940 become a steady flow. By then Germany had overrun Denmark, Norway, Holland, Belgium and, with the collapse of the Siegfried Line, part of France, as well of course as Poland and Czechoslovakia. The British Expeditionary Force was in full retreat. Dunkirk started on 26 May and by 3 June 338,226 service personnel had been brought safely back to England – mainly BEF but also the French soldiers who would soon form the core of the Free French.

With the fall of France three weeks later Greece was now our only functioning European ally left. The German army was only 23 miles from the English coast. Invasion seemed inevitable. And before it got underway, the Germans would bomb our cities to bits and maybe use gas. No wonder more and more people were doing their best to send their children to places of safety overseas, while there was still time. No-one knows precisely how many went, as no official record of privately financed passages was made. 40,000 or so seems to be the generally accepted estimate.

Individuals and agencies of one sort and another in the United States, Canada, Australia, New Zealand and South Africa offered to take British children and passenger liners were crammed with them, in many cases accompanied by their mothers. This rush to safety was at first entirely an affair of the affluent middle and upper classes, as most people could not possibly afford the fares, let alone living expenses in distant lands. So, inevitably, it became a matter of deep social division, with the press and MPs voicing their resentment that only rich children were being evacuated.

This led to the establishment of an official body, the Children's Overseas Reception Board ('CORB') to provide a free, public scheme, even though Churchill was opposed to the whole idea of evacuation overseas, as foolhardy and unpatriotic. The scheme's proponents carried the day, arguing that the fewer children there were needing to be fed, educated and generally cared for, the better for a country that was likely to be fighting for its life. And certain children, particularly Jewish ones, would be at particular risk if the Germans invaded.

Within days of its establishment, CORB had received a quarter of a million applications, but only 2,562 children sailed under its auspices before the scheme was brought to an abrupt end after the *City of Benares* was torpedoed on 17 September. 77 children died, nearly all from CORB, together with 121 crew and 57 adult passengers, most of whom were the children's carers.

The *City of Benares* was not the first ship with children on board to be sunk. A Dutch liner, the *Volendam*, was torpedoed on 30 August, but all six hundred passengers, who included 321 CORB children, were rescued. However, even earlier, on 2 July another liner, the *Arandora Star*, had been sunk with enormous loss of life; 682 of the 1571 people on board died. They had been on their way to safety in Canada, but this incident aroused little of the horror and outrage that followed the *Benares* one, despite the far greater number of casualties, simply (and sadly) because they were 'merely' German and Italian internees – paradoxically almost all of them opposed to the fascist regimes in the countries of their birth.

Some of the Petronilla's Plat clientele became repeat guests and, in due course, my parents' personal friends. It was one of these, a Canadian journalist called Marjory Grant Cook – known always to us as plain 'Cook' – who arrived unheralded one summer morning in 1940 at my parents' cottage in Chipping Campden. They hadn't seen her since leaving Winchelsea a year earlier, so they were all the more astonished by what she had to say, which was that she had decided, as her 'war work', to take Elizabeth and Richard out of harm's way to Canada – provided of course that my parents agreed. She had provisionally booked a cabin for three in a ship leaving Liverpool in a fortnight's time and she would have to confirm the reservation within the next twenty-four hours, or lose it. And with that she pushed off, promising to be back the next morning when she hoped my parents would have had long enough to make up their minds whether or not to go along with her plan.

My mother and father sat up all night agonising over Cook's offer. By the time she returned they had decided to accept it. This was June 1940. The Germans had overrun much of Europe, the British army had been rescued from Dunkirk, France had just fallen and invasion seemed inevitable. My father's new job meant that he might at any time be moved to another part of the country, quite possibly a good deal less safe-seeming than the Cotswolds.

There followed ten days of frantic preparation. Passports had to be arranged, suitable clothing somehow procured (not easy in wartime, with everything rationed) and packed. My father got time off from his job and we went to stay for the last two or three days with my grandparents in Blackpool, where my grandfather's civil service department had been evacuated from London. Then all too soon a youngish couple (they were 32 and 33) entrusted their two children into the care of a Canadian friend who would take them to Quebec where, she said, she would look after them 'for the duration'. They had no idea if they would ever see them again. No wonder my mother was upset when she tucked me into bed in that upper bunk.

Our ship sailed on or about 30 June. Again, exact sailing dates were kept secret, to make it more difficult for the Germans to position their U-boats. On 2 or 3 July my parents, along with the rest of the population, learned that a passenger liner a couple of days out of Liverpool had been sunk, with great loss of life. For the next four or five days, they were convinced that this was our ship, as were all their friends and neighbours, who did their best to console them. Then, on 7 July, Elizabeth's eighth birthday, they heard that we had arrived safely in Quebec, on-board RMS *Duchess of Richmond* and that the ship that had been torpedoed was called the *Arandora Star*.

Cook soon tired of life as a foster mum and persuaded some friends of hers – a middle-aged married couple called Dobell – to try taking us on. This experiment was a failure and it was not long before we were back with Cook, who was no doubt beginning to regret her impulsive act of generosity, particularly as she had realised almost as soon as we got to Canada that she wanted to be back in London, where the action was. Fortunately for us and for her, more friends materialised – another married couple, but much younger than the Dobells. They wanted children, but had not been able to produce any of their own. They were called Mary and Lex Smith and they and Mary's mother Suzie Atkinson (my foster granny), proved perfect.

We were lucky. We lived with loving foster parents and also in my case a loving foster granny, who treated us as their own family, in adjoining comfortable suburban houses on the edge of Quebec. The Smiths were part of the English-speaking minority – a kind of Quebecois plantocracy – and were comparatively well off. They had masses of friends and relations, including many children of our own age. Each summer the whole tribe would decamp for a month or more to a resort called Tadoussac, one or two hundred miles down the St Lawrence River, an all-day journey by river steamer. Mary and Lex had a house there, where we spent the whole school summer holiday, with friends and cousins dotted about the village, many of them in an imposing and attractive establishment called Dufferin House, which had been built by Lord Dufferin as his summer residence when he was governor-general of Canada in the nineteenth century, but later owned by successive generations of Smiths and Prices, the *haut monde* of anglophone Quebec. There were picnics and bathing and fishing and outings in no-relation 'Uncle' Arthur's yacht. And, in the winter, back in Quebec, there was snow, with plenty of winter fun. There most of our neighbours, and therefore my playmates in the street, were French-speaking, so I became more or less bilingual, an advantage that unfortunately, I lost after my return to England.

We were able to keep in – tenuous – touch with our parents, by letter. Sea mail was available and cheap, though desperately slow. A letter could take weeks, or even months, to reach its destination and much mail was lost at sea when ships were sunk by enemy action. Airmail had been in its infancy before the war and had been more or less suspended at the outbreak. But then, in 1943, *airgraphs* were introduced. These were expensive but generally reliable. You wrote on a quarto sized airletter form which you posted in the normal way. This was then subjected to censorship, with chunks invariably blacked out, after which it was reduced photographically, to five inches by four unfolded, to save space and weight and sent by air. My parents kept some of these tiny airletters from us for the rest of their lives.

Many children, especially those in Canada and the USA, were able to broadcast to their parents by radio and sometimes even to hold two-way conversations. In our case, these broadcast sessions were arranged in theory once a month, but in practice, they were far less frequent. The broadcasts were recorded and parents were later sent a 78 containing most of what had been said. My parents played theirs so often that they wore them out. I can, however, remember hearing one of them after the war, through all the scratches and hisses. It took the form of an interview, with my sister Elizabeth asking me what I had been up to. I told her what I had had for lunch – roast chicken and blueberry pie – and suddenly I sneezed, whereupon Suzie, my foster granny, interrupted to assure everyone that I didn't have a cold. I concluded my contribution by announcing suddenly and apropos of nothing in particular, that my wife didn't love me anymore. Again Suzie felt obliged to intervene, to assure my parents that I had not been married off (I was four or five) and that the wife was my little friend Pennie, one of Mary and Lex's nieces.

Pennie and I must have made up on our tiff as, in a neat role reversal a few years later, she used to stay with us during the holidays from her English boarding school whenever she could not join her diplomat parents, who were then in Cuba. And, more than seventy years on, we are still in touch, as are many other former evacuees and their hosts. Elizabeth and I have both revisited Canada and members of 'our family' – more than once, and they have been to see us in England.

It was only natural, once the invasion scare was over, that parents wanted their children home again. But children in wartime were not very far up the priority list as far as space on ships was concerned; in fact, they were just about at rock bottom. Ships were needed to carry food, planes, vehicles, arms, ammunition and, as D-Day approached, troops. But the Forties were still very much an age of rank and deference and even though there was a war on, many of the children of 'top people', including for instance the Mountbattens, were brought home long before its end, some as early as 1942, often as passengers in warships. Another favoured route was by neutral owned ship to Lisbon in neutral Portugal and then on by RAF Sunderland flying boat, overnight and low, below effective radar cover.

My parents were not in any position to pull strings, though they tried hard enough. So did a certain Dr Hensman, a London GP whose two children, Nigel and Celia, were on the other side of the Atlantic, like us. His appeals to various authorities to get them back fell on deaf ears, as did those of my parents. One day, however, he happened to mention his predicament to a friend who was 'in shipping', which in this person's case meant that his family owned a small fleet of tramp steamers. He assured Dr Hensman that these ships had the usual priorities, with no space for returning evacuee children, but then asked him why he didn't buy a ship of his own. The good doctor just laughed. How on earth could he buy a ship, organise a crew and so on? He was a GP, not a shipping magnate. Whereupon the friend sold him one of his, complete with crew, fuel, cargo commission, what-have-you, for five shillings, provided that he could buy it back later, again for five shillings or whatever the insurance would cough up if it were sunk. Dr Hensman signed on Celia, aged six, as a stewardess, with Nigel, eight, as the third mate. This ruse was possible as owners were permitted to sign on family members irrespective of age or qualifications. Nigel got to steer the ship, but forty years later Celia told me that she did not remember enjoying any special privileges!

Our return arrangements were more prosaic. At some stage, during the summer of 1944, Mary and Lex told us that we would be going home in the autumn. Neither of us was particularly keen to do so; Elizabeth, in fact, was adamantly opposed. We were happy in Quebec and we thought of ourselves as members of the Smith family, now reinforced by a baby 'sister', Susan – our foster sister, with whom we remained in touch till her death in 2015. My parents tried bribery, which was reasonably persuasive in my case, by assuring me that I would be the proud owner of a gasoline-powered model boat once I'd got back to England. I cannot recall what they offered Elizabeth, but whatever it was, it had no effect on her attitude. The sad goodbyes were said, at school and in the extended family, and off we went by train to Montreal where, as a final treat, we stayed in a big, grand hotel and Elizabeth went out to her first grown-up dinner (she was twelve) with Mary and Lex, while Suzie looked after Susan and me. The next evening, we were more or less shovelled into the sleeper train to New York, into the care of Red Cross volunteer escorts, with Elizabeth kicking and screaming and me with a horrible lump in my throat, before waving a final goodbye to our wonderful foster family left standing on the platform. I would not see any of them again till, seventeen years later, I spent a few days with them, bizarrely enough, during the Cuban Missile Crisis.

And so, after a few days spent sitting in a dock in New York and then ten days at sea, Elizabeth and I were reunited that October morning with our parents. After the greetings and, in my case, introductions, we plodded up the hill to the Adelphi Hotel where we climbed over people still asleep in the lobby to find some breakfast – our first taste of wartime British food. And by that evening we were home in Chipping Campden, where I found that my parents had misled me.

The promised model boat was powered by steam, not gasoline. But I forgave them.

We soon lost our Canadian accents and my French followed not long after, as I was too young to retain it. But Elizabeth, six years older than me, kept most of hers.

Hardly surprisingly, this upheaval in our young lives had some negative psychological effects, more so for Elizabeth than for me. She never really got on with our parents, for she went on feeling Canadian and uprooted. Being so much younger, I was more adaptable and on the whole, I rubbed along pretty well with them, though perhaps not as well as I might have done had I not been sent away for more than four years. Our experience was mirrored many hundreds of times over in the other families who were similarly split and uprooted.

And what of Cook? She got back to London, where she worked for the rest of the war as an accredited Canadian journalist. She spent the rest of her life in England and remained a great family friend. She died in 1965.

Chapter 3
Back in Blighty

When Elizabeth had finished introducing me to my parents that October 1944 I do not remember whether we said How-do-you-do, or shook hands, or just trundled along. Perhaps we kissed each other, though that might have been a bit odd, for me at any rate, for these two grownups were strangers, with funny accents. And it was almost pitch dark.

We were after all on a Liverpool dockside and it was very early in the morning, with blackout restrictions still in force. The act of disembarkation from the *Rangitiki* had finally drawn a line under our time in Canada, which had lasted well over four years. I had probably asked my parents for news of the gasoline-powered boat I had been promised as an inducement and I expect my ever bossy and almost grown-up sister had hushed me, as it was very bad form to ask for presents.

No doubt my parents had proposed breakfast in the nearby Adelphi Hotel as an opportunity to sit down and talk to us and to see what we looked like, since there would be at least a few lights on indoors. So we had stumbled past all the dockside impedimenta and climbed the hill to the hotel's entrance. There were indeed some lights on inside, though not very many, and all the chairs and sofas in the lobby and lounges, as well as a good deal of the floor-space, were occupied by recumbent forms, some of them just beginning to wake up.

I do not remember breakfast, nor how or even whether we were reunited with our luggage, though I know that it somehow reached our cottage in Chipping Campden. I do, however, remember the train journey, which seemed to go on forever, passing through drab stations all called either Ladies or Gentlemen or both. (All other signs had been removed 'for the duration', in order to fool the enemy.)

At some stage, we arrived at wherever it was that my parents had left their car; perhaps it was Birmingham, or maybe somewhere much nearer home, like Evesham. The car was a severe disappointment – not a bit like our Hudson Terraplane back home in Quebec. It was small, scruffy and black, smelling of mould and petrol. And it was shamefully old-fashioned, in that after my father had ushered us all into it, he got out a starting handle and spent the next ten minutes fiddling about with the controls and things under the bonnet, between bouts of energetic cranking and the odd expletive. Once the engine had, at last, spluttered into life and my father had deemed it safe to remove the handle and stow it tidily away, I pointed out that the Terraplane started itself, like all other cars in Canada. I do not recall his reply.

The cottage was rather more up-market than the car and I approved of my bedroom. The model boat was awaiting me, but its steam-age propulsion system was yet another indication of how far behind Canada England was technologically, as well as a disappointment for someone who had been looking forward to handling gasoline power. And it was decidedly second-hand. But it grew on me and over the next seven or eight years, it was my Favourite Thing. It might still be, had my parents not decided, when I was about fourteen, to give it away while I was away at school.

Within a few days of our return 'home' (if I had known about inverted commas I would have used them in this context) my parents decided that some of my Canadian equipment would have to go. First on the list was my wonderful Business Suit, bought by my Canadian foster parents as a farewell present, rather before time, as small Canadian boys in the 1940s usually had to wait until they were eight before graduating to such sartorial splendour. But leaving Canada and the Canadian family for good was a special occasion, so I skipped a couple of years. This marvellous outfit, which I was enormously proud of, was a tweed knickerbocker suit in loud, bright tan, check. My parents binned it and thenceforward I was clothed, for the next seven years, in the standard mid-twentieth century uniform of middle-class English boys: grey scratchy shirt, grey pullover, grey jacket for best, grey shorts, grey knee socks, grey everything, even grey garters to keep the socks up. Proper English boys, I soon learned, wore their knees bare, in all weathers. Not until I became a teenager – an aeon away – would I have the slightest hope of owning a pair of long trousers. Sub-teens in 'longs' were a species of Little Lord Fauntleroy.

Not content with this outrage, my parents then decreed that my bike was unsuitable – my gorgeous, chunky, bright red Canadian bike. It was too big, they said (I could ride it perfectly well, having mastered the art of two-wheeling on it earlier in the year) and it was undoubtedly dangerous, as it had Back Pedal Brakes – an evident heresy for my ultra-English parents. So it went too and in due course, they bought me a fairy bike, a silly, sissy object with miniscule wheels. But it had proper English brakes.

In Canada, I had gone to the local primary school. But the Campden version of this option was deemed unsuitable and I was sent to a horrid little 'dame school' next door but one to our cottage. It smelled of cats and cabbage and I do not remember learning anything during the six months that I spent there.

My parents were amused by our Canadian accents and did not order us to dispose of them, though I think they faded pretty quickly. They made vague arrangements for us to keep up our French, by encouraging us to speak it for an hour or two every now and again. Within a year mine had disappeared completely – a pity, given that I had been virtually bilingual and, years later, could have done with still being so when I joined the diplomatic service. Elizabeth had reached some kind of linguistic age threshold and retained most of hers, lucky thing.

No doubt my parents acted with the best of intentions and probably never realised how much their little programme of re-anglicisation had hurt me at the time. It all washed off later. But Elizabeth was six years older than me. As far as she was concerned she was a Canadian girl, with Canadian friends and family. She had not enjoyed her return to Blighty and was never fully at ease with our parents, for the rest of their lives.

Elizabeth and I still keep up with 'our' kind Canadian family, or what's left of it. Our foster sister Susan died in 2015, a few years after at long last visiting England and staying, mainly, with Elizabeth and her family. She was determined to somehow to get to Brussels, to see where her Belgo-Canadian grandmother – my foster granny Suzie – had come from, and we were able to arrange this, by Eurostar on a day trip.

We spent barely a year in Campden, but that was when the war finally came to an end, in two instalments. The end of the war in Europe in May 1945 ('VE Day') was marked by cheerful celebrations. One of the high points was watching Elizabeth dancing around a maypole with other girls from the Grammar School. Everyone was in high spirits, including our local Italians, no longer prisoners of

28

war, though still billeted in what had been their prison camp nearby, who were now working as agricultural labourers pending repatriation.

Three months later we were on holiday at Pett, beside the sea a couple of miles from the old family stamping ground of Winchelsea. A small area of the beach had been cleared of mines and was deemed safe enough for swimming and making sandcastles, but all around were massive concrete 'dragons' teeth' and barbed wire entanglements, labelled 'KEEP OUT – MINES', with pictures of skulls and crossbones. The war was still going on in the Far East and we wondered whether 'Wardie' (my great uncle Wilfred Ward), interned in Changi Camp in Singapore, was still alive. Then suddenly that bit of the war was over too, but this time there were no maypoles and my parents seemed remarkably subdued. They explained that the war had been brought to an end by a couple of huge bombs – 'the Atom Bomb' – that had killed thousands and thousands of people, ordinary civilians, families, children, in a couple of Japanese cities, and they didn't feel in a particularly celebratory mood.

Wardie, we later learned, had survived, starved and half-blind. He eventually made a full recovery and resumed his duties in the Malayan civil service.

My father's services as West Midlands NABC gofer were no longer required. But his role as drama adviser had mushroomed and our time in Chipping Campden soon came to an end.

Chapter 4
Grandparents

I was rather in awe of my maternal grandmother. So was everyone else. (She was Granny; the other one, a ghastly woman, was Grandmother.) I preferred my grandfather, a small, friendly retired civil servant, who liked tinkering with cars and playing homely tunes on the piano, a Fabian – whatever that was – and a friend of HG Wells, evidently some fellow-Fabian. I was rather more interested in his friendship with Charles Wade, as that was a potential entrée to playing with trains on a grand scale at Snowshill Manor, near Broadway in the Cotswolds, now owned by the National Trust.

My grandparents lived in a substantial house in the Hampstead Garden Suburb, good progressive territory, and whenever we were homeless, which was quite often, we lived in it too. My father was not only in awe of Granny, but he also resented having to be bailed out by her whenever I needed new shoes or the school fees were due, or we had nowhere else to live for a bit. For Mr and Mrs Bourne (never Tom and Barbara) were comfortably off, which my father most certainly wasn't. And they believed in hard graft, whereas in their eyes my father was a bit of a feckless artsy-fartsy type, who had made off with their daughter just when she was embarking on a solid career as the PA to the secretary to the Women's League of Suffrage.

Granny was ahead of her time. Throughout her married life, she ran a successful business, with her old school friend Elsie Blumer. The term 'entrepreneur' had not come into general use, but that is what she was. Blumer and Bourne was a manufacturing and wholesale haberdashery business, with a factory in the East End and a shop in Old Cavendish Street where representatives of the rag trade came to commission and buy their various flounces and furbelows. In the run-up to Princess Elizabeth and Prince Philip's wedding and then to the Coronation, Norman Hartnell himself was a regular habitué, buying and commissioning bits and pieces for The Dresses. And the Chartwell accounts reveal that Winston Churchill bought something there on 24 October 1938 for 2s/8d. Whatever can it have been?

The shop was an Aladdin's Cave for a small boy, sent down to the basement to visit the 'girls' in the steam and heat of the dyeing department or allowed to work the press that spat out buttons somewhere up in the attic. But for Spedan Lewis, the paterfamilias of the John Lewis Partnership, it must have been a thorn in the side, for as long as Granny refused to sell her shop's freehold it was impossible satisfactorily to complete the rebuilding of John Lewis's blitzed Oxford Street headquarters. To this day there is a kind of cave in the Old Cavendish Street end of the store, manipulated by a clever architect to function as the goods entrance, where Granny's shop used once to stand and defy the Partnership's threats and blandishments, with the new building squashing it in, above and beside.

My parents were starting a school at the time and Spedan Lewis was one of their financial backers. They had to keep very quiet about their family connection with Blumer and Bourne. Only when Granny died did it become possible for John Lewis at long last to buy that last little bit of real estate, for so long occupied by her shop. And Elsie Blumer did very nicely out of the results of the transaction.

Granny was not just a businesswoman. She had a husband and two children and she believed in the benefits that healthy exercise and travel would bring to their upbringing and to that of a good many other Hampstead Garden Suburb children. To this end, during the 1920s, she organised, and I dare say largely financed, what would now be called adventure holidays. My parents' old photograph albums are full of pictures of treks by horse-drawn caravan across Dorset, Devon and finally Brittany. Goodness knows how many children and young people were involved; the photographs are crammed with them, tending to the horses, putting up tents, carrying buckets, or just hanging about – seemingly always watched over by a stately, long-skirted woman whom a generation later I regarded as alarming, but who in those far-off days must have seemed some sort of fairy godmother. The occasional fellow parent can be glimpsed among the children in some of the pictures and even – just once – my grandfather, dressed in a suit and looking out of place. His enormous Austin can be seen parked in the distance. Perhaps he'd nipped down from Whitehall for the day. And my father, looking about fifteen, must, in fact, have already been a student, because one of the photographs is of his sports car, an improbably named Bean, hood folded away and rear dickie seat open – an indication that he must have had at least two passengers. Perhaps he and whoever he had had with him were also only part-time caravanners, down from London for the odd day of roughing it.

Granny was a keen collector of antiques and these holidays always yielded booty, some of it massive. Long after she was dead, 'Granny's chest' dominated my parents' sitting room, an enormous piece of oaken linen fold furniture, with wrought iron hinges and locks, that would once have contained a fifteenth-century Breton bride's trousseau. It was nine feet long and weighed, almost literally, a ton. My parents eventually sold it, but we still have another of my grandmother's trophies, a seventeenth-century set of fire irons and curling tongs hanging from a delicately worked iron *fleur-de-lys* frame, also Breton. Were these things crammed into the caravans?

Granny was a clever girl, with a gift for languages, the daughter of a senior executive in Crosse and Blackwells, a manufacturer of tinned foods and suchlike. Her parents had new-fangled ideas, including education for women and, had her father not died when she was in her teens, she might well have become a pioneering woman university student. But suddenly the family was plunged into financial difficulty and Granny went to work in Liberty, where she learned the skills that she later put to such good use in Blumer and Bourne.

To help make ends meet my newly widowed great grandmother took in lodgers. One of them was an ambitious young Yorkshireman, Tom Bourne, forging a career in HM Customs and Excise. He and my grandmother seem to have taken a rapid fancy to each other and they were soon married, only eight months before the birth of my mother. No doubt the birth was described as premature; after all, this was 1908 and *having* to get married and other suchlike concepts were not quite respectable in Edwardian England.

On the face of it, Tom and Barbara were an unlikely couple – he an agnostic, nominally Anglican, civil servant, she a catholic businesswoman. But they were devoted to each other and each forged very different but equally successful careers, while at the same time raising a family and acting as strong pillars of the growing Hampstead Garden Suburb community.

I never met my paternal grandfather, even though I was nearly ten when he died. He was evidently something of a black sheep. On the rare occasions when he was mentioned he was always referred to as HKT, as though he was a kind of cypher, not worthy of a proper name.

HKT stood for Hugh Kerr Thomas. He was a mechanical engineer, more specifically an automotive engineer. And he was not just any old automotive engineer or car mechanic; he was the President of the Institute of Automotive Engineers, which in due course became the Institute of Mechanical Engineers, housed in a grand building on the corner of Birdcage Walk, across the road from the Treasury. I wish I had met him and that he had not, for reasons that were never made clear, been virtually dismissed from the family. For not only was he an engineer of some distinction, but he was also a man of sensitivity, with an interest in the arts, especially poetry and painting. I know this from the nature of the books, some of which I still have, that he gave his children, and the inscriptions that he wrote in them.

Gradually, over the years, I squeezed little bits of information about HKT from my father, but not until he himself was an old man, half a century after his father's death. Many of them were recounted fondly, so I doubt that they could really have disliked each other. The problem, evidently, seems to have been my grandmother's, and when eventually sides were taken, my father and his two brothers took hers.

According to my father, HKT invented automatic transmission – or rather, the team at Pierce Arrow which he headed during the first world war did. The invention was more or less incidental. What the PA team were developing was some means to reduce the risk of stalling, particularly for the Allies' new weapon, tanks. This was before the days of self-starters, and a tank that stalled was a sitting duck during the five minutes or so that it took the crew to get it going again. All four of them had to abandon their fighting stations as commander, driver and gunners and sit amidships at a four-handled crank, which no doubt took a fair amount of time and hard winding before the engine fired. HKT's team developed a mechanism from which grew both the classic fluid flywheel and the pre-selector gear system. My grandfather took the latter with him when, after the war, he headed one of London's main bus companies and their manufacturer, AEC. All AEC's buses had pre-selectors, as have the venerable 'Routemasters' still to be seen today.

Whatever the truth about HKT's role in the development of automatic transmission, he was certainly the author of a number of engineering treatises, including one on worm gearing, which seems to have been something of a standard text. It remained in print until quite recently, even though it was written before the first war.

HKT retained his connection with PA after the war, which meant that he became a trans-Atlantic commuter. Whenever possible he travelled on board the Cunard liner *Mauretania*, his favourite ship. He travelled First Class, as befitted his status in the various companies which he worked for. This meant white tie and tails for dinner. One evening, over post-prandial coffee and liqueurs, as he was listening to Lady Whatnot's seemingly interminable story about Whomever and Whatever, he became aware that his handkerchief had slipped out from its accustomed slot inside his jacket's left cuff. So, while the story progressed, he gradually stuffed the handkerchief back into the cuff. When the time came for Lady W to rise to her feet, HKT tried to stand up to bid her goodnight but found that his left hand was locked to the front of his trousers, which made getting up out of his chair almost impossible. What he had taken for his handkerchief was, in fact, his shirt-tail, which was protruding from his flies, which he had omitted to do up.

I do not know if HKT was prone to this sort of absence of mind. Somehow I doubt it. But the fact that he told this story against himself reveals an engagingly self-deprecatory side, which it is clear he showed to his family. They must have been on good terms.

As well as helping lay the foundations of what became London Transport, HKT was also involved with Bean sports cars, popular and successful for a few years in the Twenties but now almost forgotten. This was handy for my father, at the time an art student – not the usual impecunious garret-dwelling type, but one equipped with a sporty Bean. He was courting my mother and no doubt the car was an added attraction. I know she was much taken with its dickie seat, a modified form of the boot which provided an occasional back seat, fully exposed to the elements. This was the car that appeared in the photograph of one of Granny Bourne's gipsy caravan holidays.

I believe my grandfather had a roving eye. Perhaps he was driven to this by impatience with his wife's airy-fairy artiness. She had been stage-struck from an early age, but a theatrical career was socially unthinkable for a girl from a good family like hers, a cadet branch of the Shirley family of a midlands stately home, Staunton Harold, which made her some sort of cousin of the Earl Ferrers of the day. So she gave vent to her frustrations by striking attitudes, writing vapid poetry, some of which she succeeded in having published, drinking and smoking too much, and above all vicariously by ensuring that her three sons were all thrust in one way or another onto the stage, as child actors. All three were sent to RADA at an early age, and for good measure my father was also sent to the Central School of Arts and Drama and to the Slade. None of them ever set foot in an ordinary school. They were taught by a succession of private tutors, and as a result whole swathes of normal learning, including languages, the classics, maths and science, were almost totally neglected. This deficiency must have proved a hindrance when, in his mid-forties, my father founded a school. Fortunately, my mother had been conventionally educated, at the North London Collegiate School, and was usually able to help him hide the gaps in his learning.

My father was a bit of an afterthought, eight and ten years younger respectively than his two brothers. They were already more or less grown-up when they realised that he too was being subjected to the same indulgent but inadequate teaching arrangements as they had enjoyed at the hands of their mother. So, during one of HKT's visits home from America, they formed up to him and demanded that he insist on proper schooling for young Tony. No-one now knows whether he tried to reason with his wife. If he did, his arguments did not prevail. More likely he did not even try.

My father, like his two older brothers, learned an impressive amount of English history and was well versed in the English classics, but the gaps in his knowledge were even more impressive. I was alarmed to hear him one day, when he was in his fifties and teaching drama at a London school, holding forth on Shakespeare's amazing ability to express so much and so forcefully with a vocabulary of only two thousand words. It took me some hours of argument, with recourse to commentators whose works were not all readily to hand, to persuade him that he had got hold of the wrong end of the stick. Perhaps, I suggested, he was thinking of Racine or Corneille? But the mention of these foreigners, of whom he had scarcely heard, only increased his embarrassment still further.

And, of course, my grandmother, Shirley, in deference to her illustrious but distant ancestry (her real name was Mabel, which she detested), did her best to make her youngest and favourite son a child actor, without much success. He was already going on twelve when the war ended and opportunities began to increase, but most of them were in the cinema rather than on the stage and he did have small parts in two or three films, in one of them with Ellen Terry, something that must have filled Shirley's pride to bursting. This association, sedulously maintained over half a lifetime, was to prove handy when, in the 1960s, the National Trust appointed my mother as curator of the Smallhythe Ellen Terry Memorial and franchised my father to run a theatre club in the Barn Theatre in its garden.

Shirley was one of Ellen Terry's greatest admirers. Family legend held that the two ladies were personal friends, but I suspect that the feelings were mainly one way and that my grandmother was more of a groupie than a chum. She is not mentioned in anything that I have ever read by or about ET. But one thing is fairly certain. So strong was Shirley's admiration and perhaps determination to become a real friend, that she acquired a weekend cottage in Winchelsea near Rye in East Sussex at the turn of the century, only a couple of hundred yards from where Ellen was already similarly established. But no sooner had she achieved this than her heroine upped sticks and moved to Smallhythe, fifteen miles away.

The part-time move to Winchelsea did, however, prove enduring. My grandparents lived in Upper Cheyne Row in Chelsea and later in the newly established Hampstead Garden Suburb, but Shirley spent more and more time in Winchelsea, particularly during the war when she became alarmed by air raids in London. I do not know when she gave White Cottage up – possibly not till my parents, married two years and more or less jobless, moved to Winchelsea in 1932 and set up a tea shop which gradually expanded into a guest house, which they called Petronilla's Plat, after the daughter of friends who lived across the road. (A *plat* is local dialect for *plot* and Winchelsea is full of them.) According to my mother, Shirley came for a weekend in 1936 and stayed till we moved to Chipping Campden in 1939, taking up valuable letting space. My mother couldn't stand her.

By this time my grandparents' marriage had come completely unstuck, but they never divorced. When HKT died, in 1947, he was apparently living in reduced circumstances with a girlfriend in Liverpool. My grandmother lived in a room in Kensington, supported by her three sons. She used to come and stay now and again, to my alarm and distaste, as she was always critical of whatever I might be up to and never stopped smoking. She died in 1952, shortly before her eightieth birthday. I was, secretly, rather relieved. I expect my mother was too. But it was many years before I ever heard the faintest criticism from my father. His mother had been one of the most beautiful and talented women on earth, prevented only by convention from becoming one of its leading actresses and so on and so on. It was not till almost the end of his life that he finally confided to me that she had been a dipsomaniac and a pain in the butt.

Chapter 5
Bakers Cross

For four years just after World War II, Bakers Cross House was the centre of an astonishing social and educational experiment. It was the Arts Training Centre of the National Association of Boys' Clubs (NABC). There, teenage boys and club leaders from NABC clubs all over the country attended residential courses, to learn about, practise and enjoy drama, painting and music. Most of the courses ran for a week or ten days; some, which were mainly for adults, were weekend affairs. My father had resumed full-time duties as the NABC's drama adviser and had been deputed to head Bakers Cross with my mother. There was no longer any need to live near the West Midlands. They set the Centre up and ran it together.

Bakers Cross is the name of one end of Cranbrook, a small, picturesque town in the middle of Kent, a few miles from Sissinghurst, with its well-known garden and 'castle' (actually the ruins of an Elizabethan country house). Cranbrook is surrounded by typical Wealden countryside, full of orchards, small farms, woods and hop gardens. With its neat tile-hung and weather-boarded shops and houses and general air, even in the late 1940s, of peaceful prosperity, it must have seemed unreal to the club boys, most of whom came from grim, war-torn, industrial towns. To complete its image of fairy-tale serenity, Cranbrook's huge white weather-boarded mill was still powered from time to time by the wind.

The Centre's origins lay in a boys' club travelling theatre, an enterprise thought up by my parents in the early months of 1941. Twelve boys from clubs in South Wales put on a show of one-act plays and songs on a 2,000-mile tour, with performances in a different town almost every night for five weeks, a logistical and organisational nightmare at the best of times, let alone in mid-winter in wartime. Three of the boys were unemployed; the rest were a mix of schoolboys and pit and errand boys. They learned to act, paint and build scenery, to put up and take down sets almost nightly in nearly thirty different places the length and breadth of England and Wales and above all to live and work together as a team. For this was the main purpose of the enterprise: to broaden their horizons through exposure to the arts rather than just to football and ping-pong, hitherto the standard fare of boys' club activities, and to show as many people as possible what could be done. It was never my father's or the NABC's intention to turn these boys into professional actors, and all but two of them returned to 'normal life' after the tour, all the richer for their experience and in due course keen proponents of arts activities in boys' clubs. The exceptions were a young miner called Donald Houston and his brother Glyn. Donald went on to a successful career in films (The Blue Lagoon and most of the Doctor comedies) and on radio and on the stage (Under Milk Wood, for instance), while Glyn pursued a similar career, though with a greater emphasis on television.

By the time the first Travelling Theatre had run its course all thoughts of a second one had had to be put on hold. But the enthusiasm for art and drama in clubs had caught on and during the war my father was able to run three or four short residential training courses, culminating in 1944 in one in a theatre at Great Hucklow in Derbyshire, generously lent by the playwright and amateur theatre guru L du Garde Peach, during which my father evolved a means of teaching adults and boys simultaneously. Under this scheme, club leaders were able to learn something of the technique of play production while the boys provided the raw material. This was followed by a drama producers' course at Glyndebourne, also kindly lent by its founders and owners, John and Audrey Christie.

My parents remained in occasional touch with the Christies. One day, when I was about eleven, they took me to tea with them. I cannot remember if Mr Christie was there, but his wife, the opera singer Audrey Mildmay, was most hospitable and kept pressing me to more sandwiches and cake. Then, out of the blue, she suggested that I should sing. At that stage, a year or so before I changed course and became a keen choirboy, I was decidedly against singing, which I regarded as a sissy activity fit only for the music master's pets. I resisted Mrs Christie's blandishments; in fact, I refused even to try to sing, which was something I Did. Not. Do. The tea party came to a rapid conclusion and I was removed by my embarrassed parents. I believe they never saw the Christies again. I had ruined a beautiful friendship.

As a result of the success of these two courses the NABC, which had recently benefitted from a national appeal, bought Bakers Cross in 1945, to provide a permanent base for arts training. A couple more courses, on Great Hucklow and Glyndebourne lines, were held there the following year, followed by half a dozen in each of the ensuing four years, which in the event proved to be the extent of the Centre's permanence.

Bakers Cross proved ideal for my parents' purposes. It consisted of a largish house, with extensive outbuildings which had once been the malt-house, stores and stables of Winch's Brewery. The actual brewery had been pulled down and replaced during the war by the Cranbrook fire station. The former stores and stables, rebuilt as living accommodation by the wartime National Fire Service, were redundant and empty, as the fire service had returned to peacetime operations, with part-time and volunteer firemen. They were exactly what was needed for the boys' dormitories. One room in the old malt-house was in use as the town's scout hut, an arrangement that continued amicably throughout the NABC's tenure, but the rest of the building was empty and in next to no time the upper floor had been converted into a theatre.

The only direct way from the dormitory block and the theatre to the house lay through a semi-derelict room in the malt-house, the floor of which was showing signs of collapse into the void beneath, of uncertain depth. While the route from one door to the other seemed sound enough, it was only too clear that to stray from the path could be dangerous, as there was evidently a deep cellar below the half-rotten boards, the suspect end of which sagged a foot below the skirting. I rolled marbles down the slope and it seemed a long time before I heard a clink after they had disappeared over the edge. My parents rigged up a rope balustrade to deter the unwary and put up a notice underlining the need for caution. And that is how things remained for the next couple of years, some decades before people began to worry too much about Health and Safety.

The main house provided space for the music and art rooms, a common room, a dining room large enough for all the members of a training course to eat at one sitting, my father's office, the Thomas family's quarters, a dormitory, and accommodation for staff and tutors.

The house had about four acres of garden and woodland, including a kitchen garden and greenhouses where Mr Penfold and his assistant George grew most of the vegetables. A former tennis court was turned into a potato patch. Food was still rationed, even though the war was over, so vegetable production was important. There were also seven hens, nominally my sister's property, which also did their bit, assisted from time to time by some rather less productive ducks.

The hens were called Flocci, Nocci, Nauci, Ni, Hili, Pili and Fication, a slight misunderstanding of the composition of what Elizabeth had been told was the longest word in the English Dictionary. The ducks were just The Ducks.

Part of the garden sloped down to a pond and in due course was turned into an outdoor theatre, complete with its own waterfront for Viola and Prospero to land on in productions with local amateur actors of Twelfth Night and The Tempest. These were a foretaste of my father's annual Shakespeare productions some years later at Smallhythe, during his thirty-year tenure of the Barn Theatre and directorship of the Ellen Terry Theatre Club.

An enormous amount of work had to be done to get Bakers Cross ready. Builders did the basics, but all the decorating was done by volunteers, especially members of the Brenchley Boys' Club, led by Stanley Garner, who was the headmaster of the Brenchley primary school and club leader. Once the Centre was functioning Stanley became one of the volunteer drama tutors.

By August, all was ready for the grand opening, which was performed by Somerset de Chair, a well-known writer and politician at the time, who was chairman of the Kent Association of Boys' Clubs and squire of Chilham Castle. A selection of local arts grandees attended and in one of my parents' scrapbooks, there are photographs of Ellen Terry's daughter Edie Craig enjoying a cup of tea with a professional pageant master called Gwen Lally and Mr de Chair chatting to Vita Sackville-West – who later, as my parents' good and helpful neighbour, provided much useful gardening advice. I have clear memories of a somewhat intimidating person popping over now and again in her Austin Seven, always dressed in breeches, with secateurs stuck in the top of a boot and wisps of raffia dangling from various pockets.

My parents were appointed joint wardens. In practice, this meant that my father was in overall charge, in management and teaching terms. He taught most of the drama, but during the larger courses, he was assisted by one or two others, who were generally unpaid. They included the Cranbrook curate, Douglas Remington, who had worked as a professional actor before switching to the Church, Stanley Garner from Brenchley and my uncle, Charles Thomas, who was the head of drama in the Yorkshire West Riding education authority. The NABC's music adviser, Frank Daunton and his art colleague, who I believe was called George Bradney, looked after their respective disciplines. Philip Cole, the principal of the Hastings College of Art, provided a lot of voluntary help.

My mother, the other joint warden, ran the domestic arrangements. She was matron and did all the catering, and at times much of the cooking, with the help of two young women whom my parents had employed in their guest house in Winchelsea before the war, Rose Hill and Margaret Munn. This small team cooked and cleaned for a household of anything up to thirty people. The boys, many of whom came from disadvantaged backgrounds, enjoyed good and plentiful food, at a time of stringent food rationing. At the end of each course, my mother would pop her head through the serving hatch and say, "There is a little more." This became her by-line.

My mother knew a good deal about the history of costume and was a skilled seamstress. She must have made literally hundreds of costumes during a lifetime of amateur drama and drama in education.

With the opening out of the way, courses and then rehearsals for the second Travelling Theatre began in earnest. This followed much the same pattern as the first one in 1940, but with boys chosen from all over Britain, not just Wales. Two of them went on to professional careers on stage and screen: Yorkshireman Brian Roper (The Secret Garden, various Just William films and many more) and a young shipping clerk from Bristol, Bob (later Sir Robert) Stephens, of the RSC and the National Theatre.

There were two more Travelling Theatres, in 1948 and 1949 and twenty or thirty training courses, so some three or four hundred boys benefitted from the Bakers Cross experience. They had to pay to attend, but even though the fees were little more than tokens and came nowhere near meeting the Centre's running costs, some of the students could not afford them. They were helped to do so with discreet subsidies funded by generous individuals, including Donald Houston, who felt that he owed his acting success to his inclusion as a teenager in the 1940 Travelling Theatre.

At least two more participants in these later events went on to professional careers in the theatre. Exceptionally, one of them, Richard Pilbrow, was not a club boy. He was a boarder at Cranbrook School and got wind of what was going on down the road at Bakers Cross, so he asked if he could join in. He was particularly interested in stage lighting and went on to found Theatre Projects Consultancies, which became the world's leading theatre lighting consultants, which he ran well into the twenty-first century. The other was Alan Dobie, spotted by my uncle Charles in a West Riding production when he was 14. Alan enjoyed a long and distinguished career on stage and screen. He was Prince

Andrei in the original BBC serialisation of War and Peace, opposite Anthony Hopkins as Pierre and in the West End, he starred, among many other roles, in Look Back in Anger and in Waiting for Godot. He spoke wonderfully at my father's funeral in 2001.

Sadly, the Bakers Cross venture came to an abrupt end in the autumn of 1950, when the NABC suffered a funding crisis and chose Bakers Cross, rather than any of its other activities, as its budgetary saving. My parents were given very little notice and plans for another Travelling Theatre and more courses in the following year had to be abandoned. The news of the impending closure spawned outraged articles and letters in the press, including The Times and its Educational Supplement. But the NABC really did prefer football and ping-pong to the arts and the house was sold in October of that year. My parents tried to buy it, in order to turn it into a school – to be co-educational – which would continue some of the work that they had pioneered, but they were not given enough time to organise funding.

My father soldiered on for another year as the NABC's drama adviser and even ran one more course, at the NABC's training centre for club leaders in Monmouthshire, but then he resigned, to found the school that he and my mother and some of their friends, had envisaged. It was not in Kent and it was not at first co-educational. But Stanbridge Earls School flourished until 2014, near Romsey in Hampshire.

While it lasted, Bakers Cross was a good place to be a child. There was lots of room, with plenty of outbuildings and nooks and crannies, lawns, a walled garden, a wood, a stream and the pond, which soon became 'the Lake' and other more unusual amenities, including a couple of theatres, one indoor and one outdoor.

We had moved in during the first few weeks of 1946, as soon as the NABC had completed the purchase. The house was big, icy cold, very empty to begin with and shabby. The war had ended only a few months earlier and everything was in short supply, including coal. There was no central heating, but there was running hot water, provided that the boiler was alight, which it frequently wasn't. There were basins in the larger bedrooms, and two bathrooms. One of them was tiled from floor to ceiling in antique Delft tiles depicting Dutch sports and pastimes – a blue and white picture gallery that amounted to an invitation to linger in the bath, as they were endlessly fascinating. Next to that bathroom was a magnificent loo, with a mahogany panelled WC called – in curly polychromatic lettering – The Improved Health Pedestal.

I was a few weeks short of my eighth birthday and I was promptly enrolled at Coursehorn, which in those days was the preparatory school for Dulwich College. I had missed the beginning-of-term, as well of course as the beginning of the school year. So I floundered, out of my depth, trying to keep up with subjects that I knew nothing about. Luckily we soon acquired a lodger, in the person of the curate, Douglas Remington, and he kindly initiated me at home into the mysteries of Latin and other arcana. My parents were far too busy to help as they were setting up their arts training centre. And in any case, I doubt whether they knew much more Latin than I did.

At Coursehorn I was told that I was a Mohican. This had nothing to do with my hairstyle, which was unremarkable, and in any case punk fashions had yet to be invented. The school was divided into four Red Indian tribes and when on day one I was told which one I belonged to I was outraged. "I'm not American," I said. I had misheard the word, pronounced in those days with the stress on the first syllable and I had assumed that a tell-tale remnant of my Canadian accent had identified me as a Trans-Atlantic foreigner at a moment when I was determined to blend seamlessly into the background. Even though I had spent the war years as an evacuee in Canada, I had been home for more than a year and was sure that my accent had quite disappeared.

Elizabeth was six years older than me and therefore rated more or less like a grown-up. She went to Maidstone Girls' Grammar, commuting by bus, an hour each way. We saw each other for more than a few minutes only at weekends. As a mere girl, she didn't qualify in my parents' eyes for fee-paying education. Or that is how she saw it and still does. So for much of the time, I was left by my busy parents to my own devices.

I walked to school, a distance of about a mile, sometimes on my own and sometimes in the company of Williams, a boy who lived somewhere up the High Street. No doubt he had a Christian name, but this would have been a closely guarded secret, known only to a few privileged people such as his parents. In the same way, I was plain Thomas. And our gardener was addressed as Penfold, not Mr Penfold, certainly innocent of any other name. But his assistant, the garden boy, aged probably about 15, was George, with no known surname. Someone could do a PhD dissertation on the subtleties of nomenclature and titles, or lack of them, in a mid-twentieth century middle-class English household.

I doubt whether anyone worried in those days about children walking on their own to school. There was scarcely any traffic and what little there was went very slowly. The word 'paedophile' had yet to be coined (the earliest citation in the OED is 1951), perhaps because such people scarcely existed. But I knew about not accepting sweets or a lift from a stranger and I would have been in the scattered company of a steady straggle of schoolboys ambling down the dead-end road that led to Coursehorn, as many parents would not have had cars and petrol was rationed.

Williams and I gave ourselves plenty of time, as there were things that we had to examine en route, as well as the theoretical prospect of Mr Leakey's cane if we were late. He was the headmaster and he made us all aware of the cane's existence, *pour encourager les autres*. Fortunately, I never made its close acquaintance.

Our most interesting port of call was the sluice at the outlet of a pond just over the road from Bakers Cross. This was right by the verge and there were things in the water that glinted, like gold. They were half-buried in the mud at the bottom and in rainy weather, when the water was cloudy, they were invisible. Investigating these intriguing objects and if possible retrieving some of them, was going to be a tricky business, with the risk of mud and water all over our clothes and ourselves and we had to be quick so that no-one else saw what we were up to, as this was our private treasure. But we achieved it and the golden objects proved to be brass ammunition rounds – live ones – and plenty of them. Goodness knows how they came to be there. Luckily for us, Mr Leakey or one of his assistants discovered our hoard, hidden under a pile of exercise books and Kennedy's Latin Primers, before we had quite worked out a way to hammer in the percussion pins, and the whole lot were confiscated. But the authorities did a poor job of clearing the remaining rounds out of the sluice. We used from time to time see a tell-tale glint, though from then on we left well alone. Perhaps there are still a few second world war 303 rounds buried in the mud there to this day. If there are, they must be mightily unstable.

Parents in the 1940s lived in dread of their children contracting polio, epidemics of which cropped up most summers. There was one in Cranbrook while we were living there, but luckily it did not affect me. Instead, that summer term, I had measles. And then, along with most of the school, I had dysentery, presumably gastro-enteritis. Unimpressed by what they took to be Coursehorn's lax health precautions and alarmed to be told by me that Mr Leakey had a cane, my parents removed me and sent me to board at a school forty miles away, where our temperatures were taken every morning by a formidable woman permanently dressed in white armour plating called Sister Webb and where corporal punishment was unthinkable. So that was the end of any hope of real integration into Cranbrook life. I lived there another four years, but only during school holidays.

In these new circumstances, I was thrown further back on my own devices. Bakers Cross House offered a wide range of diversions to a pre-teen boy and I think I benefitted from them. There were the training courses for the NABC boys, at least three of which took place each year during the school holidays, which meant that the house and its associated buildings were full of busy people, many of them not much older than me and all living a communal life in which I had to join (or starve). At the end of each course, there was a show, consisting of a clutch of one-act plays leavened with the odd mini-opera or ballet. Once or twice I was allowed a bit part, as a page (static and mute) perhaps, or a juvenile passer-by. And I always insisted on being in the group photograph.

The fire station next to our back yard was generally worth watching for the odd half hour. The siren that summoned the firemen was right outside my bedroom. It frightened my cousin when he was staying, because it reminded him of the blitz that he had lived through in Cardiff while I was safely tucked up in Canada. But for me it was a signal to run and watch the firemen rushing in to start cranking up the fire engines, ready for a quorum to jump on once the motors had fired and then to race away, bells clanging and brass gleaming. There was generally the odd chap who had arrived too late. With the engines gone, all he could do was mooch about and tidy up.

And then there was my bike, the fairy-cycle's successor, a sturdy, black sit-up-and-beg Norman, made in nearby Ashford. I went for a ride most days in good weather. My favourite route was a three-mile round trip through the neighbouring village of Benenden. As far as I remember, I was always alone.

We had a boat on the pond, a clinker-built sailing dinghy minus its mast and sails, but still equipped with oars and a rudder. Together with my cousin, who often came to us during the school holidays as his family were in Germany, where his father was with the Allied Control Commission, I spent hours going on long voyages round and round the pond, which cannot have been more than thirty yards across, if that. Neither of us could swim, but that does not seem to have worried anyone and we certainly did not have life jackets.

I was in charge of the ducks during the holidays. They spent the night in a hutch near the pond, safe from foxes, and were let out for a swim once they had laid a few eggs, or at 11 am, whichever came first. Once a week I had to clean out the hutch, a filthy and very smelly job that I did not care for. Whenever Elizabeth was away I also looked after her hens. They were far better behaved than the ducks, with less disgusting habits.

Once I had left Coursehorn I did not have any real local friends. I do not know what became of Williams. My parents' friends included members of the teaching staff at Cranbrook School (at that stage an independent boys' public school) and the farmers up the road, (Colonel) Robert and Catherine Cheeseman. The Colonel had been in Mesopotamia – modern Iraq – in the 1914–18 war, where he had taken part in a number of archaeological digs. I remember admiring his most cherished possession, a beautiful duck carved in jade which he had dug up in Ur (and then presumably pilfered). Catherine was a world authority on beef cattle, forever off to exotic places like Bolivia or Uruguay to judge prize cattle, at a time when most people could not get as far abroad even as France, owing to the £25 foreign exchange limit – which presumably did not apply to business travellers. She was the daughter of Billy Winch, the last brewer at Bakers Cross before the brewery was sold when all but the malt-house was pulled down. So she had been brought up in our house.

Once when Vita Sackville-West had dropped in to offer advice on the garden she told us about the secret passage which legend said Bloody Baker had dug from Sissinghurst Castle to his old house at Bakers Cross, through which to escape if ever things got too hot at home. Two miles seemed rather a long way to dig a tunnel at any time, let alone in the sixteenth century, but the story lodged itself firmly in my mind and I was determined to see if I could find the Bakers Cross end.

We knew only too well that there was a cellar below part of the old malt-house, beneath the half-collapsed floor of the way through the building from the theatre entrance and the dormitory block, where my parents had installed the rope balustrade to keep people clear of the worst of the sagging boards. Eventually, however, the NABC decided that a safer and more permanent arrangement had to be devised, a properly supported corridor. This meant that the old floor had first to be removed. While this was going on we were able to climb down the builders' ladders and, armed with torches, my father and I explored. The cellar turned out to be even deeper than we had suspected –

fourteen or fifteen feet. It was dry and led to another one, under the garage. Shining the torches around, we were relieved to see that the joists above us, supporting our faithful Hillman Minx, appeared sound and we were surprised also to see, eight or ten feet up, the remains of a couple of mullioned windows, now some feet below ground level. They appeared to be Tudor, as did much of the cellar brickwork. My father reckoned we had stumbled on all that was left of Bloody Baker's original house – perhaps a basement or semi-basement looking out on to what was now the fire station, where the ground level had been built up several feet. This could have occurred when the nineteenth-century brewery, since demolished, had been built where the fire station now stood. The cellars which we were exploring were clearly far older than the nineteenth-century malt-house now resting above them.

There was no sign of a tunnel and all too soon the builders wanted us out of the way, ready to seal the cellars up again. Curiously no-one thought of putting in some kind of permanent access.

During the summer of 1950, a few months before the NABC pulled the rug from under my parents' feet and consigned its much-admired arts training centre to the dustbin of history (and us to homelessness), it proved necessary to take up the drawing-room floor. 'Drawing room' was an ambitious misnomer for a small and almost windowless room squeezed between the communal dining and music rooms, but it was a true withdrawing room in that it was my parents' private space and as such low on the NABC's priority list for maintenance and repairs. There must have been something seriously wrong with the floor for them even to think of taking it up. But up it came and behold, beneath it was another deep cellar, hitherto undetected. Once again my father and I climbed down the builders' ladder, to discover more Tudor brickwork and another underground mullioned window. The drawing-room was about as far away from the malt-house as you could get and still be in the same complex of buildings, but the cellar seemed to be part of whatever it was that we had seen a couple of years earlier.

In the corner of the cellar furthest from the malt-house and nearest to Sissinghurst, was the entrance to a passage or tunnel. We crept into it but gave up after a few feet because the structure had partially collapsed and was clearly dangerous. I was very excited; had we found our end of Bloody Baker's secret passage? Surely we had? My father was less certain, reminding me that two miles were an awfully long way to dig an underground passage, and that any intended secrecy would have been fatally compromised by the effort and numbers of people who would have been needed for such a task. He suggested, prosaically, that perhaps the collapsed tunnel had once led to another cellar.

A few days later I went back to school, never to return to Bakers Cross and soon forgot all about its cellars and legendary secret passage, only to be reminded of them nearly sixty years later when I read Adam Nicolson's *Sissinghurst*, in which he mentions the Castle's end of the story which his grandmother had told us about in the 1940s.

Chapter 6
Two Headmasters

At the beginning of every term, the Headmaster of my new prep school, Betteshanger, gave us a short pep-talk. No doubt this was common practice at the time among prep school headmasters and may well still be. Mr Stocks's went something like this: "Now boys, remember when you are climbing trees always to have at least three limbs attached to the tree at any one moment. Two hands and a foot, or two feet and a hand. Never fewer. Now run along and have your tea." That was all and I am fairly sure that it resembled few if any other prep school beginning-of-term pep-talks.

But then Charles Lancelot Stocks CB resembled few other headmasters, of whatever kind of school. To begin with, he was immensely old. When I arrived at Betteshanger in 1946, aged 8, Mr Stocks was already 68, which was older than my grandfather. And yet, despite his evident antiquity, he understood us all and never, ever, talked down to us. He was an inspired teacher, mainly of the classics, but also of English literature and of extra-curricular subjects such as billiards and snooker (and 'slosh' an amalgam of the two which I think he may have invented), astronomy, and, above all, of architecture. In what other prep school could one have learned about the history of architecture and so enjoyably? Everything I know to this day about it I owe to Mr Stocks, from the four classical orders to Arts and Crafts and even Bauhaus – though he wasn't entirely sure that he approved of the latter. We went on outings to study the difference between Flemish and English bond and to learn to distinguish between pastiche and the real thing. And we loved learning about these things, probably because we loved the way we were treated by this remarkable man.

Mr Stocks was a believer in a rounded education. While he realised that it was important for his pupils to master the standard fare of a prep school, it was equally important to balance the maths and history, Latin and English, French and scripture, with painting, music and drama and plenty of all three. The school was liberally decorated with big bright pictures done by the children, among them several John Craxton juvenilia, and every now and again a book would be published featuring the best of the pupils' recent writings and paintings. I still have one, entitled *Fantasy and Fun*, wrapped in its original book jacket designed by a promising young artist called Richard Bennett, later better known as the composer Richard Rodney Bennett. This same chap can't have been listening once to the beginning-of-term homily, for he fell out of a tree and broke his leg, which meant that I had to deputise for him as Ophelia in the annual play. Mr S saw nothing odd in demanding renderings of the world's greatest and longest dramas from his pre-pubescent charges, or for that matter in expecting their parents to sit through them.

And Mr Stocks was a joiner-in. He would appear from nowhere to join in on a game of football, always in a suit and sporting a trilby hat, which he doffed when heading the ball – something he was very good at. He played the double bass in the school orchestra and sang bass in the choir. He abhorred violence and consequently forbade corporal punishment and came down heavily on any sign of bullying. Punishments were meted out when necessary, but they consisted mainly of a long and thorough talking-to, rarely of extra work or detention. He could spot unhappiness a mile off and was expert at getting to the bottom of whatever was causing it and at cheering up the victim. Schools that forbade corporal punishment were rare in the 1950s. This special characteristic at both Betteshanger and my Quaker public school, Leighton Park, was a key factor for my parents when the time came to choose a school for me after my false start at Coursehorn. In more ways than one Mr Stocks seemed to embody goodness and common sense.

Mrs Stocks, on the other hand, was something else. She had a long thin nose, which she used for copious sniffing, often disapprovingly. Like her husband, she too had a habit of turning up unexpectedly, but in her case, these appearances were usually unwelcome intrusions into whatever fun we might be enjoying. Whereas Mr Stocks's circular countenance bore a more or less permanent expression of beatific radiance, her thin and pointy one was often sour. But gradually, as we grew older, we came to understand that these impressions were largely superficial and that beneath a grim exterior lurked a warm, though saddened heart.

Charles and Olive Stocks married latish. She had been the manager of the YWCA in London and was rather younger than her husband, who was a successful civil servant in the upper echelons of the Treasury. Against all the odds they had a child, Christopher, on whom they doted. They sent him to an amazing new 'progressive' prep school founded and run by friends of theirs down near the Kentish coast, in wooded hills behind Deal and Sandwich. This was in 1937 when he was nine. Before long he had become the school's golden boy, good at everything. But in the summer term of 1939, and so suddenly that his parents were unable to get down to the school in time, he died of a then untreatable streptococcal infection, aged just eleven.

A few weeks later, on the outbreak of war, the school's premises and grounds were requisitioned by the military. The School Council, of which Mr Stocks was a member, managed to rent Dodington House, the seat of the Codrington family near Chipping Sodbury in Gloucestershire. Pupil numbers dropped to thirty, far too low for the school's financial health and bankruptcy loomed. In 1942, just when things could hardly get any worse, in the middle of the summer term, Howard Evans, the headmaster, died. So Mr Stocks, aged 64, newly retired as Commissioner of Crown Lands, stepped in with his wife, to run a failing prep school. As they put it, they had lost their own son, so now they would look after thirty of other people's, a number that soon grew under their tutelage to a healthier sixty. And four years later the school moved back to its real home in Kent, where it still flourishes, though now renamed Northbourne Park, much bigger and co-ed. Just some of these events could have accounted for Mrs Stocks's melancholy disposition.

Over the next few years, Mr Stocks made a couple of attempts to retire. Both replacements proved unsatisfactory and it was not until he was in his early eighties that he succeeded. He lived on, in a cottage on the estate, still full of vigour and participating with his wife in a number of school events, till he was well into his nineties. And, in a neat conclusion, two of our children, by then pupils at the school and members of the choir, sang at Mrs Stocks's funeral; she had outlived her husband by a few years.

John Ounsted, the Headmaster of Leighton Park, was a very different kettle of fish. For one thing, he was as young as Mr Stocks was old. When I arrived there in 1951 he was only thirty-two, yet already in the third year of his tenure. He was rather distant, well suited to the LP headmaster's traditional soubriquet of The Duke. He was a Wykehamist and formidably bright, having been Senior

Wrangler at Cambridge. He and his wife, who did not involve herself much with the school, had five children. They lived off the Park – in other words, in decent privacy away from the campus.

But there were some resemblances. While the Duke did only a little teaching in his own subject, mathematics, he was in sole control of a kind of creative writing for the whole of the Sixth Form, in a subject known as Headmaster's Essay, to which he attached great importance and for which I have ever since been hugely grateful. Once one got into the Sixth Form – and I was in it for three years, so I got more than my fair ration – one had to write three essays a term, or roughly one a month. There was no choosing a subject; if The Duke prescribed, say, "Friendship", then 'Friendship' it was and of a minimum length. The Duke marked all the essays himself and he did not spare the criticism, on logic, grammar, marshalling of arguments, appropriate use of quotations, the lot. Then we all sat at his feet for a double period once a week, going through them all and criticising each other, for three or four sessions, by which time we had embarked on the next essay. The main object of the exercise was to teach clarity, in thought and drafting, a skill that I would need throughout my career. And what I learned from those sessions has stayed with me ever since.

To give him his due, the Duke also did quite a bit of extra-curricular teaching, but in subjects or pastimes in which I was not involved, such as Russian, poetry and the strangely entitled pond microscopy, which presumably meant small wriggly things that lived in the School Pond. Later, as a cub diplomat, I wished that I had had the nous to opt for his Russian lessons. A basic groundwork would have been a great help later on.

And it was not all solemnity. One great exception took place in 1953 or 54, on Speech Day, an annual occasion when, as at most other public schools, a worthy notable delivered some improving thoughts to an audience of pupils and their parents. On this occasion, the advertised speaker was to be Christopher Fry, the poet and dramatist, whose son was at LP at the time and a sufficient draw to attract my parents, normally distinguished by their absence. When everyone was seated, in the brand-new gymnasium – which held more than Peckover Hall – the Duke ushered in Christopher Fry and a glamorous woman; Mrs Fry perhaps, but why was she on the platform? "Friends," (the standard Quakerly salutation) said the Duke, "it gives me great pleasure to welcome our two speakers today, Christopher Fry and Marlene Dietrich." The surprise was total and the speeches were excellent.

The Duke headed Leighton Park for 22 years, with great distinction. He made the school, true to its Quaker ethos, an exemplar of 'progressive' education, while at the same time keeping up very high academic standards. In one year while I was there, for instance, it won more Oxbridge scholarships than any other school in the country, more than far bigger and better-known academic powerhouses such as Manchester Grammar School and Winchester. And the arts were not neglected. Acting, painting and music were well taught and much encouraged. Richard (Rodney) Bennett, his leg mended and like me, an ex-Betteshanger LP scholarship boy (thanks to Mr Stocks, who greatly approved of both the school and its presiding Duke), shared the viola front desk with me in the school orchestra, where he made all the right sounds while I whirled my bow back and forth half an inch clear of the strings.

John Ounsted went on to be an HMI – Her Majesty's Inspector of Schools – again, according to his obituaries in The Times and elsewhere, with great distinction. I was very lucky to have been at LP during his time as The Duke.

Chapter 7
Teenage Adventures

I was in the choir at Betteshanger, which appeared on the map as a village, but consisted only of a large Victorian mansion housing the school, hidden away in the middle of its sizeable park, together with a dozen or so estate houses and cottages. It had been a settlement since Doomsday, so it rated a parish church, even though no trace remained of the true village that must once have existed. It also rated a coalmine, a couple of miles away, with its own modern miners' village, called Betteshanger Colliery. Apart from the occasional rumble from deep underground, which now and again reminded us privileged brats of the mine's existence, it might have been on another planet, so little did it impinge on our middle-class boarding school existence. And now, thirty years or more since Thatcherism swept it and the other Kent coalmines away, it too is little more than a memory – a very bitter one for the families who still live in the mining village.

The church, a tiny Victorian Norman pastiche, lay at the bottom of the mansion's lawn, near the walled garden, surrounded by trees, cows and sheep. The school's choir was also the church choir. We wore red cassocks and were affiliated to the Royal School of Church Music. We were good enough to sing occasional services in other churches and once a year in the crypt of Canterbury Cathedral. We were encouraged to attend RSCM courses in cathedrals during the school holidays when the course members formed a temporary choir in the regular one's absence. I went on one of these, at Ely, during the 1951 Easter holidays. I was thirteen and very enthusiastic and must have caught the attention of the RSCM course director, because during the ensuing summer term I was invited to audition for a scratch choir which would fill the gap at Westminster during the Abbey choir's regular summer absence, which that year coincided with the Festival of Britain. It was apparently inconceivable for the Abbey, only a few hundred yards from the Festival's focal point on the South Bank, to be choirless at such a time, so a competition for boys to fill the gap was held throughout the country. I was auditioned in the Chapter House at Canterbury, in a terrifying ordeal during which, in front of a panel of judges, I was tested on sight-reading, pitch, intervals, chanting and a solo piece of my own choosing. This was 'Come unto Him' from The Messiah and I won a place in the Abbey's Festival of Britain Choir.

A few weeks later I left Betteshanger for good, ready to go on after the summer holidays to my public school, Leighton Park. The Abbey venture was to fill most of the holidays, so I had to be equipped for my new school and my London sojourn, in a rush. A sports jacket, various shirts and ties, long trousers (my first since leaving Canada seven years earlier and about time too), a grey suit, sports clothes and so on – all had to be bought, equipped with name-tapes and some of them packed away till the new term, in the space of a few days. And then I was off to London, to Westminster School, which was to be my home for the next six weeks.

We were kept very busy, with choir practice after choir practice and service after service. We slept in centuries-old dormitories; or at any rate, they certainly seemed centuries-old. We ate in a kind of refectory. And we were given a very good time, with plenty of sight-seeing, free entry to the delights of the Festival, especially the Dome of Discovery, and evenings at a number of Promenade Concerts at the Albert Hall. The dean himself, a skeletal man called Dr Don, showed us round all the bits of the abbey normally closed to the public, and the organist introduced us to the console and workings of the enormous organ. And of course we sang, which is why we were there.

But after two or three weeks, I developed a sore throat. Well, as I explained to Edred Wright, the choir master, it wasn't exactly sore, it just didn't seem to work properly when I was trying to sing. Sometimes it was very husky and at others, it produced curious squeaks or even nothing at all. Worst of all, I could no longer rely on hitting the intended note. Mr Wright tried me out on a few scales. Hopeless. I probably had laryngitis, so take a day off and come back for another go after the vocal cords had had a bit of a rest. So, back I went a couple of days later for another test. Worse still. "Don't worry," said the kind Mr W. "Nothing serious. Your voice is breaking, that's all."

I was told to rejoin the choir, so as not to leave a gap, and to go on enjoying myself, but under no circumstances attempt to sing, or I'd wreck everything. Just open and shut my mouth in unison, so to speak, and mime my part. In fact, be a silent choirboy. And, for the rest of my time at Westminster Abbey, that is what I was. A silent choirboy, like a living ventriloquist's dummy.

I had been well taught at Betteshanger and won a scholarship to Leighton Park in 1951. Memoir writers seem prone to describing the horrors of their schools, which many of them profess to have hated. Maybe a miserable time at school is a necessary precursor to a successful and creative adult career. If this is so, I failed. For I was happy at both my schools. Of course, there were moments of gloom, but there weren't many of them and the only serious one was when I failed my Greek A-Level at the end of my fourth year at Leighton Park.

During my fifth year, I sat the Merton College Oxford post-mastership exam in classics (Mertonese for scholarship) and was admitted as a commoner, A-Levels or not. But in order to qualify for a county grant, I had to have at least three A-Levels and without a grant, my parents would not have been able to afford my various fees and expenses at Oxford. So I had to spend a full fifth year at LP, at the end of which I retook all three – Latin, Greek and Use of English – and passed.

Having a county grant meant that one's university education was virtually free. In my case, Hampshire County Council paid all my university and college fees, as well as a modest maintenance allowance, which my parents supplemented. How lucky we were in those days, unsaddled by student loans and debt. And I was even luckier, in that I had also won a leaving scholarship from LP, which covered the cost of all my initial book purchases from Blackwells in Oxford.

One of the best things that happened to me at LP was winning a travel scholarship, worth £35 (perhaps the best part of £1000 in present-day values). This enabled me to spend the summer holidays of 1955 bumming around Italy and Greece, for most of the time in the company of another LP boy, Nick Hussey. I was besotted by the romance of classical Greece, even though I evidently hadn't the oomph to master enough of its language to satisfy the A-Level examiners. Nick and I got ourselves from Calais to Brindisi by hitch-hiking, walking and taking the odd train or bus – which we reckoned was cheating, but frequently necessary in order to keep to our schedule. We went deck class from Brindisi to Piraeus, a voyage that took about twenty-four hours, including stops along the way. Once in Greece, which was still very poor and run-down after years of war (world and civil) and not always over-friendly to Brits, whose government at the time was intent on denying independence and enosis (unification with Greece) to Cyprus, we were able to slow down and wallow in antiquities, beaches, cheap food and wine. We walked across a chunk of the Peloponnese to get to the temple at Bassae (Vassi), in 1955 miles from anywhere and accessible only along donkey tracks, but now on the main road and surrounded by carparks, and even slept in the ruins, in a rather unsuccessful attempt to keep dry during a thunderstorm visited on us by an outraged Apollo, whose house we had violated.

Alfresco sleeping became almost our norm, sometimes right out in the open, or if a thunderstorm threatened, under a bridge. One night, at Delphi, I unrolled my sleeping bag in the circular Tholos. The last sightseers had gone, the museum and ticket office had closed and the whole site was completely deserted, so why not? And this time no god took offence. I very much doubt whether it would be possible to stretch out for the night anywhere in Delphi nowadays, let alone in somewhere as iconic as the Tholos.

I was away for most of the eight-week school summer holiday. My parents would have had only a hazy idea of where I was, gleaned from the occasional postcard and, twice, from urgent appeals for £5, to be sent to some Poste Restante or bank in Greece or Italy. This was long before the days of easy telephoning, let alone mobiles or email, and for most of the homeward leg I was on my own, as Nick, who was a year older than me, had had to race off home to start his national service. In deepest rural Apulia I was taken in by the family of the truck driver with whom I was hitching a lift. I shared their meals and was given a comfy hayloft to sleep in; they made it very clear that I was their guest, with no question of payment. And there were many other examples of hospitality and generosity along the way, in Greece as well as Italy. I never felt the remotest anxiety and I do not think that it ever occurred to my parents that I was doing anything risky or foolhardy. Perhaps people were nicer to each other in those days, or at least that we all trusted each other more.

A couple of years before this expedition the new Queen was crowned. Quakers aren't much given to celebrating royalty or royal events, but nevertheless the school gave us a few days off and I cycled the fifty-five miles home – my longest ride hitherto or since – ready for an exciting trip to London.

Coronation Day, in June 1953, dawned grey and wet. This didn't deter the thousands of people lining the streets, ready to watch the procession between the Palace and the Abbey. But I was more comfortable, with better sightlines than most of them, as I was watching it from a perfect viewing point, a wide-open first-floor window on the corner of Trafalgar Square and The Mall, right by

Admiralty Arch, in what was then Malaya House and is now the Malaysian High Commission.

My great uncle was the Commissioner for Malaya, which in 1953 was still a British dependency. Even so, it had its own (largely British) representation in London, headed by Wilfred Ward, aka Uncle Wardie. He had spent a very unpleasant war as a prisoner in Changi Camp in Singapore and had I suppose been given the commissionership, his final appointment before retirement, as some kind of compensation and recognition.

Wardie and my redoubtable Great Aunt Norah were giving a coronation party. I don't know if there were any Malayans present; I hope there were, but all I remember were a number of old stuffed shirts and their consorts – hugely antique in my estimation but probably with an average age of around fifty – and assorted unknown relations. I was fifteen and very lucky to be there.

My sister was about to be twenty-one and Norah and Wardie had invited her to their coronation party as a twenty-first birthday present. I had not been invited and was insanely jealous, but at the last minute, they relented and invited me too. Maybe there was a spare place, because their son Michael, a doctor and mountaineering freak, was unable to attend.

The coronation procession wound its way slowly past our balcony – marching troops, military bands, dignitaries in carriages, including all the world's other crowned heads. It was still raining. Suddenly the procession came to a halt. Below us, in an open landau, a small man dressed in gold braid and medals and wearing a kind of tarboosh, was engaged in an energetic altercation with his travelling companion, a mountainous lady who I learned was Queen Salote of Tonga, the crowd's number two favourite, number one being, of course, our own, newly crowned Queen. The small man wanted the hood up, but Queen Salote disagreed and seemed to be winning her case. Just as the small man seemed on the point of giving up and settling down to a damp sulk, Great Aunt Norah recognised him. He was the Sultan of Somewhere, Tunku Someone-or-other, known to her and many of her guests by some nickname which I have forgotten, which she screeched out, several times, till at last the poor man looked up and gave her a sad, despairing wave – the sort of wave you give when you are far from home, on public display, soaked to the skin, frozen stiff, worsted by a Polynesian lady monarch and shrieked at by a colonial memsahib who has just witnessed your discomfiture. Just then the procession's traffic jam eased and the landau, mercifully, moved off.

The adult guests settled down to discuss their distinguished Malayan friend's predicament and Queen Salote's unreasonable insistence on getting wet, when someone passed a note to Wardie, who immediately showed it to Norah. More shrieks ensued and more champagne was uncorked. They'd done it! Michael and his friends had done it! They'd conquered Everest! Michael, my absent cousin, was the expedition's doctor. And Hillary, in his immortal words, had with Tensing "knocked the bastard off".

Joy was then indeed unbounded.

Chapter 8
The French Exchange

The 'French Exchange' was a rite-of-passage in the mid-twentieth century for nicely brought up middle-class teenagers. Both Elizabeth and I were put through it when we were sixteen. I don't think she enjoyed hers much. But I loved mine.

My parents left it to Leighton Park to make the arrangements, doubtless trusting that solid Quaker institution to find me a safe and worthy family, preferably on the dull side, equipped with a clean and proper boy with whom to spend the summer holidays.

I returned home from an end of term archaeological dig in Wales to find Gérard already installed. He seemed to fit the bill. He was smallish and almost totally silent. He appeared reasonably clean, even though not over-keen on abluting – a characteristic that was only to be expected of the French who, according to my father, washed in eau de cologne, whereas we had only soap and water to offer him.

These first impressions soon proved inaccurate and once he had overcome his initial culture shock Gérard scarcely drew breath. He even had the occasional bath, generally after thrashing me at tennis. He wanted to know when we would be setting off for the Edinburgh Festival (we lived in Hampshire), which he had overheard my parents discussing and which they intended visiting once they had got shot of us to Gérard's family in France. To alleviate his disappointment, they took us on an all-day drive round much of south-west England in their Wolseley Six Eighty (a model favoured by the police and much admired by Gérard, who judged it almost as good as a Mercedes). In Gloucester, my father, with chauvinistic pride, pointed out the factory where the world's first jet fighter had been built. As we hurtled across Salisbury Plain he asserted that Stonehenge was the finest prehistoric monument in the world. And somewhere, no doubt, we had a picnic.

Gérard bore all this stoically. He must have been bored rigid because we lived miles from anywhere in a Jacobean mansion in which my parents had started a school and of course, in August the house was more or less empty. He cannot have met anyone apart from the three of us and perhaps Elizabeth, who had flown the nest but popped back now and again. Maybe he also caught a distant view of the gardener. But I made sure that he knew how privileged he was to be spending a few weeks in so magnificent and historic a house.

When the time came to swap countries and families, the two of us caught the overnight ferry to Cherbourg and the train to Paris, where we spent the best part of a day. Gérard proved an excellent tour guide and I became uneasily aware that we should at least have taken him to London. At the Gare d'Austerlitz, Gérard suggested a drink and a snack. At his suggestion, I had vermouth and pizza, both of them novel and woozily agreeable experiences, which set me up nicely for a slow overnight train to Poitiers. Next morning, we changed onto a branch line to Montmorillon, where we were met by Gérard's older sister, Geneviève, with whom I very quickly fell in love. She must have been eighteen or nineteen and consequently well beyond my reach. But she was everything that I thought a girl should be: kind and jolly, efficient without being bossy and very easy on the eye. There were also a couple of Gérard's numerous younger siblings, one of each variety as far as I remember.

We somehow all piled into a minute Simca and set off for Grand'mère's house, somewhere out in the country. On the way through Montmorillon, I could hear Gérard telling his brother and sisters a story, in French of course, which I thought contained the word Gloucester. He then switched to English and told me solemnly that we were at that very moment passing the pâtisserie where the world's first macaroon had been made – an announcement which, though undoubtedly interesting, did not greatly impress me. It was followed by an explosion of poorly suppressed giggles, quickly shushed by Geneviève. We did not pass any prehistoric monuments.

A few miles further on we encountered a sign announcing that we were entering a village called Bourg-Archambault, where Geneviève turned smartly right, over a bridge, through a fortified gate and into a courtyard surrounded by towers and battlemented walls, with a grand and turreted house along one side, in front of which we came to a halt. Either Grand'mère lived in a château, or I was being treated to some more tit-for-tat sightseeing.

But this was Grand'mère's house all right, because there she was, the de Peslouan matriarch, greeting her grandchildren and holding out a welcoming hand to me. She was spherical, roughly four foot six in diameter and almost entirely encased in black bombazine. At least, I assumed that it was bombazine – a fabric about which I knew next to nothing – because that was what my parents said French peasant women were generally encased in. The only flaw in this logical deduction was that, judging from the scale and manner of her dwelling, Mme de Peslouan was clearly not a peasant.

Gérard was told to show me to where I would be sleeping, a draughty attic lit by tall dormer windows, running the full length of the house, four or five storeys up. It smelled musty and dirtily sweet. Dotted around here and there were beds and this was where the boys slept – Gérard, two or three younger brothers and me. There was a wash-stand, with bowls and jugs of water, together, I was relieved to note, with an enormous bottle of cologne, and in a side turret a garderobe, none too inviting, the origin of the unpleasant sweetish smell. It gave directly on to the moat, the waters of which twinkled prettily fifty feet below.

It was soon time to go downstairs for lunch. We gathered in the salon, a grand room full of gilt and fussy furniture. Gérard instructed me on no account to touch the curtains, lest they fall to pieces. There were several framed photographs dotted about, most of the same severe-looking man. All of them were signed and I learned that they were of the Comte de Paris. This meant nothing to me, but Gérard explained that the Comte was the pretender to the French throne. The de Peslouans were ardent royalists. It had not occurred to me that such people existed in France and I wondered if they had to keep their views under wraps.

Grand'mère led us into the dining room where, as the guest, I was seated on her right. Someone had laid my cutlery the wrong way up. I was about to put this right when I noticed that the same mistake had been made right around the table, so I thought it best not to intervene. Grand'mère had no English and my French was schoolboy level. It was enough, however, to understand, after I had received a painful slap on my left arm, that nice children in France never put their hands on their laps when seated at table. Who knows what they might be getting up to? Hands were to be kept visible at all times. But after this unpromising start, Mme de Peslouan and I got on famously, with the help of a fair amount of interpretation by Geneviève and Gérard.

So far there had been no sign of Gérard's parents, so after lunch I asked when I would meet them. The answer was Never. They were in Germany, where Papa was a colonel in the French army and they were not due for any leave in the next few weeks. Grand'mère and Geneviève were in charge, information which suited me well enough.

Several days passed, in agreeable though slightly boring idleness. Every morning I read aloud from *Lettres de Mon Moulin*, an improvement on the excerpts from the Readers Digest which I had inflicted on Gérard in England. He half-listened, corrected my pronunciation, asked me a few questions about what I had just read and then proposed tennis, or boating on the moat. Swimming was judged inadvisable, owing to the nature of the drainage system from the château's oubliettes. Once or twice we went into Montmorillon for supplies. Mercifully there was no further mention of macaroons.

Then suddenly consternation reigned. Geneviève had learned that *les oncles* were on their way. Not only did this mean that unspecified numbers of *tantes* and *cousins*, as well as *oncles*, would soon be joining us, but also and in consequence and more worryingly, there would be intolerable pressure on the tennis court booking arrangements. There was only one solution: escape. This was accomplished within a day of the arrival of all the relations, who, true to their reputation, immediately commandeered not only the tennis court but also the moat's only rowing boat.

Geneviève packed me and as many of her siblings as would fit into the Simca and despatched the remainder, under Gérard's supervision, by train. We were off to the family's holiday house near Tours, La Ravinière in Rochecorbon, a village a mile or so from Vouvray on the Loire. And there we remained for the rest of my time in France, a fortnight or so of teenage bliss, unsupervised by any adults apart from Geneviève – and she didn't really count as she was still technically a teenager herself.

The sun shone every day, we got out of bed when we felt like it, Geneviève somehow conjured up delicious things to eat, very occasionally we had another go at Alphonse Daudet's improving letters from his windmill and then in the afternoon, we joined a pack of the local kids for swimming in the river, lazing and larking about, with no doubt a little dalliance on the side.

Some or maybe all of our local friends must have had parents in the background, but I have no recollection of any tedious adult interference in our activities, not even in the frequent evening parties held, by candlelight, in the wine caves in the hillsides around Vouvray. There was wine, and grenadine for the more timorous, and there were cigarettes and dance music played on wind-up gramophones, and above all – a fascinating novelty – plenty of charming and cheerful girls, so different from the young ladies from the nearest girls' school who were imported to Leighton Park for the odd debate and the annual sixth form dance. I had surely arrived in heaven. I was also, without realising it, learning quite a lot of French.

All too soon it was nearly time to leave. At the very last minute, Geneviève decided that I should be subjected to a bit of culture and my last day was spent, on my own with her, my idol, on a coach tour of half a dozen Loire châteaux. I still have a few dim and grainy impressions of Blois and Azay-le-Rideau and various others, taken on my Brownie Box. But none of Geneviève.

Chapter 9
Student Years

I left Leighton Park in the summer of 1956 and went up to Merton College Oxford that October. Merton is by most standards – teaching fellowships, a Royal charter and so on – Oxbridge's oldest fully fledged college, having been founded in 1265. Some of its fabric dates from soon after the foundation, including Mob Quad with its famous mediaeval library and parts of the enormous, only half completed, chapel. My rooms were in Mob, backing on to the chapel. Every quarter of an hour the clock in the tower which loomed above the quad boomed out its mournful, minor key, mediaeval sounding ditty, known now to the millions who have watched the television series Morse and Lewis and spine-tingling in a way that the even better-known Westminster chimes are not.

I was impressed, but at the same time almost overwhelmed, by the atmosphere of antiquity and scholarly gloom that seemed to pervade my new surroundings, including my thirteenth-century cell. Fortunately, Merton was one of the richer colleges, able to afford post-mediaeval amenities such as a washbasin with hot and cold in every bedroom. The nearest baths, however, were in a basement across three quads and the nearest – unspeakable – loos were behind Mob, squeezed between the chapel's buttresses. It is perhaps unsurprising that, immersed in so much history, I opted for a decidedly mediaeval slant to an English degree, with Chaucer as the sole, not over-convincing, concession to modernity, and lashings of Old and Middle English, garnished with Old Norse and Mediaeval Welsh. My sole extra-curricular activity was music, in the form of membership of the college choral society and rather inaccurate participation in the second row of the violas in one of the lesser university orchestras.

But any thoughts of a life of reclusive scholarly calm were swept aside when the term was barely three weeks old. Britain and France had invaded Egypt in a collusive pretence of halting an Israeli attack, a last gasp exercise in aggressive imperialism and duplicity which outraged progressive-minded students of the sort that I sometimes reckoned I was and dismayed our closest allies, headed by President Eisenhower. At the same time, the Soviet Union and its Warsaw Pact clients were busy putting down an insurrection in Budapest, a cruel and bloody activity that outraged the slightly less progressive-minded, among whom I was numbered whenever I forgot how progressive I now was. Already activists in the latter faction were preparing to drop everything and head for Hungary, equipped with medical supplies and a determination to help man the barricades, while the more progressive faction had the rather easier and far cheaper option of taking the train to Paddington and joining in a demo or two.

I was torn, but simple economics won the day and I soon found myself in Conrad Russell's rooms, with a bunch of eager activists busily planning Merton's, or maybe Oxford's, part in the next day's demo. Conrad was Bertrand Russell's son, a circumstance which we reckoned lent our activities philosophical respectability and gravitas which they might otherwise have lacked. One of our numbers said he was a member of the Communist Party (I forget his name), but the rest of us were just a politically heterogeneous bunch of liberal-minded young people who were deeply unhappy with what Eden and his government were up to, as were probably half or more of the population. I was probably the youngest, having gone straight from school to Oxford, while all the others would have done their National Service and were, therefore, two or three years older than me and much more worldly and sophisticated. I had to work doubly hard, to appear as mature as the rest of them.

We made some placards and banners, which had to be concealable in bags and briefcases so as not to draw attention at the railway station. Someone said that he had acquired a supply of ball bearings, to throw under the police horses' hooves so that they would slip and fall over. This proposed tactic did not meet with general approval (cruelty to animals) and, though plenty of ball bearings were indeed thrown, I doubt whether any of them emanated from our gang.

The next day we went to the station in dribs and drabs, as we reckoned that a large party would arouse any prowling Bulldogs' suspicion ('Bulldogs' were a kind of university police force), and we managed to get to Trafalgar Square undetected. There we joined what soon became an enormous crowd, urged on by Nye Bevan and other fiery speakers before setting off down Whitehall, chanting a number of slogans including one based on the voting figures in the UN General Assembly resolution, proposed by the Americans and carried 64–5, with a few abstentions. (The five opposers were the UK, France, Israel, Australia and New Zealand.) The centre of the crowd halted in front of Downing Street, in those days a public right of way but closed off by the police that day and roared out its disapproval of Anthony Eden and all his government.

I do not recall whether we joined any of the follow-up demos, but my taste in extra-mural activities had certainly been affected. Politics seemed far more fun than trying to play the viola, an activity that was put in cold storage for the next twenty-five years.

Events in Hungary, however, had a contrary, more positive, effect on my music-making. Many Hungarian students fled the country once the uprising had been crushed and found refuge in universities throughout the West. Merton welcomed a scientist, George (now Sir George) Radda and a musician, Laszlo Heltay. Laszlo had been studying under Zoltan Kodaly and he immediately took our slightly lack-lustre college choral society in hand. It was soon renamed The Kodaly Choir and I was proud to be a founder member (and in due course one of its bit-part soloists, as a baritone). The Kodaly Choir still flourishes, I kept up my singing in choirs for many years and Laszlo went on to forge a distinguished career all over the world as a choral and orchestral conductor.

People in novels who go to Oxford tend to have a gorgeous, dreamy time, lounging around in punts, falling in love, acting in plays, getting drunk, attending the odd lecture and occasionally doing some work at the behest of a wonderfully sympathetic tutor who becomes a friend for life, before acquiring a degree and drifting off into the real world of careers, families and so on. Much of this did, in fact, happen to me, though not the tutor bit. I sat at the feet of an alarming South African martinet called Geoffrey Smithers, a man devoid of empathy or humour, who appeared to enjoy spending an age fiddling with his pipe while his victim squirmed and stuttered to find the right words about Grimm's Law or the forty-eighth crux of Beowulf. When one alarming day I explained that I didn't know any German and would, therefore, struggle to read Herr Professor Someone-or-other's 5,000-word essay on the semantics of Deor, printed in 1856 in gothic type, he shrugged and said, in that case, I'd better learn some German and be quick about it, as he'd be expecting me to demonstrate easy familiarity with the Herr Professor's wisdom once the long vacation was over. Fortunately, I did Old and Middle English in tandem with a generous friend called Chris Ball, who later went on to be Warden of Keble before, as Sir Chris, somehow turning all the polys into universities. Chris did understand German and cheerfully

68

helped me to write my essays and fend off the worst of Mr Smithers' sallies. Merton's Old and Middle English boss, the Merton Professor, was J R R Tolkien, a bluff and hospitable soul who occasionally had the likes of me to tea but, alas, didn't do any teaching. Perhaps he was too busy writing about Middle Earth or Hobbits.

On the other-hand tutorials in Mediaeval Welsh, with an inscrutable Welsh gnome in Jesus College called Professor Idris Foster, and in Old Norse with Professor Edward Turville-Petre in Magdalen, were fun, even exciting. These kindly men taught me, set their respective papers for Finals and probably marked them. There were only four of us doing Old Norse and I was the university's sole candidate in Mediaeval Welsh. I got alphas in both. I got various shades of beta and gamma in all the Old English papers. Maybe they were marked by Mr Smithers.

Those same Oxford students in novels do amazing things in the 'Long Vac', the empty space between June and October. These people usually have lots of money, which propels them to Greek islands or Tuscan villas. I had next to none, but nevertheless filled both summers positively and enjoyably, first as tutor to a couple of small boys in the Scottish Highlands and then the following year on a twentieth century version of the Grand Tour. The tutoring stint led to a lifelong friendship with the Sisson family who employed me. The piece that I wrote about George and Andrea for the family's memorial book can be found as an annexe at the end of this memoir.

Some lucky young gentlemen during the eighteenth century went on the Grand Tour, visiting classical sites and renaissance cities around the Mediterranean, mainly in Italy and Greece. This was almost a rite-of-passage, a necessary culmination of a proper Enlightenment education. It was also an opportunity for the acquisition, by fair means or foul, of many of the artefacts, from the odd altarpiece panel to classical Greek statues, which were in this way being added to the national art collection. These same young gentlemen were mostly very privileged and very well-heeled aristocrats. They were followed, or perhaps augmented, in the nineteenth century by people with other motives, often a good deal less well-heeled – poets, painters, romantics, including Keats, Lear, Byron and many others.

Aged twenty, I followed in some of their footsteps financed and organised by an elderly peer to whom I had been introduced a couple of years earlier by another student and who evidently enjoyed the company of young men – though to give him his very considerable due I never heard of anyone with anything to complain of in this regard. As far as I was concerned, he was simply a generous – very generous – patron or friend and of course I was flattered to be entertained at his house or club in London. He was, after all, a Lord, a wounded war hero who had lost an arm at the Battle of Jutland and a former Cabinet Minister. He had also been married to Captain Scott's widow, by whom he had had a son who was later also a distinguished politician. He was Hilton Young, ennobled as the first Lord Kennet. My parents were a bit startled and made enquiries, but were assured by friends in the know that he was harmless.

There was strict exchange control during the 1950s. After you had bought your tickets you were allowed to take out of the country only £25 spending money per head, later increased to £50, or rather over £1000 at today's values. Lord Kennet owned a villa at Lerici, on the coast just south of La Spezia, where he liked to go every summer and, by inviting a number of visitors from the UK, whose foreign currency allowances could be pooled, this was feasible. His preferred guests were male undergraduates, mostly impecunious, but that was not a problem as he paid for everything, including our tickets and a sum with which we could buy up to the maximum permitted currency allowance. On arrival at the Villino San Carlo we handed over any lire for which Lord Kennet had reimbursed us in England, and from then on everything was paid for. One was invited for about four weeks and I think that two, or possibly three, parties visited each summer. I believe there were five of us in mine.

The Villino was perched on a cliff overlooking the Gulf of La Spezia and almost everything about it was a delight. The only exception was the lack of a decent, easily accessible place to swim. There was a slightly sinister cove a couple of hundred feet below the house, reached by a precipitous path. But otherwise one had to go across to next door, two or three hundred yards away, where we had permission to swim at certain times of day from a pleasant private beach. Next to this was the big house, Gli Scafari, where the literary critic and biographer Percy Lubbock lived the year round. He was a widower and, because he had in later years gone blind, he was accompanied by a live-in reader, usually a recent graduate from either his Cambridge college, King's, or Trinity (Lord K's), who, unsurprisingly, much looked forward to the few weeks' company afforded by the annual migration of Lord K's young men. One of our numbers was Lord K's selected travelling companion, and by dint of this privilege acted as de facto senior prefect. Since Lord K had only one arm, he needed a bit of help with dressing and with getting in and out of his berth in the overnight sleeper train. This chap was expected to see out the whole season, but once at Lerici, he was at liberty to join in our various activities, apart from any which took us away for a night. I managed not to be appointed to this exalted position.

In the 1950s, it was still the custom for Oxbridge undergraduates to go on reading holidays, often in the company of one or more of their tutors. The idea was that during the morning one 'read', i.e. studied, while in the afternoon one indulged in suitable manly activities such as walking or climbing (the Lake District was a favoured location). The evenings were given over to eating, drinking and – supposedly – lofty conversation. Lord Kennet's arrangements followed much the same pattern, with him playing the part of tutor. Afternoon activities included visits to various local churches and museums, walks, tennis and swimming, always in a trusted gaggle without Lord K, who stayed at home in the Villino. The best of the walks was an all-day one, when we walked and trained the length of the Cinque Terre, excused our morning's reading. These five territories are a string of improbably picturesque villages squeezed in coves along the Gulf of Spezia, reached only by foot or by a train which runs through a series of tunnels, emerging briefly at each terra.

The eating, drinking and discussion part of the day began with drinks on Percy Lubbock's terrace, where we would sip our aperitifs, gaze out over the waters where Shelley had drowned and try to think of intelligent things to say to the two great men and the occasional extra guests. Then we would repair to the Villino for supper and early bed. Occasionally we would be treated to a bath, with water heated in a 'chippy', a sort of miniature volcano, clamped onto the wall above the bath, into which were fed dry twigs and out of the top of which issued a hurricane of flame and sparks which shot up into an open chimney. But otherwise, we managed with cold showers and mugs of water heated over the stove for shaving.

After a week or two of this agreeable existence, Lord K asked whether any of us had brought an international driving licence. Two of us had, so we were appointed expedition leaders. A minute Fiat was hired and we were instructed to proceed to Florence via Pisa, Lucca and San Gimignano, where rooms had been reserved for us in a hotel. From there we were to go to somewhere outside Florence (probably Fiesole) where we were to stay four or five nights at a guesthouse, from where we were to sally forth each day on cultural expeditions, including one to Siena.

In Fiesole, if that is indeed where we stayed, we were billeted in a kind of cultural boarding house run by a posse of intense English ladies dressed in flowing Seicento-ish robes who, despite their wafty Botticelli-style appearance, were determined martinets, tasked by Lord K to keep a close eye on us and to ensure that we kept to a pre-arranged programme of intensive culture absorption, on which, each evening, we were examined over a – very good – dinner.

"Today you will do the Uffizi. Tomorrow the Duomo and the Pitti. Tell me, Mr Thomas, now that you have been to the Academia, what was your chief impression of the David?" And so on, with the one out-of-town excursion to Siena. Facetiousness was definitely not on; never for a moment did I consider suggesting that my chief impression of the David was of its overwhelming nudity.

A day or two after our return to Lerici, where we were subjected to another *viva voce* by Lord Kennet, I dropped out and headed off on my own to Greece, via Milan and steerage on a boat from Venice. I do not know if Lord K was affronted – and he had every reason to be – but he did not show it. My fellow guests, who were all from Cambridge, put this crass behaviour down to my Oxford provenance. But at that stage, I was besotted by Greece and everything to do with it and I reckoned that, as I was halfway there and had now more or less done the Italian Renaissance, I owed it to myself to pay a second visit to the country where it had all started – it being, in my not over-original view, civilisation, art, culture, you name it. I cannot now remember what I did for money, but I suppose the ever-generous Lord K let me have a bit of my foreign currency allowance back. And once I got to Athens I sponged off a Greek friend who, fortunately, was the scion of a rich shipping dynasty and happy to provide for me for two or three weeks, during much of which I wandered around southern Greece and a few of the islands, on my own.

I managed to inveigle myself into another Cambridge bunch, who had a spare place in a group booking on the Tauern Express back to Ostend and Dover. This inaccurately named weekly service took three days over the journey, probably because it went at little more than walking pace through Tito's Yugoslavia. When we reached Ostend we were without any form of travel documentation, apart from our passports, as our group leader, travelling free by dint of this position, had decided he could afford a couchette for the last night. His bit of the train had been detached during the small hours and had veered off to Copenhagen, with our group ticket in his pocket.

"Group leader gone off to Copenhagen with your tickets?" asked the ticket inspector guarding the gangplank to the Dover ferry. "Don't worry. On you get. Happens every week."

A few days later, I was back in Oxford for my final year, which was followed, despite all my attempts to avoid it, by National Service, something that seemed while I was still a student scarcely worth enduring now that it had been announced that it was being brought to an end.

Chapter 10
Tunes of Glory and Other
Stellar Encounters

By the time I left Oxford, in 1959, national service had more or less ground to a halt. Only those whose service had been deferred while they attended university, or completed articles or apprenticeships, were still being called up, which is what happened to me in November that year. I was summoned to a recruiting office in Brighton, where a sergeant asked me what I wanted to do my time in. I suggested The Buffs or the Royal East Sussex, the two local regiments.

"Service Corps," replied the sergeant, so did I want to be a driver or a clerk? I said I wanted to learn Russian.

"Driver," said the sergeant. "The bleedin' Russian course stopped last year." So it was as a trainee truck driver that I spent my square-bashing months in the RASC, before managing to get commissioned as a second lieutenant, in charge of the ambulances dotted around Northern Ireland.

My intake started its square-bashing in early November 1959. As we had all been at university, or apprenticed, or serving articles, we were a homogeneous bunch of moderately well-educated young men who had accepted that we would never have been able to wriggle out of our two years' service. But only a month or so later the government changed its mind and announced that there would be only two more intakes and that then the whole system would come to an end. We heard this news on the billet radio while we were bulling our boots. We were virtually the last national servicemen. We had so nearly escaped. So we downed tools and went and got drunk in the NAAFI. The next morning, we were all on a collective charge for dirty boots and general sloppiness.

I was potential officer material. Goodness knows why. Perhaps it was just because I did not speak with a regional accent, for I had few other qualifications. We did not have Officer Training Corps at my Quaker public school, where in any case I had signed on as a prospective conscientious objector, while at Oxford I had taken an enthusiastic part in anti-government demonstrations in London during the Suez crisis, written to Bulganin or Khrushchev or both denouncing British imperialism (though, to be fair, also pointing out the error of Soviet ways in crushing the Hungarian uprising, an episode that helped prompt me to forget about being a conscientious objector) and had had letters published in the Manchester Guardian while I was still at school attacking British colonial misdeeds in Cyprus. These qualifications would not have counted in my favour and might not have gone completely unnoticed. But if they had been noticed, I had been forgiven.

One of the characteristics of the potential officer lifestyle, once initial square-bashing was over, was hanging around waiting for something to happen. For several blissful weeks of this enforced idleness, I was a hut orderly. This meant what it said, in that, I spent my days in a hut, where my duties were to keep it clean and to keep the stove alight. Otherwise, I was free to read, which I did, book after book. So I was mildly upset one day to be rounded up with some of my mates by a drill sergeant, who told us that we were all off to be bleedin' film stars and quick about it. We were bussed every day to Shepperton studios, where we did a good deal more hanging around for a fortnight or so, dressed in trews and Scots bonnets, though required every now and again to form up in front of a cardboard castle, where we came to attention whenever Alec Guinness or John Mills walked past. They were dressed as colonels, one nice (Guinness) and the other less so (Mills), whose daughter (Susannah York) was in love with Guinness's son. This character distinction was reflected in real life. Alec Guinness spent a good deal of his spare time chatting to us and standing us bacon butties and cups of char in the canteen, whereas John Mills and Susannah York shunned our company, preferring to skulk in their caravans.

In due course, *Tunes of Glory* became something of a classic. I am discernible – just – as Third Man Front Rank. Many years later – many, many years later – I encountered Susannah York at an arts festival where she was performing a one-woman show. I greeted her as one Tunes of Glory star to another. She was not impressed.

For two or three years running, while I was in my late teens, my parents took me to Stratford where we saw a couple of Shakespeare plays, usually directed by someone whom I thought of as an uncle, even though we were not related. He was, however, married to someone, one Angela Baddeley, who had at some stage been married to a genuine uncle and who therefore counted as a sort of aunt by marriage. So, by extension, her current husband, Glen Byam Shaw, just about counted as an uncle by (former) marriage. This connection, though tenuous, was deemed strong enough by my parents to justify bed and board chez Byam Shaw, as well as free tickets. I do not know what Glen and Angela thought about it, but they fell in with my parents' plans and always with good grace. They usually invited other people to a meal while we were staying, presumably to dilute our self-invited company. On one occasion, one of the guests was the prettiest girl I had ever seen. She was French and apparently about my age – or so she seemed to my besotted eye, though I learned later that she was seven years older than me and therefore in a completely different league. I was struck dumb, which was probably just as well for her and for everyone else, including her husband, who it turned out was that other, definitely grown-up, chap at the table. She was Leslie Caron and he was Peter Hall, a guest director that season.

One September morning in 1955, a year or two before the Caron encounter, I rang the doorbell of a flat in Rome. I was coming to the end of my travel scholarship adventures, having been bumming around Greece and Italy for several weeks and was now on the homeward leg, back to school in ten days' time. I was filthy dirty, equipped with an enormous rucksack and seventeen. The door was opened by a concierge who looked me up and down with every sign of disapproval. She was on the point of shutting the door in my face when I managed to summon up enough phrasebook Italian to explain that I wished to speak to Mr or Mrs Cardiff. I heard her explaining on the intercom that '*uno bambino inglese*' was asking to be admitted. *Bambino,* my eye! I was a bloke, a man, not a child. But my indignation was short-lived, as the concierge beckoned me in and told me which button to press in the lift, from which I emerged to be greeted by a puzzled person whom I took – rightly as it turned out – to be Mrs Cardiff.

Mrs Cardiff was evidently hoping for some kind of explanation. This was disconcerting, as I had assumed that I was expected. The Cardiffs had a couple of sons at my parents' school – and indeed I could see them lurking in the background, looking none too friendly, despite a cheerful wave from me – and my father had promised to write to their parents to ask if they would be kind enough to put me up for two or three nights on my way back from Greece. It was uncomfortably clear either that he had failed to do this, or that the sons had briefed their mum to have nothing too much to do with me. As I was broke and had been planning to explain this sad state of affairs to the Cardiffs and had nowhere else in mind to go, I had in the next few minutes to devise some means of arousing Mrs C's sympathy, while at the same time explaining who I was. So I said that I was just passing by, hoping that there would be a letter from my father, who was stuck for the summer at Stanbridge working out next term's timetable for Masters Johnny and Jo, or whatever their names were, and that the letter would contain sufficient funds for me to continue my journey.

Luckily, the penny dropped and even more luckily, Mrs C turned out to be a warm, motherly soul. After she had finished berating her sons for failing to explain who I was and sent them off to buy things for lunch, she said that I must be wanting a bath and could she do any washing for me? Neither offer was entirely altruistic, as even I could appreciate, and both were eagerly accepted. By the time Mr C got home from work, I was clean, reasonably sweet-smelling and enjoying being cosseted.

Jack Cardiff was a cameraman. In fact, he was one of the world's leading cameramen and he was at that stage shooting War and Peace at Cine Città, which was why the family were living in Rome. He and his wife made a great fuss of me, with sightseeing trips around Rome and a day at the studios, where I was to be introduced to Audrey Hepburn, who was starring as Natasha.

The great day dawned. I saw all over the various Moscow streets and palaces, met technicians and assistant cameramen, best boys, gaffers and grips and eventually was ushered into the presence.

"Why, hullo, you must be the boy who's walked all the way from Greece!" she said, extending a long thin arm, on the end of which was a gloved hand, which I shook, very carefully. More of this insulting and inaccurate boy/child business, but I swallowed my pride and played the bashful young ingénu, acknowledging the praiseworthiness of my endeavours with due modesty, while at the same time confessing that I had accepted the odd lift. And then she was gone, elfin and gorgeous, but taller, far taller, than I had expected. I watched as she disappeared into a cardboard ballroom, for she was wanted on set. I had met a film star and the best of the bunch at that.

That evening, about my fifth or sixth, the Cardiffs took me out to dinner. When we got to pudding, zabaglione as far as I recall, they signalled to the band. One of its numbers detached herself from her colleagues and came over to our table, where she sang specially for me, looking deep into my eyes. This was better. No more of this boy business, just straight adult-to-adult romanticism. But gradually my satisfaction subsided as I realised what was happening, for the song she was singing was *Arrive'derci Roma*.

I got the hint and left the next morning, a few minutes after the arrival of a letter from my father which, fortunately, contained a couple of pound notes.

Some years later, one wet weekend in the summer of 1963, I went with a couple of friends to visit a stately home in the Midlands. We parked the car and headed off towards the drive leading up to the house. There were very few other people visiting; in fact, the only ones we were aware of were, somewhat bizarrely, two or three men standing around, each on his own – lurking, almost.

We were just starting to comment on this strange behaviour when suddenly there was an almighty racket and our fellow visitors, plus a number of others who had materialised from the surrounding shrubbery, shouted, "Stand back! Stay where you are! Don't move!" and similar bits of advice, all in American accents. A helicopter was landing right in front of us and in next to no time out stepped Jack Kennedy, thirty yards away.

Unsure of the correct protocol required on such an occasion – after all, none of us had ever encountered the president of the United States anywhere, let alone on a damp driveway in the English Midlands – we tried clapping. The feeble noise that the three of us managed seemed to do the trick, however, for the president flashed us his famous smile and said, "Hi guys," or words to that effect. But any opportunities for further conversation were stymied by the arrival of a car. At the wheel was the Duke of Devonshire, who jumped out, swept up the president, and disappeared back up his drive, to Chatsworth.

We followed, on foot, paid our two and sixpences and continued with our visit, marvelling at what had just transpired and gradually realising what it was all about. We knew that Kennedy had been paying a state visit to Ireland at the time and we guessed – rightly as it later turned out – that he had slipped away to visit his sister's grave. She had been married to the Duke's elder brother, the Marquis of Hartington, who had been killed in the war and had herself later died in an accident and been buried beside her husband in the churchyard at Edensor.

Back in London a few days later, I encountered the Duke in the office, doing his day job as minister of state at the Commonwealth Relations Office where, as private secretary to the parliamentary undersecretary, I inhabited part of the adjoining suite of offices.

"Good weekend, Richard?" he asked.

"Wonderful," I said and told him what had happened.

"You silly chump," replied the Duke, "you should have made yourself known. Then you could have joined us for tea and met him properly." And he meant it because that was the way he was – the friendliest and most considerate of men.

Four months later four of us were drinking tea in Ghana after our afternoon swim in the surf at Labadi, the main beach at Accra. I was keeping the residence aired pending the arrival of the new high commissioner, living in the lap of luxury, which I shared nearly every afternoon with Michael Shea and a couple of girls, called Agnes and Mary. Agnes was German and Mary was English. All three were PhD students at Legon University's Institute of African Studies and Michael, later the Queen's press secretary, was a fellow member of the diplomatic service. The BBC World Service was hissing and crackling on short wave in the background.

Suddenly we were all four stunned into silence. Kennedy had been shot. He was dying and very soon it was confirmed that he was dead. Could it really be true? The girls began to cry. Michael and I stared at the floor. We were in our early twenties and the world had become a better place with Kennedy as US president. And now all that was over.

Over forty years after that I queued up at a literary festival to ask the Dowager Duchess of Devonshire to sign her book of letters exchanged with Paddy Leigh Fermor. I explained who I was – that I had recently been in touch with Leigh Fermor about the still unpublished, possibly still unwritten, account of the last part of his famous walk across Europe in the early 1930s, including the whole of the Bulgarian bit, and that I had been in her late husband's ambit in the CRO and coincidentally had witnessed Kennedy's visit to Chatsworth a few months before his death. Although she was rising ninety and must have been tired after addressing a large audience and fielding their questions, she cottoned on without missing a beat.

"Yes, an extraordinary day," she said. "You could almost hear the visitors' jaws dropping when Andrew and I passed them on the stairs with the president in tow."

Chapter 11
Private Secretary

My appointment as private secretary to the CRO's parliamentary undersecretary of state, Bernard Braine MP, took place in the spring of 1962. He was the most junior of the department's three ministers, the other two being the secretary of state, Duncan Sandys and the minister of state, the Duke of Devonshire. For this advancement, my pay went up 23%, from £600 to £740 pa, on the strength of which I bought a newish dark red Mini and moved into a flat in Agincourt Road in Hampstead, which I shared with the Duke's PS, an arrangement that saved both of us money and helped us cover out of hours on-call duty.

I had done nothing to deserve this preferment, other than to tell the CRO's head of establishments that I was bored with doing next to nothing in west and general Africa department and was minded to try my hand at more stimulating employment elsewhere. This was an idle threat, as I had not the faintest idea how to begin to look for another job and I was not foolish enough to swap a secure position, however boring, for the uncertainties of unemployment. But it stirred this mild and kindly man, into action. A few days later, I was installed in a grand outer office on the ministerial floor, without any training or other preparation apart from the six months I had spent sorting Foreign Office Congo telegrams into date and time order. The chap I was taking over from, Brian Gilmore, said not to worry as he was moving only a few yards down the corridor to become Sandys's assistant PS, where he would usually be available to tell me what to do. And besides, Helen would look after me.

Helen was Helen Bateman, the minister's PA and mine. She had seen more PSs come and go than she'd had hot dinners. She had red hair, a powerful cockney accent and a formidable reputation. She thought little of most of the ministers she had served, apart from a certain Lord Alport, whom she had held in high regard and always cited when a wise or suitable precedent was sought.

She looked me up and down, told me to take a seat – my seat from now on – opposite her across two massive facing desks and said I'd better learn how to "go through" right away. 'Going through' meant switching an incoming telephone call through to the minister, with a kind of lever sticking out of the special Private Office telephone. It had to be done smoothly and in perfect sync with whoever was at the other end, usually another PS in another part of Whitehall, but sometimes – alarmingly – an actual minister or some other kind of bigwig who would not take kindly to being cut off. Once I had done a couple of dummy runs to Helen's satisfaction I was a fully trained PS, ready to go. This on-the-spot training had taken about ten minutes. It was also the only training of any kind that I had received up till then at the hands of the CRO.

Fortunately for me, Bernard Braine was an easy-going and forgiving person, though given to short bursts of confected rage when he wanted to get his way in a hurry. He knew that I knew more or less nothing and, like me, he was in awe of Helen, who knew more or less everything. When in doubt, ask Helen. And if she didn't know, she knew who did.

"Ask Colonel Hugo," (the protocol officer).

"Send a minute to Sir Algernon," (Rumbold, the deputy secretary; mandarins had suitably impressive names in those days). Or:

"The Duke'll probably know."

"The *Duke?* We can't ask *him.* He's the minister of state, for heaven's sake, *and* a Duke."

"Why ever not? And if you don't want to, I will." And off she would go to see the Duke who, amid guffaws and laughter, would as predicted provide the answer.

The Duke was a kind and thoughtful man in a number of ways, some of them quite unexpected – at least to me. He had permanent use of a box at the Albert Hall. He was not very interested in music, but he realised that some CRO officials were, so he used to lend the box out whenever there was a good concert. He lent it to me for the London premiere of Britten's War Requiem. This was only the second performance, the first having been at the dedication of the new cathedral in Coventry, but this one was the first at which Britten had managed to get his whole intended cast together. So I sat with a friend, gratis, in the ducal box, to hear Galina Vishnevskaya, Dietrich Fischer-Dieskau and Peter Pears, together with the LSO and assorted choirs, perform that marvellous work, intended as a musical reconciliation between Britain, the Soviet Union and Germany.

Helen's husband was a policeman, a mounted policeman. Every now and again he would hitch his horse to a railing in Downing Street, next to the side door into the CRO where the doorkeeper could keep an eye on it, and come up for a cup of tea by the fire, where we were usually joined by Bernard. The central heating was selective and creaky and many rooms had open fires, kept fuelled and stoked by a small army of ancient men, most of them retired soldiers, who doubled as messengers and doorkeepers. Their boss sat in a stately padded and hooded throne, a kind of giant coquille St-Jacques, just inside the main entrance. He was the principal doorkeeper and just about all the security we had, and in those days Downing Street was an open public thoroughfare. Teatime by our fire was a pleasant social occasion, interrupted only now and again by work.

Once a month the CRO was 'Top' for PQs, Parliamentary Questions, which meant that oral answers had to be prepared, for the questions themselves and for any likely follow-up supplementaries. The secretary of state answered the more eye-catching ones, while the more mundane, and some of the trickier ones which Sandys preferred to avoid, were allocated to the Parly US of S, which was the clumsy abbreviation for Bernard Braine's job. The private secretary had to ensure that the relevant departments drafted the answers and provided some guesses at a range of supplementaries, ready for the minister's red box the evening before the great day. On the morning of the day itself the minister's parliamentary private secretary, or PPS (the bottom rung of the ladder leading to a ministerial position for an ambitious MP), would spend a couple of hours firing possible supplementaries at his boss in a hectic rehearsal. (Once the PPS failed to turn up and I had to stand in for him, not over convincingly.) And then shortly after 2 p.m., we would walk over to the House of Commons (I had a pass, but there was little serious security) where I would join two or three other PSs in the officials' box in a corner up behind the Speaker's Chair.

When it was Bernard Braine's turn to answer I would sometimes have to scribble last-minute notes to be passed down to him and when it was all over I would have to go to the Hansard office to try to ensure that the department's line had survived the cut and thrust of quick-fire debate. This was not always as straightforward a task as it sounds. Once, when he was still very new, Braine's successor said the precise opposite of what he had been briefed to say, on a matter of some constitutional importance to a newly independent Commonwealth country. The permanent undersecretary told me to do my best to persuade the Hansard officials to record what we wanted and not what the minister had said.

At first, they refused. Their job was to record what had actually been said, not what we wished had been said, implying that it was somehow my fault that the minister had not done as he was told. But in the end, they relented and weasel-worded something that more or less passed muster.

Bernard Braine confessed that he was looking forward to a bit of overseas travel and commissioned me to trawl the geographical departments to see if there was anywhere in need of a ministerial visit. This was something that had to be carefully managed, preferably so that it appeared that the minister had to be persuaded to find enough time in his busy schedule to squeeze in a quick visit somewhere. Once the need for a visit had been established, it could gradually turn out that there would, after all, be a little more time available than had originally been envisaged, and on this occasion the scene was soon set for a ten-day 'familiarisation' visit to Cyprus.

Emboldened by this demonstration of ministerial free-loading, I asked Bernard whether he thought it might be possible for him to drop me off in Athens on the way home, so that I could have a little much-needed R and R in my favourite foreign country, without the inconvenience of having to pay my fare. He readily agreed. So, after an agreeable and virtually pointless official visit to a still undivided Cyprus, I spent another ten days bumming my way around northern Greece, visiting monasteries and out of the way villages, in the company of a friend who had good Greek. This was just as well, as mine was merely a mish-mash of what I remembered of my schoolboy classical Greek, updated with a bit of twentieth-century vocabulary and pronunciation.

I managed another of these fare-free holidays when Braine's successor, John Tilney, agreed to drop me off at the end of a coast-to-coast tour of Canada, which was pretty decent of him given that we had found ourselves on the wrong side of the Atlantic just when the Cuban missile crisis reached its peak in 1962. I remember driving into Montreal, with our side of the road more or less empty, while the other side was packed with traffic fleeing imminent urban nuclear Armageddon. I spent the next ten days catching up with the kind people who had looked after me and my sister during the war and by the time my holiday came to an end, the crisis had been defused.

While Tilney was a proper Tory toff, Eton and Oxford, Braine most certainly wasn't. He was a grammar school boy who had had a 'good war' and worked hard, in business and politics, to reach his position in the Conservative Party and the MacMillan government. He was popular in the House of Commons and eventually became its 'Father'. When Tilney succeeded him, as an outcome of what became known as MacMillan's Night of the Long Knives, I was dreading the change, a dread that wasn't lessened when I got into the office good and early for Tilney's first day, only to find him already sitting at his desk, having been there since 7:30. Fortunately, this display of enthusiasm was never repeated. And he proved just as understanding and kind a boss as his predecessor, with the added dimension of greater involvement in his domestic arrangements, as he lived just around the corner, in Victoria Square, whereas Bernard lived in his constituency where London merged into Essex.

Tilney's constituency was Wavertree, in Liverpool, which is where he went most weekends. We had a system whereby his ministerial boxes travelled back and forth by train and when Helen or I opened up the one that had just arrived we usually found that it contained his Dictaphone, complete with an urgent recorded request to go and look for his Mini, which he vaguely remembered having left somewhere near Lady Whatever's house in Mayfair, where he and Guinevere had been for a dinner that had apparently proved a trifle too alcoholic for safe driving home. This was in the days before comprehensive parking restrictions and I had a spare key ready for emergencies of this kind, which cropped up fairly frequently. So off I would go, to search the designated bit of London, in order to return the car to its usual space in Victoria Square. It was also before the breathalyser had come in, so it was to the Tilneys' credit that they didn't try driving home on those occasions.

Often there would also be a request to order flowers to be sent to a hostess from the florists Moyses Stevens. And just occasionally there would be a query or quibble about one of the papers sent up for signing off. This was a rare occurrence, as Tilney was a most amenable minister. And he proved even keener on overseas travel than Braine. We did not go just to Canada. I accompanied him on trips to all the CRO posts in West Africa, to Trinidad (for independence) and, most memorably, to India in 1962, in response to the Chinese incursion into Assam. The secretary of state should have gone, but he had flu and at the last minute, Tilney stepped into the breach, to provide a bit of political leavening to what was otherwise an entirely military delegation, led by the CIGS, field marshal Sir Richard Hull. When we got to Delhi in our VIP RAF Comet we were joined by the US delegation for the next leg of the journey, to Calcutta, as they preferred the luxury of our Comet to the austere furnishings of the USAF troop carrier in which they had flown from Washington. The field marshal discovered that I shared his interest in mountaineering, so we diverted a bit to the left, to get a better view of Everest. Goodness knows whether the Nepali air traffic control were aware of this high-powered incursion into their airspace, or cared, but the Indian liaison officers on board assured us that it didn't matter if they did or didn't.

By the time this show of Anglo-American support for India had materialised hostilities had ceased. But the military went ahead nevertheless with their visit to the front, high up in the Himalayas and even managed an evening in Sikkim, at that time still an independent state, where they were entertained by the Ruler and his American fiancée, Hope Cook. Meanwhile, Tilney held meetings with some of the more excitable British expatriate businessmen in Calcutta at which they discussed scorched earth contingency plans in the event of a full-scale Chinese invasion. The deputy high commissioner (the CRO equivalent of a consul general) was out of town. When he got back and found what had been going on he was not best pleased. I had taken a note at the meetings, which then had to be watered down and generally fudged, as the last thing the British government wished to be seen to be doing was to encourage alarmism. Tilney had jumped the gun, but fortunately for him (and maybe for me too), the DHC was able to retrieve the situation.

At the time of our visit to the CRO's West African posts, the High Commissioner in Accra was a former Labour MP, Sir Geoffrey de Freitas. He had given up his seat at the behest of his (Tory) friend Duncan Sandys, in a practical and ultimately fruitless demonstration of the advantages of bipartisanship, for the edification of Kwame Nkrumah, the Ghanaian president, who was showing signs of dictatorial behaviour by for instance locking up opposition politicians, just six years into independence. Only a few months after this visit I arrived back in Accra for my first posting, as a second secretary, just in time to attend Sir Geoffrey's farewell party before his departure for Nairobi, where he was to enact a similar demonstration for the edification of Jomo Kenyatta. There was a shortage of accommodation, but as there was to be an interregnum before the arrival of the new high commissioner I was told to move into the residence, where I had stayed earlier in the year, to keep it aired as it were – and naturally, I was only too happy to oblige.

When my eighteen-month stint as a private secretary came to an end I still had not received any formal training. By being thrown into the deep end, to work for two very different, but fortunately very kind, junior ministers, I had learned the hard way how Whitehall and Parliament worked. And, as a very considerable added bonus, I had visited eighteen CRO posts, including the one where I was to work, off and on, for the next two and a half years. I had even stayed with the governors of two of our then remaining colonies, Aden (on the way to India) and The Gambia. I was a very lucky new entrant.

Chapter 12
Szamuely

I spent the winter of 1964 – 65 in London, studying economics in an institution which later became the Civil Service College.

When Harold Wilson became prime minister in 1964, he promised the electorate modernisation through the white heat of technology, whatever that might mean, which was probably very little. He also discovered that most of his A-branch civil servants, while no doubt bright enough chaps with a sound background in Latin and Greek and maybe even a bit of history, knew next to nothing about economics, let alone technology of whatever hue or temperature. So it was decreed that, as a start, the younger ones should be put through an intensive course of economics, from which they would derive as much benefit in six months as they would have done in three years if they had studied the subject at university. Junior A-branchers in the Foreign and Commonwealth Services were included in the scheme and I was one of the latter's guinea-pigs. My mid-tour leave would be brought forward, to begin in September 1964, so that I could have three weeks to prepare myself for a six-month stint as a kind of mature student.

The high commission in Accra was deemed to be generously enough staffed to be able to manage without a second secretary for a while, a wholly reasonable assumption from which I was to derive considerable benefit. I had after all been doing next to nothing, other than enjoying myself, living it up in all manner of ways including sailing, drinking, socialising, exploring Ghana's slave castles and all on decent pay, with comfortable accommodation thrown in. I had done a fair amount of travelling in the region and had got to know some interesting people, including Jo and Peggy Appiah in Kumasi. Jo was a politician, who had fallen foul of Nkrumah and consequently spent longish periods under house arrest, watched over by his wife Peggy, the daughter of Sir Stafford Cripps. I still have the antique kudzho pot (an Ashanti funerary urn) that they gave me after the last of the weekends that I spent as their guest. I do not remember doing much in the way of work.

However, things were about to change. Shortly before I was due to go on leave, our kindly old high commission 'SLO' (security liaison officer) was replaced by a slicker, smarter 'political officer', cross-posted straight from the 'action' in the Congo. Ghana, under its Osagyefo (Redeemer) President, Kwame Nkrumah, was reckoned by our masters in London to be heading towards the Soviet camp and it was time for the BHC to focus its political work accordingly. Just when I was about to be whisked away I suddenly found that I had more, and more challenging, work to do. The new political officer was encouraging me to get to know more about young Ghanaians, especially educated, politically motivated, ones, at Legon University and above all at the secretive Kwame Nkrumah Ideological Institute along the coast at Winneba.

Legon was easy enough. It was completely open, with masses of expatriate staff and students, including my diplomatic service colleague Michael Shea, who was doing a PhD on African trade unions. Through him, I already knew plenty of people there and could visit as often as I liked, without arousing any attention. But Winneba was different. It was surrounded by a barbed-wire fence, with just one entrance, across which was a barrier manned by guards who were said not to be over-friendly.

Winneba was a half-hour drive to the west, near an attractive beach. I parked my car at a discreet distance, hoping that the guards would not notice the CD number plates and strolled up with as much nonchalance as I could muster and explained that I had been invited to a lecture on *Consciencism*, Nkrumah's newly invented ideology. To my relief, they accepted this fabrication and let me in, whereupon I had to find a lecture hall – any would do, provided it was in use – and slip in, preferably unnoticed, an optimistic aim given that I was white and everyone else was black.

I must have looked lost, because someone asked if he could help – a fellow European, with just the faintest trace of a foreign accent and therefore, as he was almost certainly a communist, necessitating extra vigilance on my part. He led me into a lecture hall, sat next to me and then, when the lecture was over, asked me who I was. There seemed to be nothing to be gained from outright dissimulation, so I explained that I was a junior official in the British high commission, doing my best to learn about the new Ghana. This bit of disingenuousness amused him. If that was the case, why not come again, perhaps for tea? This was an alarming prospect; did he wish to brainwash me? Presumably, he didn't intend to kidnap me, or he would have done so straight away. I said that would be lovely and could I bring a friend or two? (Safety in numbers.) Certainly. The more the merrier. We exchanged names and telephone numbers. He explained that he was a Hungarian academic on secondment and that he and his wife would enjoy some more normal socialising than they had so far experienced at the Ideological Institute.

When I reported back to the new political officer, now officially known as the counsellor external affairs, I confessed that I hadn't got to know any of the students, but that I had been invited to tea by one of the academic staff, a Hungarian called Tibor Szamuely. Should I go ahead, or was this a sting, leading to the sort of potential compromise which I had been strongly advised during my pre-posting briefing to avoid? "Go ahead," said the counsellor. "And if he shows any sign of wanting to come and meet any of us here, don't discourage him."

I took Michael and his fellow Legon PhD students, Agnes and Mary, along to the tea party. We all got on well with the Szamuelys and their two children and just before it was time to leave Tibor steered me into the kitchen to tell me, out of hearing of the others, that he was planning to attend a conference in London and would need a UK visa. Maybe I could put him in touch with the right chap in the high commission? I passed this request on to my counsellor colleague, who from then on took control of all contact with Tibor, whom I did not see again till some months later, when I had embarked on my economics course in London. By then he and his family had been granted political asylum and were living in Reading.

And what a tale he had to tell. He had been to school in England, first at Bertrand Russell's establishment in Hampshire – the one at which the front door had been opened to the local vicar, who was attempting a pastoral visit, by a stark naked child who, when the startled chap exclaimed "Good God", replied that there was no such thing as God, before shutting the door in the cleric's face – and later at the famously progressive Summerhill School in Suffolk. Hence the near-perfect English. He had spent time as a political prisoner. On release, he had been permitted to become an academic at Budapest University, where he had been at the time of the 1956 uprising, in which his passivity had later been rewarded by his appointment as vice-rector. In his now accepted guise as a regime trusty, he was in due course offered the Winneba job, which he accepted on the condition that he could take his wife and children, a gamble that, to his surprised delight, paid off. He had insisted that he would need his collection of academic books if he was to do a proper job and was permitted to ship them to a holding address in Ghana pending his arrival at Winneba. At last, by arrangement with our political counsellor, the entire family – and the books, which had never left the holding address – were whisked to London and eventually to Reading, where Tibor was taken on as a lecturer at the university and his wife worked on OUP's new Russian dictionary.

Tibor assured me that he had planned and carried out this whole episode, beginning with his conspicuous failure to join in on the 1956 uprising, as his only feasible means of escaping to the West with his family and the tools of his trade (the core of his library) intact – however long it might take, which in the event was eight years. He had assumed – almost certainly correctly – that he was under surveillance by the Hungarian and Soviet embassies in Accra, which meant that his meetings with our political counsellor had to take place in secret. This explained why I had never set eyes on him again in Ghana once I had put the two of them in touch.

And the rest, as they say, is history. Tibor soon became well-known, for his scholarly writing, broadcasting and journalism. The family were granted British citizenship. But alas he died all too soon, in 1972, aged only 47.

Chapter 13
Mariage à la Mode

I returned to Accra in April 1965. Michael Shea had left Legon and returned to London, to a desk job in the CRO's West Africa Department. His two Legon friends, Agnes and Mary, had also left. Fortunately my friends Helen and Rosie Odamtten were still around, but their brother Solomon and brother-in-law Francis Nkrumah, the president's 'love-son', had also gone abroad, in pursuit of their medical studies. My social circle was much reduced.

I had arrived back just in time for Anzac Day and I had been invited to the Australian high commissioner's reception. I joined a gaggle of blokes on the far side of the stoep, as I had recognised some of them. They were the usual Saturday night crowd from Shell, the Crown Agents, Cable and Wireless and so on. The focus of their attention was a girl, fair-haired, smiley, pretty, giving as conversationally good as she got, backed up against the stoep's balustrade. I had never seen her before, which I soon learned was unsurprising, as she had been in Accra only a couple of days. She was the newest member of the Australian high commission staff and her name was Catherine Hayes.

We arranged to meet again and I took my leave, explaining – and I hope that this is apocryphal – that I had to rush as I had three or four other parties to get to. Even if it was not apocryphal it was certainly untrue. If it was intended as self-promotion, it failed to impress Catherine. Nevertheless, we did meet again, more than once, more and more often and for longer and longer.

Early in December 1965 Ian Smith, the prime minister of Southern Rhodesia (later Zimbabwe), then still a British colony and a very tiresome one at that, announced that he and 'his' country had declared themselves independent, a decision that came to be known as 'UDI', standing for Unilateral Declaration of Independence. A number of African countries registered their displeasure by breaking diplomatic relations with the UK. Among them was Ghana.

When relations are broken the head of mission and most of the staff are given a few days to leave, after which they will each be regarded as *persona non grata,* or PNG. Arrangements can be agreed to exempt some of them by attaching them to another mission as members of an Interests Section, but PNG'd people are not permitted to remain in or re-enter the host state. About a third of the staff of the British high commission was to be transferred in this way to the British interests section of the Australian high commission, as Australia had been accepted by Ghana as the protecting power. But I was not one of them and at first, it looked as though I would be shipped home in the next few days, along with the high commissioner and everyone else who had been PNG'd.

Ghanaians are famously genial people and Jimmy Aggrey-Orleans announced that there was no need for us to rush, as no doubt we'd all like to stay on over Christmas when, he knew, a number of parties were planned. Jimmy was the chief of protocol in the Ministry of External Affairs and therefore the official charged with the implementation of the break in relations. He had been invited to many of these parties, for he was much liked by the diplomatic community. Then a few days later he announced that, since we were going to stay on for Christmas, we might as well stay on into the New Year, so as to be able to go to all the other parties that he knew had been planned. So Catherine and I had plenty of time to get our affairs in order.

By this time we were what would nowadays be termed an item. We spent most of our free time together, though not as many nights as we would have liked, for this was the mid-Sixties and times were not as permissive as they now are, particularly for diplomats in a foreign posting. We had been in this state for over six months and neither of us was looking forward to the impending separation, in which Catherine, as an Australian, would remain in Accra helping to protect British interests, while I would be back in London, not eligible for any kind of Australian protection. Naturally, we had both had other relationships before we met, but this was the one that had really stuck. We spent what started as a miserable evening trying to face up to our predicament, but by the end of it, our gloom had been replaced by something quite different, for we had decided to get married. Just quite how this would be accomplished we left till later – maybe the next day when our heads would be clearer. What mattered now was that there was no longer any question of being parted.

Having come to this important conclusion I returned to my flat in another part of Accra where, as possibly misconstruable luck would have it, I was putting up a couple of English girls, VSO teachers from the sticks visiting the great smoke for a couple of nights' R and R. Fortunately they were due to leave the next morning, a work day, when Catherine was to come to lunch.

Some days earlier I had invited a Ghanaian contact for a business lunch *a deux*. I could not put him off. So when Catherine arrived and found me doing my best to be agreeable to an unknown third party she almost turned around and left, assuming either that I had turned out after all to be an s-h-one-t or that she had dreamed the night-before's proceedings. But something unusual caught her eye; Anthony, my steward, had included wine glasses in the three place settings, which suggested, just possibly, that something rather more festive than a routine business lunch was planned. And so it proved when we sat down and I asked my official guest Francis to be the first to drink to our health, as Catherine and I were now engaged.

There then ensued a period of hectic and fairly bibulous activity. Catherine was well supplied with Great Western (Australian) champagne – this was before the days when the French laid exclusive rights to this denomination – Jimmy had arranged a stay of execution, the weather and beaches were just what the doctor ordered and I had not yet managed to sell my Ford Cortina, so we still had a means of transport. Catherine's boss, who in those unemancipated days was *in loco parentis,* had no personal objections to our plans and plied us with more champagne, but warned us that he might have a hard time persuading Canberra to waive the costs of what would now prove in their bureaucratic eyes an aborted posting. At the worst, Catherine would have to refund the cost of her first class Sydney-Accra airfare, a mere two years' salary or so. But in the end, human-kindness prevailed and Canberra's only demand was that their blessings should be heaped upon us.

Then we had to deal with London. They were rather less accommodating. They ruled that, unless we had managed to become a married couple in time for my return to the UK, they would be unable to pay Catherine's fare. But, in order to give us a bit more time, they also ruled that I would be cross-posted to the embassy in next-door Togo to cover a leave absence for a few weeks. And my boss, the British high commissioner, who had not yet left, happily gave us his blessing. For, again in those unemancipated days, a member of HM Diplomatic Service had to have permission to get married, permission that would generally be refused unless the officer's intended was British or at least from a Commonwealth country.

My mother had just been appointed curator of the Ellen Terry museum at Smallhythe Place near Tenterden in Kent, a small National Trust property with which she and my father had long had links. This appointment carried with it a tied cottage, which would leave my parents free to sell their house in the nearby village of Wittersham, about seventy miles from London. After remarkably little thought or discussion, Catherine and I decided that this was too good an opportunity to miss, so I sent a telegram which read: *'HAVE BEEN PNG'D STOP AM ENGAGED BE MARRIED STOP WISH BUY YOUR HOUSE STOP LETTER FOLLOWS STOP RICHARD.'* In due course, we became the owners of Queens Head Cottage. This impulsive purchase set the pattern of our lives for many years to come, with a lonely rural existence for Catherine and an absurdly long and costly commute for me during our periods of home postings. Most of our friends and colleagues chose to live in London. Sensible people.

Straight after Christmas, I was transferred to the embassy in Lomé, barely a hundred miles from Accra, but with hopeless communications reflecting the former colonial allegiances of Ghana (ex-Gold Coast) and Togo. All telecommunications were routed via Paris and London, priced accordingly. The border crossing functioned only intermittently. British United Airways, which ran an efficient and relatively inexpensive milk-run service along the coast of West Africa, ignored most of the francophone towns, including Lomé Air Afrique, its French-owned equivalent, was almost equally uninterested in anglophone stopping points. It did, however, run a weekly service between Accra and Lomé – on Thursdays, both ways. Catherine used it twice, one way only, from Accra to Lomé. She had to return on Sunday in an overcrowded shared taxi, with a long wait at the ferry crossing over the Volta River.

When I left Accra, we had still not managed to make any wedding arrangements, but assumed that I would be able to organise a consular marriage in Lomé Just in case this proved impossible and I wanted to return to Accra, Jimmy Aggrey-Orleans provided me with an impressive-looking document, complete with a seal and an embossed letterhead, which read something like: 'The bearer of this document, Mr Richard Thomas, formerly second secretary at the British high commission, Accra, is *persona non grata* in the Republic of Ghana, but may enter and leave the Republic as often as he wishes.' I treasured this amazing piece of paper for many years.

The embassy in Lomé was tiny, barely more than a mini-mission, with a total UK-based staff of five. It was headed by a friendly counsellor grade ambassador called Bill Wilson, who lived with his wife Monica in a pleasantly shambolic flat (the 'Residence'), above the chancery offices, in an undistinguished concrete villa a few hundred yards from the Ghana border. The atmosphere of the whole set-up was one of cheerful improvisation, resembling something in a film version of a Graham Greene novel. It was very different from the soul-less modernity and bureaucracy of the high commission in Accra. Office hours were flexible, as were office methods. There was no machine cipher, so all classified material had to be enciphered or deciphered (unbuttoned in Bill's expression) manually, using one-time pads. Enciphering presented few problems, as Bill reckoned that very little that happened or was worth reporting in Lomé needed to be classified and could, therefore, be sent *en clair* (once a day, from a telex machine in the Post Office). It was the incoming stuff that was the trouble – yards and yards of ticker tape printed with nothing but groups of numbers, all of which had to be unbuttoned. This material consisted mostly of repeats of telegrams from the Foreign Office and from other FO and CRO posts in Africa, all of which were bigger than the embassy in Lomé and were therefore equipped with machine cipher. These missives were invariably repeated all African posts, or given UDI distribution and there were plenty of them as UDI and its consequences were very much still current. Bill reckoned that the only moderately civilised way of coping with this deluge of ciphered bumf was for a couple of us to take it down to the beach with that day's one-time pad, find a reasonably secluded bit of shade under a palm tree and settle down to a couple of hours' grind before being relieved by the next pair. One of us read out the cipher groups and the other worked them out with the help of the one-time pad. Everyone took their turn, including Monica. The FO's Security Department would have had a fit if they had known what we were up to. But they didn't and the world didn't come to an end.

Ninety-five per cent of what we read need never have been classified. I remember one seemingly interminable telegram from the hugely grand ambassador in Addis Ababa, Sir John Russell, which began, 'As I was lying in my bath this morning, I thought, given that what promised to be a beautiful day was dawning in the African sky, I would, once I had completed my morning ride, seek an audience of my old friend the emperor – a wise old bird if ever there was one – and chew the fat with him about what was to be done about…' and on and on and on in this vein, or something like it – all in cipher. We never discovered what the wise old bird might have advised should be done about whatever it was that had crossed Sir John's mind while he wallowed in his bath, for it was this missive, or maybe one very like it – and there were plenty to choose from – that prompted Bill to declare that enough was enough. He scooped up yards and yards of undeciphered tape, shoved it into a diplomatic bag with a covering note to the department in London suggesting that if there was anything in this garbage worth deciphering perhaps they would do it for us and send it back *en clair* in the return bag. And we never heard another word.

Bill and Monica did their best to help us get married. Many an evening was spent ploughing through Foreign Service Regulations and when that great tome proved unhelpful, Consular Regulations. But each time it seemed that we had at last mastered the complexities of a consular marriage, helped along our way by a soothing flow of beer or whisky and gradually increasing fits of the giggles, we would come up against a barrier. The banns had to be displayed for six weeks (but we didn't have six weeks), or they had to be nailed up (but the embassy was made of impenetrable concrete), or they had to be somewhere where the entire British community would be able to read them (but there was no British community) and so on. More seriously, even consular marriages had to abide by local law and Togolese law demanded a number of intrusive and possibly dangerous premarital health tests, tests which also ruled out a Togolese civil ceremony as far as Catherine and I were concerned.

So we eventually plumped for a special licence in Ghana, relying on Jimmy Aggrey-Orleans' magical document to permit me, still PNG'd, to re-enter the country – which it did. We were to be married at 11 am on Saturday 12 February 1966 at the Black Star Square register office, a wooden shack leftover from colonial times, only yards from the ceremonial heart of the New Africa and next to the stadium where Kwame Nkrumah held his military parades and political rallies. Our tickets for the voyage 'home' to Liverpool (Catherine had never been to England) on 16 February had been purchased and our luggage had been despatched. Catherine was to stay with her boss, the Australian high commissioner John Ryan and his wife Patsy, while I was to spend my last night as a bachelor with his deputy and my best man and witness, John Trotter. Catherine's fellow PA, Claire Savage, would attend as bridesmaid and witness.

At about 10 a.m. on the day of the wedding, the registrar rang the Ryans to explain that Nkrumah had ordered a political rally that morning, to start at 11 am next door to his office in the Black Star stadium. As a public servant, he would have to attend. So the wedding as far as he was concerned was off. John Ryan somehow managed to persuade him that he would not lose his job if he stuck to his post and conducted a wedding for which authority had been given at the highest level (a fabrication) and that as a mark of the Australian government's esteem he would be an honoured guest at the reception immediately following the ceremony. The registrar said he would see what he could do, but could not make any promises.

This unsettling news was relayed to John Trotter and me, together with instructions to await the arrival of the high commissioner's official Buick, which would, contrary to all diplomatic custom, be flying his flag – something that officially could happen only if he were present. Catherine and Claire would be in the car and we should join them and to hell with traditional nonsense about not seeing the bride before the wedding. Catherine ('Cathy' to John Ryan) had been told that she was to fly the flag to ensure safe passage through the milling, pre-Party rally hordes. She had also been told to "wear the bloody ring" (made for us out of smuggled Ghanaian gold by a slightly dodgy Lebanese chap who specialised mainly in money laundering) even if she hadn't managed to get married, as John and Patsy had laid on a massive party and they didn't want to disappoint their guests.

The Buick appeared and duly conveyed the four of us to the register office, weaving its way through dutiful Party activists heading to what would turn out to be Nkrumah's last rally. The registrar was there and a photographer recorded parts of the brief ceremony. Claire was barefoot, having forgotten where she'd left her shoes in the previous night's alcoholic haze, and I was immortalised studying my watch, but we did get married and have a piece of paper to say so. The Ryans' party went with a swing and was immediately followed by another one, given by the head of the British interests section, the Board of Trade counsellor Solly Gross. This was a wedding breakfast, with speeches, led by no less than the chief of protocol, Jimmy Aggrey-Orleans. So the chap who had thrown me out of Ghana, where I was still officially *persona non grata,* played the traditional wedding part of uncle or godfather. A year or so later Jimmy stood us to lunch in a restaurant in Paris, when the three of us had a good giggle about what had surely been an almost surreal occasion.

After Catherine had changed out of her – very attractive – cream silk wedding outfit and I had done my best to sober up, we set off in a borrowed VW Beetle for somewhere promisingly called the Nyanabah Beach Pleasure Resort, a hundred miles to the west of Accra, where we had arranged to spend three nights before setting sail for Liverpool on the Elder Dempster ship *Accra*. Five miles out of Accra we were stopped by the police as I was driving on the wrong side of the road, under the impression perhaps that I was back in Togo where they drove on the right. I was also roaring drunk, but when we explained that we had just got married the policemen slapped me on the back and said that in that case I was forgiven. They did, however, suggest that I should go a bit more carefully and somehow we got to our thatched beach hut by the sea for our brief tropical honeymoon.

Five days later, by now cocooned in the ancient bowels of the *Accra*, we heard that Nkrumah had been overthrown and that diplomatic relations with Britain had been restored. Most of the high commission staff returned to post. But not us. We had left for good and a few days after arriving in England I was told that our next posting was to be to Paris, where I would be a member of the UK delegation to NATO – not bad as honeymoon postings go.

Chapter 14
NATO and Home Again

The news of the Paris posting was relayed over the phone to me by someone in the personnel operations department of the newly amalgamated FCO called Anne Warburton (later Dame Anne, the UK's first woman ambassador). This person seemed surprised that I was only dimly aware that the North Atlantic Council, to which I was to be accredited as a second secretary, was part of NATO, its governing body in fact, and that it was based in Paris. No doubt, poor Anne sighed deeply – why did the FO have to accept all these ignoramuses from the CRO and even send them off to what had hitherto been their own plum FO postings, all in the name of integration? – but she managed to conceal her exasperation. Instead, after going through all my official instructions, she said that we were to be sure not to miss out on weekends at her favourite hotel, the Gargantua at Chinon, advice that we followed enthusiastically and enjoyably over the ensuing months.

We inherited a flat near the Porte de St Cloud, between the Stade de Coubertin and the Renault factory. Since our block was in Boulogne-Billancourt, by a couple of metres and not the Seizième, it had been built a little taller than the permitted Parisian norm. We were at the top, so we could see over the whole of Paris, with the Eiffel Tower in the middle distance. In a small street at the back lay Chez Carmen, a friendly workmen's café, much patronised by the carmakers from across the road, where we ate well for next to nothing and were eventually admitted to the select band of customers who were allotted their own bespoke pigeon-hole for their table napkin. And we were only a couple of hundred metres from the Porte de St Cloud market, with its dozens of stalls laden with fresh produce of every kind. That was also where the Metro station was, together with the bus stop where I caught the PC (Petite Ceinture) bus which took me straight to the Porte Dauphine, dominated by the huge A-shaped building which was the seat of the North Atlantic Council, aka NATO. (Its A-ness was discernible only from above, presumably for the benefit of Soviet bomber pilots, according to the *Canard Enchaîné*.) The PC also took us past the Château d'Auteuil, the headquarters of the Organisation for Economic Cooperation and Development, in the basement of which diplomats from OECD member countries could buy duty-free champagne, a perk that we made ready use of – though generally with the car, which was better than the PC for the transport of bulky provender.

With the flat, we had also inherited from my predecessor a certain Mme Rigaud, as cleaning lady, counsellor, adviser and friend. She told us where to get the best meat, what to do when the electricity fizzled out, how to cook some of her favourite dishes and even when the time was drawing near for our departure, had us to dinner in her own house. We also inherited Mme de Wardener, our very grand landlady – though not too grand to insist on being paid in cash.

Our time in Paris coincided with de Gaulle's disenchantment with NATO, which took the form of France's withdrawal from the Alliance's integrated military structures and the expulsion from its Fontainebleau home of Supreme Headquarters Allied Powers Europe. While SHAPE was hurriedly reinstating itself in Mons in Belgium the French insisted that they had no objection to the continued presence in Paris of the (civilian) North Atlantic Council. But this didn't wash with the other fourteen members of the Alliance; if their military colleagues were no longer welcome they would leave too. The only question was where.

There was a strong preference for London on the part of almost everyone working in the Porte Dauphine building. The exceptions were the French, who affected lofty disdain, and ourselves, the UK delegation, who had no desire to have to work from home and lose our overseas allowances. And as it happened it was difficult to see how two or three thousand foreign diplomats – international staff and national delegations – could be shoe-horned into London. There was only one remotely suitable building with vacant possession, the Euston Tower, and it was probably too small and inconveniently sited from a security point of view. So attention began to be focussed on Belgium where, after all, SHAPE had already found refuge.

George Brown, the FCO's secretary of state known for sometimes 'suffering from fatigue and emotion', was definitely in favour of Brussels, as he pointed out in more than one forceful intervention in favour of the 'Tour d'Amour', as he termed it, an empty skyscraper in the centre of the city actually called the Tour de Namur. So that he should not become too tired and emotional before one of those many ministerial meetings began, I was tasked by our permanent representative, Sir Evelyn Shuckbrugh, to keep him occupied in any legitimate way that would keep him out of the building's bars, for something like two hours. This struck me as a formidable task, given that I was a mere second secretary and he, my boss of bosses, a full-blown secretary of state, with a well-known penchant for a drink at any time of day. The Porte Dauphine building was full of bars, but somehow I managed to get him to admire something else in the opposite direction whenever we passed one, and even succeeded in steering him into the barber's shop for a haircut, followed by a (complimentary) cup of coffee.

The NAC agreed in 1966 to move to Brussels. The Belgians offered a disused military airfield at Heysel, on the way out to the airport, and the 'relocation committee', on which I was the British member, had its work cut out to ensure that a building would be ready for occupation by the autumn of the following year. The eventual result was an enormous three-storey prefab, with spines radiating from a central block. National delegations and international departments were accommodated in wings jutting out from the spines. Plumbing and drainage ran along each of the spines and ten metres or so into each of the wings, to allow for washrooms, canteens and so on. But this arrangement wasn't good enough for the UK delegation, which would need plumbing right out to the far end of its wing since all British heads of mission were entitled to their own private loo, en suite with their offices, which in this case had to be at the extreme end of the wing, as far away as possible from the hoi polloi in the spine and the lowlier, more communal, parts of UKDel territory. None of the other delegations insisted on such a refinement, soon dubbed the British Clochemerle, and I was left with the unenviable task of defending this ridiculous requirement in the relocation committee. But it was achieved and Sir Bernard Burrows, who by now had succeeded Evelyn Shuckbrugh, moved into his brand-new office, complete with private facilities, in October 1967.

The new building was intended to be temporary, with a maximum life of ten years, during which a more grandiose, permanent headquarters was to be built on the other side of the city, next to the Atomium. But it lasted till early in 2018, enlarged and titivated, but at heart the same gargantuan prefab that a bunch of second secretaries on the relocation committee had commissioned half a century ago. Only now has it been replaced, by a new building nowhere near the Atomium.

NATO, including most of UKDel, moved to Brussels in the first week of that October, but we were left behind in Paris, as Catherine was due to give birth any day. Phoebe arrived on 8 October, in the splendour of the Château de Belvedère maternity home, once the property of Empress Josephine, around the corner from us in Boulogne, which is where her obstetrician insisted Catherine should *accouche.* Our recently recruited Danish au pair was hugely impressed by Catherine's evident celebrity status, judging from the hordes of press photographers and heaps of flowers in the corridor outside her room, only to learn that the object of all the attention was Sacha Distel's wife in the next room. But from then on she sought every opportunity to visit her new boss, in the hope of catching sight of the great man himself. She never did, poor girl.

Phoebe's arrival coincided with the *Prix de l'Arc de Triomphe,* France's greatest horse race. Pierre Vellay, Catherine's obstetrician and France's leading natural childbirth guru, only just made it on time to the delivery room, as he had been watching one of his horses win the race. By the time he arrived, I was already intoning '*un, deux, trois, poussez*', as instructed in a dozen ante-natal classes, under the supervision of the *monitrice.* (I thought it would be friendlier and more spouse-like, to say *pousse*, but we had been taught to stick to the formal mode of address.) Once Phoebe had been safely delivered and somewhat callously dumped on the scales where she snuffled and gurgled politely, Dr Vellay and I celebrated both the birth and his horse's triumph with the whisky that he had earlier suggested I might care to provide. An exhausted Catherine asked for a cup of tea, to the near consternation of the *monitrice* and her nurse assistant, as tea-making equipment was not part of a French delivery room's equipment. Their improvisation skills were put to the test, but they soon managed to brew up an acceptable cuppa in the steriliser, with a tea bag that I had brought along with the whisky. And the next day, I managed to persuade the *Mairie* that Phoebe was a suitable name for our first-born, but only provided that she was also furnished with a pukka saint's name, which I was allowed to select from an enormous tome. I chose Elizabeth on the spur of the moment (my sister's name). So much for French secularity.

Catherine remained in the Château de Belvedère for several days, in the greatest luxury, feasting on dainty delicacies like quail breasts, receiving visitors and attending to Phoebe, who was wrapped in mediaeval-looking swaddling clothes. One of the visitors was an astonished Lois Burrows, the day before she left for Brussels.

"Things must be looking up for the wives of second secretaries," she said. "I had my first baby in an Egyptian shack, when Bernard was a second secretary in Cairo."

We moved to Brussels when Phoebe was ten days old, accommodated in a carrycot on the back seat of the car, unsecured by any of the safety apparatus that has since become mandatory. We had been allocated a respectable semi in Woluwe-St-Pierre, furnished by the Ministry of Works in a manner deemed suitable for a second secretary. Not long after we had arrived, Catherine was called on by a MoW functionary bearing a gift, a tea trolley. When she explained that she neither wanted nor had space for a tea trolley, the functionary seemed hurt, as what he was offering her was something to which only first secretaries and above were entitled and she should be flattered by the acquisition of so magnificent a status symbol. She accepted it.

The new NATO HQ was not well served by public transport, which meant that I had to get there by car. Catherine had not passed her driving test, but as the Belgians didn't believe in such bureaucratic nonsenses this would not prevent her from using a car of her own. We bought a fourth hand ramshackle two-stroke contraption called a DKW – closely resembling but apparently no relation of the East German Trabant – which sat in the road outside our house for the next ten months, used only now and again, in clouds of blue smoke, by our guests, but never by Catherine. But then came the Warsaw Pact invasion of Czechoslovakia, one of the less important results of which was that I had to go into work at about 5 a.m. on 21 August 1968 and did not return home till nearly midnight – when I noticed that the DKW must have moved, as it was no longer in its accustomed position facing downhill. Bored by my seemingly interminable absence, Catherine had driven her car around the block – and from then on never looked back.

Astonishingly, the invasion had caught NATO on the hop. Most of the more senior people were on their summer break, including Bernard Burrows and most of UKDel, leaving the minister, Fred Warner, in charge, with only me from the teeth staff to help. The other delegations were in similar holiday mode, as were the international staff, including the secretary-general, Manlio Brosio. So it was the second eleven which manned the Council, drafted resolutions and Alliance statements, took instructions from governments and reported back, during a long and frenetic day. And that was the day when I suddenly acquired the confidence to become a moderately useful diplomat. Fred galvanised me into action, dividing the work between us, cajoling, steering and now and again congratulating me, forcing me to believe in myself and have the guts to forward my own views, even if they conflicted with those of my superiors, and above all to share his enthusiasm.

By the time my posting came to an end, in May 1969, I was a first secretary. I had attended the Alliance's 20th anniversary meeting in Washington and we had made a number of good friends, in other delegations as well as our own and in the international staff. And Catherine was pregnant, too much so to be able to exercise her newly honed driving skills for the journey home. So friends from the international staff, Peter and Vera Pooley, drove the Ford Taunus – which had succeeded the smoky DKW – while Catherine, Phoebe and I followed in the Austin 1800. Our two cars constituted 67% of the cargo of the Silver City Bristol freighter which whisked us from Le Touquet to Lydd in about fifteen minutes flat. Crossing the Channel was quicker and easier in those days.

Alexander was born on 2 July, in a modest country nursing home outside Tenterden. His arrival was supervised by a midwife, with our GP on call if required (he wasn't) and with me once again chanting '*un, deux, trois, poussez*', to the surprise and confusion of the midwife who, assuming that Catherine was married to some sort of foreign doctor, kitted me out accordingly in an important-looking white outfit. And then it was baked beans on toast, not quail breasts.

Two or three weeks after Alexander's arrival Dame Sybil Thorndike was staying with my parents down the road at Smallhythe, where she was due to appear in the Barn Theatre. She was alarmed to learn that they did not have a television (they were cultural snobs and affected to disdain such vulgar fripperies), as she wished to watch the moon landing. It was arranged that she should spend half the night with us, as we were moderately up-to-date and had a TV set. This, however, was located in the sitting room, which was at the very top of our strange little house, in a kind of attic, approached by a near-vertical ladder-like staircase. Dame Sybil was going on for 87, but she assured us that she was quite used to going up and down ladders and she was glued to the screen for hours, while we kept her fed and watered and Alexander bellowed his objections just below.

I was assigned to the trade relations department, which was housed, along with the FCO's other economic departments, in the Treasury, on the other side of Great George Street, in rooms overlooking St James's Park. I was desk officer for a mixed bag of international economic organisations, including the OECD in Paris, the UN Economic Commission for Europe (ECE) in Geneva and the shadowy Coordinating Committee (COCOM), also in Paris, which policed the West's strategic embargo against the communist world. All three involved a certain amount of travel, both to meetings at their headquarters and also to bilaterals elsewhere, including Washington and Prague – the latter because we were paired with the Czechs in the ECE, in a practical demonstration of UN-sponsored East-West cooperation.

The COCOM job was the most fun. The organisation's members (NATO plus Japan) were outwardly one hundred per cent committed to maintaining a rigid embargo, but each was equally intent on outwitting the others in a perpetual game of gaining exemptions for their own manufacturers, at the expense of their commercial rivals in other member countries. During my time in TPD, we won two great victories: Trident passenger jets for China (at the expense of the USA's Boeing 727s) and ICL 1906 computers for the USSR's Serpukhov research centre (at IBM's expense).

COCOM issues sometimes had to be resolved at the highest level and most of the more important submissions had to go up to Number Ten, bypassing a few intermediate steps on the way. Once, when I was working late, alone in the department and getting ready to make a dash for the train home, the phone rang. Should I answer and risk missing the train? It could be Catherine, hit by some kind of crisis. I picked up the receiver, to be told by a Number Ten private secretary that the prime minister couldn't quite follow something I had submitted about Serpukhov. I did my best to elucidate, but the PS said it would be easier all round if I explained the point directly to the PM and I found myself talking to Ted Heath. He was friendly, easy to talk to, grateful for my help and apologetic for keeping me after hours – not at all the disobliging grump of general repute.

A couple of years after Alexander's arrival and a year after we had moved away from the impractical cottage in Wittersham, a third child was on the way. The run-up to her arrival was far from straightforward and deserves a chapter of its own.

Chapter 15
A Near Thing

In May 1971, I was given three weeks' convalescence leave after a minor operation. Catherine was seven months pregnant, but in robust health, and there was clearly no longer anything the matter with me. We couldn't believe our luck.

Friends of ours owned a cottage at Glenelg on the coast facing Skye – the one, as it happened, where I had been staying with my parents ten years earlier when I learned that I had passed the civil service exam. We made enquiries. Was it available? Indeed, it was, for two weeks, starting in a couple of days' time. We were off like a shot.

We were blessed with good weather. Phoebe and Alexander played on the beach and made friends with the local children. The sun went on shining many hours after they had been put to bed and we longed to be able to escape for an evening walk, but we knew no-one whom we could ask to babysit. Then one day we met another couple in precisely the same predicament and we arranged to take it in turns to babysit for each other. We were released that very evening.

We decided to explore Sandaig, the Camusfearna of Gavin Maxwell's book Ring of Bright Water about the years when he lived in a cottage on a lonely beach a few miles south of Glenelg, at times with only his tame otters for company. He had died a couple of years earlier, not long after his beloved cottage had burnt down. But the ruins would still be there and we were assured that the old jeep track down to it from the road was still walkable, though certainly no longer drivable.

We parked the car and started down the mile-long track. After about half an hour's rough downhill walking we reached all that was left of Camusfearna, which sure enough proved to be right on the beach. It was a beautiful evening, still and warm, with the sun lighting up the westward-facing hillside and shoreline. We explored the sad little ruin, found the waterfall that had served as

Maxwell's shower, saw some seals but no otters and then, after an hour at the bottom of the hill, reckoned that it was time to start the climb back up to the road, five hundred feet above us. We reckoned it would take us at least an hour to scramble back to the top, as the path was very overgrown and quite steep in places, not really suitable terrain for someone in Catherine's state.

Halfway up, Catherine stopped, hesitated and then sat down.

"I think I'm having contractions."

Surely not? She was not due for another couple of months. But if the baby had really decided to come now, we were in serious trouble. We were still two or three hundred feet below the road, half a mile down a steep rough track. It was late in the evening. There wouldn't be any passing traffic, as all the road did was to lead five or six miles around a high headland to Kinloch Hourn, where it came to an end by a couple of cottages, whose inhabitants would by now be ready for bed. We would have to drive back towards Glenelg to reach any kind of help.

Catherine stood up. "It's stopped. Probably just a bad stitch. Come on." Brave words. Not very convincing however, and a few minutes later she sat down again. There was no doubt about it. She was at the start of labour, two months early, on an exposed mountainside, miles from anywhere, with no-one to help apart from her husband, who was trying to appear calm, even resourceful – but with nothing at all to be resourceful with. I suggested that she should make herself as comfortable as possible and stay put, with my pullover and maybe also my shirt, for a bit of extra warmth, while I headed back to Glenelg as fast as I could to fetch help.

But no. Understandably, she had no wish to be abandoned, all by herself, on a lonely mountain path gone ten o'clock in the evening. The light was beginning to fade and it would soon be dark. She would keep going, between contractions. She was sure she would be all right if only we could get back to the car. And somehow we did, with me in a near panic, encouraged by my amazingly calm and tough wife to keep going.

By great good fortune, Glenelg had a doctor, the only place for miles around to have one, and I hammered on his door shortly before midnight. It was now almost dark and Dr Dunlop and his family were all fast asleep. But within minutes he had taken over, helping me get Catherine into bed, where he gave her an injection that stopped the contractions in their tracks. Our new babysitting friends, bewildered and alarmed, were quickly reassured and between us, we disentangled the two families and got everyone back to their own beds.

Catherine would have to stay in bed, said Dr Dunlop, for a number of days, after which she would be ready to be moved, still lying down, eighty miles and two mountain passes away to hospital in Inverness, where she would have to remain till the doctors there were satisfied that she was stable enough to be transferred the seven hundred miles home to Kent. Meanwhile, our fortnight's rental was almost up, with no way of putting off the people who were to follow us into the cottage. Somebody – probably the wonderful Dr Dunlop – found us another billet, an alarming looking, but reassuringly modernised old blackhouse almost next door. Kind people – the Dunlops, our babysitting acquaintances who had been done out of their child-free evening and the couple who looked after the cottage, Iain and Cathy Campbell – rallied round and helped me look after Catherine and the children, and I spent what seemed like hours in the village phone box trying to reorganise the arrangements that we had made for the next week or two. I needed to persuade the FCO to extend my leave. And I very much hoped to recruit someone to accompany me on the two or three-day drive home with two children under four on board.

The first of these two objectives proved easy enough to achieve. My head of department, a kindly soul called Ray Britten, was full of sympathy and said that I need not return to work till I had everything satisfactorily resolved. I got nowhere with the second.

The seating in our car could be made to fold down flat, an arrangement that would enable Catherine to lie full length on the passenger side, leaving just enough room for Phoebe and Alexander on the right-hand half of the back seat. Dr Dunlop approved this DIY ambulance configuration, which would certainly have failed any twenty-first-century health and safety requirements, and we drove to Raigmore Hospital on the other side of Scotland, where the staff had been alerted. Catherine was admitted immediately.

The almoner's department gave me a list of B and B's and off I went with the children to book into one before finding a café where we could get something to eat. I soon began to know what it must have felt like to be black, Irish or a dog.

Landlady after landlady said, "Sure enough. Come right in," before spotting Phoebe and Alexander in the back of the car, whereupon they would add, "But no bairns."

Eventually, I persuaded one marginally kindlier woman to rent us a room, but strictly for one night only, as you never knew these days. She didn't explain what it was that one never knew and I was too relieved to be bothered to ask. We dumped our bits and pieces and made for the nearest café. On the way back to our digs I used a phone box to ring my parents, to be told, thank goodness, that my mother would be flying up to Inverness the next morning, to lend a hand. And when I told our landlady the good news she thawed, suggesting that maybe we would need an extra room and that of course, we could stay an extra night. Maybe what one never knew was the degree of respectability, or otherwise, of men with a couple of toddlers in tow, especially the sort who claimed that they'd just deposited their wife in a nearby hospital.

With my mother's help, I got the children back home to Kent, where she and a succession of people, paid and unpaid, enabled me to get back to work before the FCO's patience ran out. Eventually, our wonderful friend Diana Gaunt came to the rescue, all the way from Yorkshire, bringing her two children and another one she was caring for, but abandoning her husband Nicky to look after himself.

Meanwhile, Catherine prepared herself for a long and lonely stay in Raigmore Hospital. But on day two, a local volunteer popped in and turned out to be a fellow Australian. And not just that. She and Catherine knew each other. They had been fellow inmates in a student hostel in Sydney. So things began to look up and eventually, after a long and fraught sleeper-train-cum-taxi-cum-ambulance journey, she was transferred to Pembury Hospital near Tunbridge Wells. And after another fortnight of more of lying flat, she was permitted to come home (standing up), where she remained, with the baby apparently now reluctant to make an appearance. Corinna eventually deigned to arrive, after being induced as she was by now well and truly overdue, on 26 July 1971, back at Pembury Hospital.

Chapter 16
Catherine

It was customary for retiring ambassadors or high commissioners to include in their valedictory despatch a few words about their spouse. Some of these passages were fulsome, some were perfunctory, others totally absent – maybe because there hadn't been a wife or husband, or perhaps because the marriage had gone wrong. There was never any doubt in my mind that I would write something about Catherine, without whose support and longsuffering forbearance I could not have done my job. And when the time came, this is what I said:

"Finally, my wife, the traditional theme of the last paragraph of all Valedictory Despatches since time immemorial. There is not too much that I can add to the many pages which have accumulated on this subject in the last few years. (I am none too sure what I meant by this sentence, which is immediately contradicted by some hundreds of words of additional material. Perhaps I meant that there was nothing particularly original that I could add.)

"Not only am I profoundly grateful to my wife, but I am also ashamed on the Service's part that she will 'retire' no better off and no more acknowledged, than her analogues of earlier years. While I was trying to work out what we would be living on in retirement, I learned from an office in Newcastle that my wife would be entitled to the princely sum of £16.24 per week when I become 65, provided she (repeat, she) paid £3,126 in arrears of unpaid national insurance contributions by this coming April. (This was written in February 1998, when I was just about to be 60.)

"This derisory future income, financed by her from zero current income, would be all that she would have in her own right, which strikes me as a miserable reward for 32 years of hard work in support of HMG's interests abroad – work that became steadily harder the more senior her husband became. Many was the time that the show had to go on even if the caterer had let us down or whatever other crisis had intervened. She has been cook, cleaner and hotel manager since I first became ambassador in (servant-less) Reykjavík in 1983, and before that. She has also been a shoulder for innumerable members of staff and spouses to cry on and a very hard-working 'charity' worker, mainly in support of the mentally handicapped, in several posts. She has gladly done her bit week in week out, for the British Diplomatic Spouses Association and for various British women's groups. And yet she is not even British, as on occasions of particular frustration she reminds me. The Service has collectively and individually taken her for granted ever since I had the good fortune to be accepted by her as her husband. I am immensely grateful to her and the Service should be too.

"Perhaps it is time to drop some of our pretensions. Is it really necessary to go on behaving as though residences abroad, even small ones with only part-time domestic help, are regarded by the Service as some kind of Edwardian country house, but with all mod cons, available for the repose of all travelling ministers and senior officials? In reply to a recent questionnaire issuing from somewhere in the FCO (yes, my wife gets them too!) she wrote, *I am beginning now to detest official guests, who treat me as though I were part of the furniture. Can't these people be put in hotels?* I felt for her and I wish her successors a fairer deal. Spouses who elect to give up their own careers and private lives for the furtherance of HMG's business, especially spouses of heads of mission, should be paid or allowed to opt-out."

This is in fact exactly what happened, shortly after we retired. This development, which must have taken months or even years to achieve, had nothing to do with my plea, but it was a very satisfactory outcome, even if it came too late to benefit Catherine.

I could not have ended my final despatch in such a grump and Catherine wouldn't have wanted me to, so there is a final paragraph.

"But it would be wrong to end on so carping a note. I have had an enjoyable and, I hope, productive career, much of it spent in exotic places and in exciting times. Gripes about the hotel management aspect apart, my wife and I have been fortunate to have spent almost all our married life together, unlike colleagues in the armed services and many other occupations that require overseas travel. We have been supported by a system and by colleagues who cared and we have made lasting friendships all over the world, in and out of the Service. Our three children have had a tremendous launching pad for their adult lives. I would like to be starting all over again."

And now, twenty years after I wrote those words, we still look back on our time as diplomats with pleasure, pride and nostalgia. And through all the thirty-two years of our shared diplomatic life Catherine was my indispensable prop, stiffening my resolve and making me believe in myself whenever, particularly at the outset of a new assignment, I was sure I wasn't up to the job, or conversely, and just as necessary, puncturing bouts of self-importance or pomposity and covering up for my deficiencies, names and faces in particular, which I was as hopeless at remembering as she was brilliant. She was always within whispering distance, ready to prompt me, except at formal dinner parties, where custom decreed that we should invariably be seated as far from one another as the geography of the table would permit. On these occasions, she would sneak a quick peek at the table plan and brief me on the ladies between whom I was to spend the next couple of hours. Once, when she had not had an opportunity to do this, I turned to the lady on my right, introduced myself and then, with asinine foolhardiness, announced that I didn't think we'd met.

"Not since last night," the lady said, "when we sat next to each other at the Ruritanians." Further conversation after that was likely to prove difficult and there were still two hours to go.

Catherine moreover had to put up with a great deal more than enforced hotel management, particularly in the early years of our marriage. From the word go, I now realise, I was shamefully inconsiderate. No sooner had we set foot in England in 1966 and survived an initial stay with my parents than I led her off on a helter-skelter programme of sightseeing and introductions to friends, great-aunts, friends of friends, my sister, cousins, friends of my parents, all over the country. I suppose I thought I was being helpful, by slotting her into what had been my life before I went to Ghana, but it must have been hell for her. She knew none of these people; in fact, she knew no-one in Britain apart from me. She must have been terribly home-sick and would have been even more so had she known then that she wouldn't set eyes on a single member of her own family for another seven years. In the middle of all this frenetic activity, she fell ill with malaria, which at first went undiagnosed, and eventually I had to set off alone to France for what had been planned as joint language training, leaving her as the sickly and lonely guest of my sister and brother-in-law in the Cotswolds. Their GP finally twigged what was the matter with her and helped her get well enough to join me for a few days in Tours before we moved first to a hotel and then to our flat in Paris, where I began my new job in the UK Delegation to NATO. Only then, I think, could she have begun to feel that she was once again someone in her own right, rather than some kind of trophy, for we were now on a more equal footing, with both of us facing a new existence and new people.

Her private nightmare was renewed when, three years later, we returned from Brussels, where NATO had been relocated after de Gaulle kicked it out of France, equipped with a small child and another on the way. The house which we had bought from my parents was woefully unsuitable for a family. We tried to find something better, preferably in a town or village, but eventually, the only reasonably suitable place we could afford was a pair of ramshackle old cottages that someone had started to join up as a single house, midway between three Kentish Wealden villages, Benenden, Rolvenden and Biddenden, and the best part of three miles from each of them. Over the years we managed to turn this arrangement into an attractive and roomy home, but there was nothing we could do about its isolation. Each day when I set off on my ninety-minute commute to the FCO Catherine was left to fend for herself, desperately lonely, with only three small children for company and half a mile or so from all but our nearest neighbours, a crabby old couple who seemed to resent our arrival on the scene.

Years later, when we were in Iceland and the house was let, our tenants asked to buy it. By that time the children were in their teens and neither they nor Catherine had any desire, when the time came, to go back to living in a field, miles from anywhere. So we sold and in due course returned from Reykjavík, this time to London instead of a Kentish field. Catherine was happy in Tufnell Park and, twenty years into her marriage, at last got to know the capital of the country that she had been helping her husband represent.

To use one of her favourite Australian expressions, she is pretty crash hot. I can't imagine life without her and now, older and wiser, I'm astonished that she put up with so much insouciance from a husband who loved her deeply but hadn't the wit to see how unthinkingly he was treating her and how little he understood the extent of her loneliness and separation from her family and the country of her birth.

As I became more senior and better paid, it became possible for Catherine to travel to Australia reasonably frequently – roughly every eighteen months – to see her mother, sisters and their progeny. I went too now and again, for wonderful holidays and a proper chance to get to know my funny, feisty mother-in-law.

Chapter 17
Long Sea Voyages

Hundreds of thousands of people now go on long sea voyages. They go on cruise liners the size of city blocks, packaged and entertained in floating theme parks equipped with every amenity, including the most improbable – for who would only a few years ago have thought it likely, let alone sensible, to practise rock climbing techniques on a ship's funnel? – 'visiting' places that many of them have never heard of and whose treasures and amenities interest most of them only if they involve shopping. But it was not ever thus. Not so long ago people had to go by sea to get from one place to another, for it is barely half a century since aeroplanes began to supplant ships as the standard form of intercontinental conveyance. And ships, in the heyday of the great liners, were the floating epitome of glamour, luxury and, in First Class, exclusiveness.

It is doubtful whether the cruise industry would have ever existed if the shipping companies of the inter-war years had not vied with each other in the extravagance and luxury with which they cocooned their better-heeled passengers, for it was on board the likes of the Titanic, Normandie, Queen Mary and so on that so many of the present-day cruise liner staples began: the sports, the concerts, the lectures, the dressing up for dinner. And it was then that people started travelling in them for recreation rather than merely as a means of getting from one place to another.

My grandfather's travels back and forth across the Atlantic on the *Mauritania* during and after the first world war were definitely part of 'work', which for him happened in both the UK and the USA, even though these voyages had a distinctly recreational, even recuperative, aspect largely absent from today's air travel, however luxurious. He would have arrived in New York or Liverpool refreshed, maybe a bit over fed, after a week or so onboard his favourite ship.

I crossed the Atlantic twice as a very small WW2 evacuee, so maybe long sea voyages were already part of my DNA when the time came in the late summer of 1963 for my first overseas posting, to Ghana. My father had recently been to Australia and back by cargo ship. He assured me that this was a far more interesting means of travel than an aeroplane or a humdrum passenger liner and I rather envied him. So I asked the CRO's travel department if they would let me go to Accra in this way, rather than by Elder Dempster liner or, even less adventurously, BOAC. They agreed, and a few weeks later my parents saw me off from Liverpool on board the Palm Line's *Bamenda Palm.*

Palm Line was owned by the United Africa Company, part of Unilever. Its ships were pure cargo boats, not cargo-liners with accommodation for twelve passengers like the ones that had carried my father to and from Australia. Nevertheless, each was equipped with an owner's suite, presumably for the use of Lord Leverhulme should he feel in need of a little sea air, but at other times available for the likes of me. My suite consisted of a night cabin, with twin beds, a very grand bathroom, a sizeable entrance lobby, furnished with three or four chairs, presumably for the repose of any lackeys kept waiting by his lordship, and a day cabin with seating for at least a dozen. I rattled around in this splendour for over a fortnight, emerging for meals with the captain and his officers (no special dressing up), occasional stints on the bridge, or a breath of fresh air on the very limited deck-space. The *Bamenda Palm* was a working tramp ship, picking up and dropping cargo at various ports along the way, including Agadir, Dakar and Conakry, in each of which I spent a day or two.

Most of Agadir had recently been flattened by a colossal earthquake, so there was depressingly little left to explore. Dakar was agreeable and still very French even though Senegal had by 1963 been independent for a few years, whereas Conakry, ruled over by the dictator Sekou Touré, had the feel and drabness of a tropical version of Cold War Eastern Europe. Two snowploughs, a rumoured and hilariously inappropriate component of the Soviet aid programme, were indeed there, rusting on the quayside. And then, two or three days later, we arrived at Tema, Ghana's new port, a few miles east of Accra.

I thoroughly enjoyed my voyage and was tiresomely superior about it to colleagues who had travelled in more conventional ways. I visited places that I wouldn't otherwise have seen, I had plenty of time to read, demolishing the whole of Lawrence Durrell's Alexandrian Quartet as well as a number of books about Ghana and West Africa, I learned at first-hand about the work of the merchant navy and even took part in a bit of it by doing watches during quiet stretches on the bridge, and I played chess with one of the officers. I also managed to contract viral meningitis somewhere, probably Agadir, but it stayed hidden till a week or two after I had been installed as the caretaker tenant of the high commissioner's residence (we were between HCs) when I suddenly became thoroughly and painfully ill. Cargo ships don't carry doctors, so I was lucky to be back on dry land, with medical help within reach.

My posting to Accra was supposed to last three years, with home leave half way through. But my stint in Ghana coincided with a change of government in London that had ushered in the in-service training in economics from which I was to derive so much benefit, and I was snatched away mid-posting to attend the second of the new, six-month courses. There was no time for a holiday with pay with Palm Line or Elder Dempster. I went the modern way, by BOAC. But, having returned to Accra seven months later and met and married Catherine, we were accorded a sea voyage home to Liverpool – not that England was yet in any sense home to Catherine, who had never been there.

It was winter and once we'd left the tropics the sea was rough. We proved to be good sailors, which was probably just as well for the state of our marriage, less than a week old when we embarked. Rough weather in a 1960s liner, before the days of stabilisers, meant special measures. Ropes were rigged in the corridors and on the stairways to hang on to. Little flaps on the edges of tables were clicked up an inch, to stop crockery sliding off. Tablecloths were dampened to make them less slippery, for the same reason. And a dispiriting number of buckets were dotted about for people to be sick into. Once at dinner, Catherine and I were almost on our own. If a prize had been awarded for the least affected passengers, we would have won it. We lurched about, enjoying the spray on the heaving deck, where we even managed a game or two of ping-pong before giving up because all the balls had been blown away. In the cabin we read Richard Hughes's storm novel In Hazard aloud, just to show that we weren't cowed – and maybe also because it was a rollicking good read. I celebrated my twenty-eighth birthday and Catherine hurled a ring overboard, given to her by her former, Australian, boyfriend.

We lunched in the restaurant car on the train from Liverpool to London. Catherine peered through the grimy window at the grey winter landscape, her first view of the English countryside, and asked whether it ever got light in England. We had met in the glare of tropical Africa and she had been brought up in the New South Wales sun. Nothing had prepared her for the gloom of a soggy February day in the English Midlands.

Only days into the voyage we heard that President Nkrumah had been deposed and that relations with the UK had been restored. So we wondered whether we would be sent smartly back to Accra, along with the rest of the PNG'd staff. But this was not to be. Only days after disembarking, we were told of our fairy-tale honeymoon posting to Paris.

Six years later we were off on another sea voyage, my longest yet by far. We had been posted to New Delhi. We had three children under the age of four and a half. The youngest was only nine months old. Catherine couldn't face the idea of a ten-hour flight and all the mayhem of airports with such young children – and in those days first secretaries, which is what I now was, flew Economy, whatever the distance. So we chose to go by sea, an option that was shortly to be abolished.

By 1972, there was only one line still operating between Europe and India, Lloyd Triestino, which sailed from Venice to Bombay (now Mumbai). The travel people in the FCO furnished us with ferry and rail tickets to Venice and my mother drove us to Dover where she waved us off to Calais. Two of the children were self-propelled, each clasping a mini suitcase, frequently mislaid or just abandoned. The third was in a box, a carrycot with handles but without wheels. Most of our accompanied baggage had been sent on ahead to the ship, but even so we had with us three or four full-size suitcases (again, no wheels) and an unconscionable number of plastic bags, a dozen or more, filled with last-minute essentials such as disposable nappies, then newly available. We had been assured that our coach would be detached from the rest of the train at the Gare du Nord and then be shunted around Paris to the Gare de Lyon where it would fetch up across the platform alongside the night sleeper to Venice so that we would have to shift ourselves and our bags a mere twenty or so yards to our pre-booked family compartment. There would be plenty of time – at least three-quarters of an hour.

Our coach emptied out at the Gare du Nord, was duly detached from the rest of the train and then shunted out to some unpromising sidings, where it came to halt, apparently abandoned. We were alone in an empty coach in French Railway No-man's-land, trying to get to Bombay via Venice, and time was ticking by. Just as serious panic was setting in there was a violent juddering. We had been joined onto another coach, from which emerged a benign being in SNCF uniform who assured us that all was well and that we would indeed shortly be on our way to the Gare de Lyon. Our two coach train eventually set off, wending its way at snail's pace, with many a dead halt, through a post-industrial railway jungle till it slid alongside Platform 25 or so of the Gare de Lyon. We had ten minutes to find and board the Venice train, which was nowhere to be seen. Nor apparently were there any porters. With four minutes to go, we found our train, on Platform 1. Our coach was at the far end and now with less than a minute to go Catherine climbed up into it and I lifted Phoebe and Alexander up to her, followed by our mass of cases and plastic bags.

Whistles were blowing, someone was yelling: '*Depêchez-vous, Monsieur*'; the train was beginning to move and Catherine was screaming: "Corinna's still on the platform" – in her carrycot, which I had just enough time to shove up on to the coach threshold, before finally climbing in myself. Once we had managed to close the door we calmed down and spent the next ten minutes moving all our clobber, and ourselves, into our two reserved interconnecting sleeping compartments.

It was pouring with rain when we arrived in Venice the next morning. But never mind; we had come to catch a boat, not to sightsee and we made straight for the ocean terminal where we could see our ship, the *Asia*, looming above the dock. We presented ourselves at the desk, ready to be ushered into the comfort of a long sea voyage, only to be told to go and have a lovely day in Venice – it was by then not yet 10 a.m. – and not to come back before 4 p.m. Despair was setting in, only moderately alleviated by the news that we could leave our luggage in the office, as a very special concession, when salvation arrived, in the person of another passenger, a lovely helpful person called Meg. Meg proved to be a fellow member of the diplomatic service, bound for a posting in Pakistan and she immediately took us in hand.

Off we went to St Mark's Square. It was only midday, but still raining, so we went into the first reasonably priced restaurant that we could find, ready to while away the hours over a long lunch. We were encouraged by our knowledge of the Italians' well-known love of children, but the proprietors of this particular establishment seemed not to have heard of this aspect of their national psyche and promptly kicked us out, muttering darkly about *bambini*, wet clothes and so on. This discouraging experience was repeated another half a dozen times till eventually we were permitted to install ourselves in a rather scruffy dive a longish way from St Mark's. We ordered a bottle of Chianti, which we reckoned we had earned and which Phoebe promptly sent flying. We were very nearly expelled, but we were given one more chance to behave ourselves and fortunately passed muster.

The voyage, which lasted nearly six weeks, was not without incident. To begin with, it was largely sybaritic, marred only slightly by the presence of rather too many cockroaches in our two adjoining cabins. We thought of complaining and asking for a transfer to vermin-free accommodation but could not face the upheaval. Nevertheless, we admired the chutzpah of another diplomatic service couple who got themselves upgraded to a suite, having persuaded the purser that they were the British high commissioner and wife on their way to their new posting in Pakistan. (The chap concerned was, in fact, a chancery guard and the two of them understandably avoided over-close social contact with us or with Meg once they had achieved their ambitious move.)

The weather cheered up as we cruised down the Italian coast and round back up through the Straits of Messina, eventually to Marseille, where Catherine and Meg shot off to Prisunic to buy all the things that had been forgotten, in our case mainly yet more disposable nappies. From there the next stop was Tenerife, a day or two after passing a misty and mysterious Gibraltar in the early hours of the morning. The Suez Canal had been closed following one of the Arab-Israeli wars, so our route was to be Magellan's, more or less.

There were only fourteen adult First Class passengers, with about a dozen children between them, but we were dimly aware of more passengers in Tourist and could even sometimes catch glimpses of them down on the small corner of their deck visible from ours. Their quarters were strictly out of bounds, but it was not long before some of us had found a way down to their bar, where we indulged in illegal fraternisation. Our misdemeanours were revealed a few days later when the bar chits were totted up; how could First Class passengers possibly demean themselves by descending to the Tourist bar and drinking with the hoi polloi? In vain did we protest that it was mean to keep us segregated, especially when the ship was four-fifths empty and from then on we usually found our way barred. As a special concession, however, the purser, or the captain, or whoever policed these tiresome rules, arranged a 'mixed' social evening for all passengers, First and Tourist, in the First Class lounge. We could have done with more of these, for, on the whole, the Tourist passengers seemed a more stimulating bunch of people than us Firsters. Most of them were paying their own fares, as backpackers, writers, missionaries even. Whereas we were mainly officials or company executives.

After Tenerife came Lagos, where another family joined us in First Class, Carole and Ashim Barua and their two children. Carole was Scottish and Ashim, an architect, Indian and they were a breath of fresh air. But as a family, they were of 'mixed race', something with which Lloyd Triestino did not seem entirely at ease, so they were put at a table all on their own, while we continued to make polite conversation every breakfast, lunch and dinner with the German couple with whom we had been told to sit from Venice onwards. We asked the Maître D if all six of us could sit together, but were told that this would be quite impossible. (The children were fed separately and at different times, so that supervising parents – in our case Catherine – seemed to inhabit the dining saloon more or less continuously.) Only some weeks later did we realise that part of this impossibility stemmed from our German table-mates' own prejudices.

Cape Town and Durban came and went. In Cape Town, we went sightseeing and in Durban we spent a day on the beach, reserved for Whites. Carole and Ashim chose to stay on board, having no wish to be subjected, as 'coloureds', to the indignities and insults of the apartheid regime. We did toy with the idea of trying to go ashore with them, as our own small demonstration for human rights, but they dissuaded us, wisely no doubt.

The last stop was Mombasa, with another day on the beach and no racial restrictions, and then just the western half of the Indian Ocean left to cross before, at long last, reaching Bombay. We had begun to count off the days when suddenly war broke out among the adult First Class passengers, all sixteen of them. The *casus belli* was a bite, inflicted on a pure-bred Aryan by someone of mixed race. Both biter and bitten were three years old, a Barua and one of our German table-companions' two children. Sides were taken and we asked the Maître D if we could change tables, as we found it difficult to sympathise with our German table-companions' case, based entirely on racial prejudice and pressed on us to the exclusion of all other topics of conversation. Our request was refused, so for the last two days, we ate, rather sadly, in our cabin, citing sea-sickness (despite the prevailing calm weather). When at last we were tipped out on to the noisy, steamy chaos of a Bombay quayside, half institutionalised from six weeks' cosseting in all-inclusive Italian luxury, we felt a mixture of relief from tension and alarm at the prospect of fending for ourselves in very unaccustomed surroundings.

That was a long time ago and there were to be no more sea voyages at the FCO's expense. But after retirement, we went on a few, this time as passengers on cruise liners on which I had been invited to entertain the punters by delivering lectures. We went to many interesting places and some of the voyages were quite long, but somehow this wasn't the same thing as sailing for weeks on end in order to get somewhere. Those long sea voyages were Travel. These cruises were just Entertainment.

Chapter 18
India

We were posted to New Delhi in April 1972, after a three-year spell at home during which Alexander and Corinna were born, Phoebe having arrived during our time with NATO in Paris and Brussels. We had turned our pair of ramshackle cottages in Kent into a reasonably coherent and workable house, with six bedrooms, modern plumbing and central heating. We called it Barrow, the name of an earlier nearby farmhouse which had been pulled down. It was a good place for young children, with plenty of space and a good-sized garden for them to play in. But it was lonely and hard work for Catherine, as well as inconveniently far from the nearest railway station, which itself was only just within commuting distance from London. And we had over-extended ourselves financially. So we were more than ready for a posting.

But we were not at all sure we wanted to go to India. Our three years in Paris and Brussels had given us a taste for Europe and India seemed terribly far away and probably full of germs. Postings in 1972 were, however, more or less mandatory and a fear of less than perfect hygiene was not something that anyone would try to deploy as an argument against a decision by Personnel Department. We had, however, managed to persuade them that we should be allowed to travel by sea, as we were not sure that we could manage our children on a long flight. I cannot imagine what we thought would be so overwhelmingly difficult about a ten-hour flight, but our wishes had been granted.

I was to be the first secretary (economic), an alarming development that meant I was to head the aid section in the high commission. I knew nothing about aid and not very much more about economics, but I was assured that all would become clear once I'd arrived and got stuck into the job. It was suggested that, by way of preparation, I should read the World Bank's latest annual report on India during the long sea voyage. I do not recall receiving any other form of briefing. And the voyage was certainly long – nearly six weeks, as the Suez Canal was closed and the ship had to sail from Venice and out of the western end of the Mediterranean and then right around Africa, before heading across the Indian Ocean to Bombay.

I managed to read the World Bank report, even though much of it was virtually incomprehensible, and Catherine and I both read Kipling's Kim, which proved a far more digestible and effective introduction to India, written during the Raj's heyday, long before the invention of development assistance, national or international, let alone the employment of cohorts of economists and consultants sitting in offices in Washington, readying themselves to deliver their opinions and the Bank's aid programmes, in a multitude of developing countries.

It was a wonder we read as much as we did, as shipboard routine, with all its meals and repeated entertainments, had left little time for other pursuits. This routine had occasionally been interrupted by stops at ports of call, together with 'Crossing the Line' (duckings in the ship's pool by Neptune), passing in mid-ocean another Lloyd Triestino ship (much hooting and cheering) and the swell between Africa and Madagascar, which had caused Corinna's cot to trundle back and forth the length of the children's cabin until we had devised a means to anchor it. Life on the ship had been easy and predictable and even profitable, as sea travel was still regarded by the FCO as time on duty, financially buttressed by a daily shipboard allowance intended presumably to cater for all those little unavoidables, such as tips for the staff and *chota pegs* with influential fellow passengers. We had certainly had to dole out quite a few tips, but there had been no influential passengers with whom to share *chota pegs*.

We had become so institutionalised that by the time we were tipped out into the real world of an Indian port we felt almost helpless. But as we were almost certainly not the first new arrivals to feel this way, provision had been made by the high commission to take us in hand. We were installed in a hotel, woefully downmarket after the comforts of the *Asia,* and two or three days later in a train, the state of which confirmed all our apprehensions about the likelihood of germs. After another twenty-four hours, we found ourselves in Delhi, which was to be our home for the next three and a half years.

We had been allocated a house 'Off-Compound', at our request. Most of the high commission staff lived in an aseptic housing estate, surrounded by a high wall, with flats and houses ranged in accordance with the rankings of their inhabitants. The estate was well provided, with shops, community hall, cinema, mess, library, bar, garage, play-park, swimming pool, tennis courts, hospital – and even offices in which to carry out HMG's business. Everything was centrally air-conditioned, and heated in winter. There was a guaranteed electricity supply, together with artesian wells, water-purifying plant and sewerage farm. Hidden discreetly away in one corner were the 'quarters', where the only Indians permitted permanent access – the servants and their families – lived, crammed together. This mini Albion was 'The Compound' and woe betide any germ that dared enter it.

But even so, we had said we would prefer, if possible, to live in India and our wish was granted. Never mind the germs, or the power cuts, or the fluctuating water supply; we did not wish to live huggermugger with the other first secretaries in Antrim, one of four blocks of flats, each named after a county in one of the Home Nations and each graded according to rank. The poor secretaries – the 'girls', whatever their age – lived in one-room studios in Dorset, where they didn't even rate a kitchen (hence the Mess), while intermediate ranks lived in Radnor and Lanark. Antrim was the most senior block; staff above the rank of first secretary lived in a row of identical two-storey houses, called 'bungalows' nevertheless, just to show that their designers and occupants knew that they were (just) in India.

We were not the only ones who lived in the more or less real-world of suburban New Delhi. The BHC's staff had outgrown the Compound, so some twenty per cent of us were obliged, thank goodness in our case, to live elsewhere. And how lucky we were. Our house was twice the size of an Antrim flat, with a garden, a garage, a *barsati* (a roof area suitable for alfresco sleeping and hanging out the washing, monkeys permitting) and its own servants' quarters, on a street thronged with exotic people and traffic, including the occasional elephant. In the garage, the previous occupants had by arrangement left us a strange three-wheeled motor-scooter which I used for my twice-daily commute to the Compound, leaving our Cortina Estate free for Catherine and the children. This BSA Ariel, for that was its name, caused a mini sensation wherever I stopped, not so much for its third wheel, as for the space-man helmet that topped its rider. I reckoned I must have been the first person in India to wear a safety helmet and people queued up at every intersection to get a chance to give it a tap or two before peering in to see what lay inside. Despite my new-found status as a helmeted celebrity on a tricycle, or maybe because of it, I grew fond of my Ariel and enjoyed whizzing along New Delhi's grand boulevards on it – but only in dry weather. Before long the monsoon broke and I did not enjoy being half-drowned in whooshes of muddy, turdy water hurled up from adjacent puddles by Delhi's gigantic, articulated double-decker buses. So I abandoned the trike in favour of a half share in a colleague's second car, an odd arrangement that worked surprisingly well, and in due course put the Ariel up for sale.

I could not sell my trike on the open market as it had been imported duty-free under diplomatic privilege and it was worth a good deal less than the tax that I would have to pay to release it from fiscal bondage. My only option was to sell it to another diplomat, so I sent flyers around Delhi's dozens of diplomatic missions. There was no response, which I suppose was hardly surprising given that even the most junior diplomat, of whatever nationality, tended to prefer the tried and tested virtues of his Merc, or even his Cortina, to the wholly theoretical benefits of a three-wheeled scooter. But some months later I received an enquiry, couched in elaborate, third-person diplomatic language, from the Royal Bhutan Mission, typed on thick paper heavily embossed with dragons and tantric symbols. This enquiry was destined to lead to unexpected consequences.

I had scarcely heard of Bhutan and wondered why it had a mission rather than an embassy, though it was not long before I realised that its tenuous hold on independence obliged it to keep its metaphorical head down when dealing with its powerful neighbour. The Bhutanese reckoned that the Indians might regard the presence in their midst of something calling itself an embassy as provocative. After all, it was only a few years since Delhi had annexed Bhutan's neighbour Sikkim.

Before long I was in touch with a Mr Wangchuck – most Bhutanese of any consequence, from the King down, seemed to be called Wangchuck – with whom I enjoyed many long conversations, always over a cup of tea. I heard all about Bhutan and about Mr W's life history, but it was many weeks before we got down to brass tacks and faced up to the delicate matter of the scooter. It turned out that the Bhutanese wanted it as a messenger's runabout, and eventually I sold it to them for not much less than I had paid for it. The whole process, from first answering the mission's 'Third Person Note' to banking their cheque, had taken about three months.

By this time Mr W and I were firm friends, so much so that we invited him for Christmas lunch, evidently a novel experience for him, as indeed it was for us, with three small children and Catherine's mother, visiting from Australia. It was the first time that he had encountered western family hospitality, and we learned how he and a few of his contemporaries had managed to acquire a modern, secondary education, leading later to university. When he was a child Bhutan was still a closed theocracy, with just a few primary schools, run by monks. He was one of the first to go on to secondary school. This meant a boarding school in Darjeeling, some hundreds of miles away and reached only along mountain footpaths, as there were still hardly any roads in Bhutan, or in Sikkim, through which he had to pass. Every year young Mr W walked the whole way, which took him about a month and at the end of the school year, he walked home again for the summer holiday. For five years.

Mr W wanted to know what I did in the high commission. He seemed surprisingly interested when I explained that I administered the aid programme. I could not at first see how he could possibly care about project and non-project aid, maintenance grants, debt relief, capital investment loans, grants to pay off earlier loans or at least make them interest-free, project appraisals, technical assistance, IBRD terms compliance, grant elements and all the other arcane components of my job. But he pressed me for more and then, quite suddenly, said, "Wonderful. We could do with a bit of that." And that is how the sale of my BSA Ariel led to the start of the British aid programme in Bhutan.

During the wet monsoon months which had led to my abandoning the scooter, Catherine and I sank into a gloom. We felt cooped up, bored, even depressed. We were well looked after by a small fleet of servants – bearer, cook, ayah, sweeper, gardener, watchman – and were beginning to get to know some of our neighbours. Even so, we found it difficult to make an effort and stir ourselves to explore beyond our immediate surroundings. But finally we were persuaded to give a weekend in Mussoorie a try – a rather damp weekend, as it turned out. And from then on we were hooked by hill stations, many of them, like Mussoorie, only a few hours' drive from Delhi. Cool air and the smell of wood-smoke worked wonders and over the next three years, we spent weekends and longer holidays in a mass of delectable places, from houseboats on Nigeen Lake at Srinagar to the Kulu Valley, from Dharamsala to Ranikhet, from Chail to Kasauli and many others.

As we got to know more people, we went on more adventurous trips, staying in circuit houses (impossible without the help and often company of Indian friends) and *dak* (postal), forest and canal bungalows, all over north-western India, including Rajasthan during the cooler months. Networks of these places were set up during the Raj for the use of itinerant officials and they were still in working order in the Seventies – maybe they still are – and mostly bookable by the likes of us. The grandest were the circuit houses, meant for the visiting ICS – later, IAS – magistrates (Collectors) and District Officers, though even they were relatively spartan compared with hotels. But they were spacious and private, and for the most part equipped with staff who were happy to whip up rumble-tumble (scrambled egg) or some other form of sustenance. And they were cheap.

We enjoyed wonderful breaks, with colleagues and with friends including Ray and Bulbul Pillai and Mark and Maggie Tully. Ray was the IBM representative in India and his wife Bulbul was and still is, an artist, with an atelier now in Paris. Mark, later Sir Mark, was the BBC's distinguished correspondent in India, who knew and no doubt still does, absolutely everything that was going on, often to the discomfort of the Indian government. The Pillais and the Tullys had children roughly the same age as ours, which made for easy joint holidays. And Mark was a keen horseman and polo player, who encouraged me to learn to ride and even, just before our tour came to an end, to start learning to play polo. Many years later he wrote the foreword to Corinna's book on voluntary work with paralysed people in Bangladesh, *From Horizontal to Vertical,* and, even later, to this one.

One of our trips, with British Council colleagues, took place in the aftermath of the 1973 Arab-Israel War. We were aiming for Jaisalmer, on the far side of the Thar Desert, almost in Pakistan. Because of the war, there was very little petrol about anywhere, let alone in the subcontinent's largest desert, so we took enough with us for the whole journey in jerry cans tied precariously onto the roof racks of our two Cortina Estates. Because petrol was in such short supply, and therefore of great interest to thieves, we had to unload the whole lot every night and store it, gently stinking and dangerously inflammable, in our rest-house bedrooms. We also had to be sure not to add significantly to our carefully calculated mileage range. The map indicated a single obvious proper road to Jaisalmer, so we were confident that we would get there, provided we followed signposts pointing to somewhere beginning with a *Devanagari* 'J', which looks like a '5' on its side. All seemed to be going well and late in the afternoon, we were within sight of a large walled city, surrounded by desert, which was good news till we drove in through one of its great gates, when it turned out to be Jodhpur.

We were at least 100 miles off course and therefore in potential petrol deficit, as well as abashed by our shameful ignorance of the *Devanagari* script. If we had bothered to learn even a second letter we might by now be almost in Jaisalmer. It had not occurred to us that, so far from the tourist and industrial towns surrounding Delhi, there would be no signs written in English and that three of the desert's four great cities all began with a 'J', the third being Jaipur. (The non-J one is Bikaner.)

Fortunately we found some petrol, and the next day continued on our way, only to come to a hushed halt in the middle of nowhere while the Indian Army Camel Corps crossed our path. Hundreds of camels in line ahead, each ridden by a soldier with a rifle across his lap, swished past us, soundlessly, from right to left, from horizon to horizon – an unforgettable spectacle. It was as though we had stumbled into a set for Lawrence of Arabia, only better, because it was real.

Not long after this spectral encounter, we found ourselves driving past a massive construction site, with watch-towers, armed sentries, gantries, barbed wire and unfriendly notices, in English as well as Hindi, advising us to keep out, take no photographs, keep going. We wondered why drilling for oil, which is what we assumed was going on, needed quite so much security, but a few months later we realised, with a shudder, that we had stumbled across the preparations for India's first nuclear explosion, which had taken place a few weeks later, deep underground, and of course for entirely peaceful purposes. If we hadn't missed our way and taken an unplanned detour via Jodhpur we would never have gone near this sinister place. It is a wonder that we were not stopped and accused of espionage.

I reckoned that I had the best first secretary job in the high commission, in that it gave me enormous scope for travel and contact with Indian officials and business people. Maybe it did not carry the prestige of the political jobs in chancery, but it was certainly much more fun. I travelled all over India, visiting our aid projects or appraising possible new ones. One week I might be discussing progress at a fertiliser plant at Tuticorin in the far south, while the next I might be travelling deep under thousands of feet of Himalayan rock along a half-built tunnel destined to connect two of the five main tributaries of the Indus in what was then the world's biggest hydro-electric scheme. I did much of this type of work in tandem with the first secretary (economist) – I was the first secretary (economic); note the difference! – an official seconded from the Overseas Development Ministry, later termed the Department for International

Development or DfID. We got on well together and we were assisted by an ODM second secretary who handled the technical assistance programme (mostly concerned with agriculture), an FCO third secretary who pulled everything together and was, by useful good fortune, married into one of India's leading manufacturing families and consequently a source of high grade economic and commercial gossip and intelligence, and by a locally engaged statistician – five of us, supported by a couple of archivists and a couple of typists. We were nominally headed by half of the economic and commercial counsellor (the other half of whom supervised the commercial section), but in practice, we were left largely to our own devices, as the incumbent, when he was there, was mainly interested in the commercial – export promotion – side of his portfolio. But for much of the time, the poor man was absent, seriously ill (which meant that I was acting head of the section, drawing acting counsellor's pay, which was handy).

So five, or officially five and a half, officials ran the British aid programme in India. In my last complete financial year, we disbursed over £100 million, by far the biggest bilateral programme in the country – the Americans having dropped out for political reasons – accounting for something like a quarter of the UK's total global bilateral aid. This was in the 1970s when £100 million was worth a great deal more than it is now, by a factor of about twenty. Our programme was diverse and many-facetted and as far as I know, it was pretty effective. During my time it was converted entirely from loan to grant terms, a complex process. In 2006, the most recent year for which I have details, the programme was run by a separate DfID 'Devdiv' (development division) with a staff of twenty, consisting mainly of first secretaries, headed by a minister and a counsellor, with no FCO input (deemed political and therefore un-PC). No doubt the programme had in the ensuing years become even more complex, as it was mainly geared to the alleviation of poverty rather than to the encouragement of economic growth and self-sufficiency. But in real terms, it was far smaller than its Seventies antecedent. Present-day chancellors seeking ways to cut the deficit could with advantage study what must surely be an unnecessarily extravagant overseas aid administration bureaucracy, which is replicated in missions in all significant aid-receiving countries.

Catherine meanwhile had joined Rosemary Garvey, the high commissioner's wife, as a volunteer with a remarkable Indian charity called Mobile Creches. Delhi was peppered with building sites and most of the labourers were rural migrants, mainly from Rajasthan. These people came with their entire families, including large numbers of children in need of nutrition, shelter, medical services and education, little of which, if any, was provided by their employers. Mobile Creches volunteers worked hard to fill these gaps, all over the city and also to raise awareness of the dangerous and exploitative conditions in so many of the sites. Rosemary was a wonderful role model of the best sort of diplomatic wife – unstuffy, keen to learn as much as possible about the environment into which her husband's job had taken her and determined to find ways of helping in a participatory and non-patronising manner. She preferred getting stuck into hard, voluntary work to playing golf or bridge and attending coffee mornings. Which is precisely how Catherine felt.

The children attended the Playhouse School, a delightful introduction to education, run on Montessori lines, before moving on, in Phoebe and Alexander's case, to the so-called British School – so-called even though the only really British thing about it was its curriculum. It was a solid, rather old-fashioned establishment, staffed by kindly and competent Indian teachers and our children were very happy there, just as they had been at the Playhouse. And outside school hours there was an enormous amount for them to do, riding, swimming, visiting ruined cities and tombs, mountains, deserts, game parks.

Delhi was not over-endowed with children's playparks and from our point of view, it didn't need to be. But there was one on the edge of Rajpath, near the India Gate, which boasted a miniature railway, on which children could ride for a nominal fee. One day they were getting ready to do just that, with Catherine and me sitting just behind them, when we were joined, three or four rows further back, by a woman with a couple of her grandchildren. It was Mrs Gandhi. There was no fuss. We were not shooed away. We were not aware of any undue security. And when the ride was over, the prime minister of the world's largest democracy flashed us a friendly smile before scooping up her charges and walking them away to her waiting Ambassador (Indian Morris Oxford) car – an admirable but ultimately misleading demonstration of political health and stability by the woman who, only weeks later, would declare her notorious Emergency, the harbinger of the unravelling of Congress supremacy.

We were in India for nearly four years. It was a wonderful posting. My job was absorbing and fulfilling. We had a happy family life, uninterrupted by boarding school. We travelled widely. We made many friends, Indian and British. Our children grew up in a multiracial environment. It could hardly have been better.

Chapter 19
Prendy

Delhi's climate was mixed. For about half the year, from April to September, it was pretty hellish – at first dry, dusty and far too hot, then sticky and still too hot, with torrential rain, sometimes for days on end. But the other half of the year – the Cold Weather – was pretty good, even blissful for quite a lot of the time. It was only properly cold for three or four weeks around Christmas and New Year, when the temperature could drop to freezing at night and we needed our open fires or central heating, while for the rest of those six months we enjoyed balmy blue skies and grew English summer flowers and vegetables in our gardens.

The advent of the longed-for Cold Weather was presaged by hints and portents, one of the most encouraging of which was news of the approach of Prendy, at first sporadic and maybe untrustworthy, but gradually more frequent and believable. Someone resembling Prendy had been seen in Tehran. Prendy, or someone jolly like him, had crossed the Khyber and was rumoured to be in Peshawar. Prendy had crossed the border, after a fleeting glimpse in Lahore. Prendy had turned left in Amritsar and was presumably heading up into Kashmir. Prendy had definitely been sighted in Srinagar. And then yes, Prendy's arrived! This last, definitive news was generally conveyed to us all by Mark Tully, the BBC Correspondent. Once we had heard it, from this most reliable of sources, we could relax, in the certain knowledge that the Cold Weather could now begin. For Prendy was not accustomed to spending a minute longer on the Plains in the Hot Weather than was absolutely necessary, which latterly had been never.

Prendy was a retired Indian Army officer, Brigadier Prendergast. Ever since 1947, when he had been required to leave newly independent India to its own devices, he had spent the summer half of the year in Wiltshire and the winter in India, commuting in a specially constructed Prenmobile, in which he and the Memsahib, or 'Mem', lived while away from home.

The Prenmobile was a modified Bedford Three Tonner, as used by the British army as their standard truck. It had four-wheel drive and stood high off the ground, well clear of rocks, dead animals and other miscellaneous detritus of the road. The cab was more or less as it had left the factory in Luton, but the rest of the bodywork was very different. In essence, this was a large Thermos flask, triply insulated, with a small, airtight door and a couple of tiny windows. Presumably, there was some provision for ventilation or poor Prendy and his Mem would have died of suffocation, but it was not in evidence and clearly minimal. For the whole idea, as Prendy proudly explained, was that the insulation was so effective that there was no need of heating, even when camping in sub-zero conditions at high altitude in an Afghan or Iranian autumn or spring, as the Prendergasts' own body heat was all that was needed to maintain a cosy fug.

There were two spare wheels and copious tankage, for fuel (topped up dirt cheap in Iran), water, and wine (slurped in for next to nothing in Bulgaria and then tightly sealed while in transit through Muslim territory). This whole imposing vehicle was painted bright yellow – 'stands out in a snowdrift' – with discreet badges on the two cab doors which, on closer examination, proved to be the Prendergast coat of arms.

Prendy did all the driving and mechanical side of things, while the Mem was 'in charge of the commissariat'. She was evidently also the chief sentry and security guard, as Prendy spent a lot of time fishing, not always in sight. I don't remember if she was ever encouraged to voice an opinion, or even to utter more than the occasional greeting or assent. I hope she had plenty of good books with her.

The Prendergasts spent most of the Cold Weather in the Corbett National Park in the Uttar Pradesh *terai*, where the Prenmobile had its own permanently reserved parking space and Prendy 'fed the camp' with the – more or less inedible – fish that he hoicked out of the River Ramganga. Every now and again there was general rejoicing when he achieved a *mahseer*, a delicious gamefish.

Prendy made up for the Mem's silence with reminiscences of the good old days the Raj, punctuated occasionally with accounts of fishing exploits and adventures on the long road between Warminster and Corbett Park. The first hour or two around the campfire could be intriguing, but once started he was more or less unstoppable and ultimately mind-blowingly boring. Only the saintly Mark was capable of maintaining a convincing simulacrum of interest right through till bedtime. The Mem had doubtless heard it all before and had nothing to add.

One September a friend from England was staying with us, getting ready to go up to Kashmir for a few days. We told Juliet that if she saw a stereotypical retired brigadier fishing for trout this would almost certainly be a certain Prendy, on his annual way to Corbett Park. Kashmir is a big place, with plenty of trout streams, so Juliet thought nothing more of our forecast till one afternoon, as she was preparing to disappear for a minute or two behind a convenient bush, an imposing figure rose up from the undergrowth and, without missing a beat, greeted her chivalrously.

"Good afternoon, Madam. Here for the fishing?" Juliet's immediate purpose had little to do with fishing, as evidently had his presence in that exact spot, but she readily agreed and mutual introductions followed, still in the shrubbery. And of course, it was Prendy.

Soon after we had left India we heard that Prendy and the Mem had spent their final year in Corbett Park. Old age had overtaken both their energy and the reliability of the Prenmobile, which was having to content itself with trips to the Scottish Highlands, tame stuff after the four or five thousand miles of the road from Wiltshire to Uttar Pradesh. And now, what with wars and Taliban and Isis and IEDs, it seems inconceivable that ordinary civilians could drive the whole way, along good roads and in moderate safety. But that is precisely what many staff members of the Delhi high commission did, along with the NAAFI truck that used to supply the high commission shop.

Chapter 20
Kolahoi

Captain Derek Robbins RN was the naval adviser for most of the time we were in the high commission in Delhi. He was a distinguished naval aviator, a Fleet Air Arm man, once the holder of a world airspeed record and the chap who'd taught the Duke of Edinburgh how to fly helicopters. He was also a mountaineer and, for the duration of his India posting, the guardian of a store of equipment belonging to the Alpine Club for the use of its Himalayan expeditions. When he discovered that I too enjoyed climbing, he suggested that we should have a crack at Kolahoi, an eighteen-thousand-foot peak north of Sonamarg, in Kashmir. He and a couple of his sons had just trekked up the Lidder Valley as far as the foot of the Kolahoi Glacier, from where, had the weather not been misty, they had hoped to be able to see the peak and get an idea of the route up. They had, however, been assured that dainty ladies in saris and high heels regularly made it to the top, so it shouldn't be too much for us. A bit too easy, perhaps. We made a date for the next summer and I forgot all about it.

But a year later, Derek had not forgotten and, a little hesitantly, I agreed to join him in the Nigeen Lake houseboat where he and children from one or two of their more recent families (both he and his wife Cynthia had had more than one) were spending the summer holidays. I flew up, spent a night on-board *The Lady of Shalott* and set off with Derek next morning in his Range Rover, which he had pre-packed with everything we would need for our expedition. The road petered out a little way up the Lidder Valley and there, waiting for us were the porters and ponies that Derek had hired from an agency in Srinagar. I was most impressed and began to feel more like a proper Himalayan climber.

I was a little less impressed when, fifteen minutes later and after a frantic search through the mound of kit that had been unloaded from the Range Rover, Derek confessed that he'd forgotten the crampons, which would certainly be necessary if, as seemed likely, we needed to go up or across the glacier. "Still," said Derek cheerfully, "we should be able to find another route, avoiding the ice."

Two of the ponies were saddled, ready for us to ride. The others carried the kit. The men whom I'd assumed to be porters turned out to be more like syces, or grooms, in charge of the ponies. Derek rode, while for most of the time I walked, as I reckoned that I would need to get acclimatised to the altitude, having flown the previous day from Delhi's 500 feet to Srinagar's 5,000 and driven that morning up a further 4,000 or so, while Derek had had more than a week to get used to the 5,000 feet and upwards of his holiday territory. Besides, walking made it easier for me to nip off course every now and again to pick a likely looking flower to put in the press which Catherine had instructed me to fill with alpine specimens, ready for her to try to identify when I got back to Delhi. "Anyone would think you were some kind of cream puff, the way you keep picking those damn daisies," observed Derek.

We walked or rode all day till, a bit before sunset, we reached the glacier snout, a messy looking grey cliff from the foot of which gurgled the infant Lidder. Kolahoi itself was still tantalisingly out of sight, hidden behind a formidable foothill, at the foot of which the syces were starting to pitch some tents, Camp One. Our route had taken us up another 3,000 feet. We were now at about 12,000, almost above the tree line. During the day's march, we had passed a few straggly flocks of sheep and goats, but hadn't seen a soul. The syces cooked us an excellent supper and we were soon fast asleep in our sleeping bags, undeterred by thoughts of marauding bears or wolves, leopards perhaps.

We were up early the next morning, ready to start the climb up to a suitable spot for Camp Two. From now on we had to manage on our own, leaving the porters/syces to look after their ponies and various bits of unwanted gear at Camp One. Our rucksacks contained a tent, a couple of sleeping bags, rations for four days, warm clothing, all the necessary climbing gear apart from crampons, a Camping Gaz stove and lantern, cooking equipment, a couple of bottles of water and Catherine's flower press, furnished now with a few damn daisies. The sacks were very heavy.

The way up led over steep, grassy meadows, richly dotted with yet more damn daisies, some of which I was brave enough to pick, risking Derek's scorn. The sheep and goats had given way to a scattered herd of cows, each clonking its bell. After a couple of hours, we reached the top of a ridge from where, at last,

Kolahoi was fully visible. There, right in front of us, rearing up over the glacier, was a triangular-shaped precipice, as near as dammit vertical – a bit like the north face of the Eiger but twice as big. I was beginning to feel a little less like a proper Himalayan climber.

Just then we were surprised, and I was secretly relieved, to see some fellow human beings, walking briskly across the slope. They were chattering and laughing, unencumbered by monstrous rucksacks. They were Italian, on a botany holiday, looking for interesting specimens – kindred spirits in the daisy stakes, as Derek grudgingly acknowledged. When they learned what we were up to they were impressed. After all, said one of the two lean and hardened men who were evidently the group's leaders, it's only been done twice and the second time was when poor old Whatshisname was killed. After that, they'd nearly had to call the expedition off. Derek explained, modestly, that we wouldn't be attempting much of the face itself – not this time anyway – but would follow the right-hand ridge to the summit. Even so, they said and were on their way.

At lunch-time, we reached the end of the grass and the beginning of serious rock, with patches of snow. This was the obvious place for Camp Two, so we pitched our tent and ate the sandwiches that the porters had made for us. We had drunk all our water. We were several hundred feet above the glacier and there was no sign of a stream. But Derek assured me that there was bound to be water from snowmelt a hundred yards or so to our left, along a precipitous ridge, and off he went with the bottles and a mess-tin.

No sooner had he gone than the mist descended and our miniscule camp became enveloped in thick, freezing cold cloud. When, after half an hour, the mist had not lifted and there was no sign of Derek, I began to worry. I called out to him, but the only response was an echo, with now and again the faint clonking of a distant cowbell. Perhaps he had had an accident and needed help? I decided to search the immediate surroundings, but, as visibility was down to about twenty yards, I would need to follow strict compass bearings to be reasonably sure of making it back to the tent. My first couple of forays led to the edge of the precipice at the foot of which lay the glacier. If Derek had slipped down there, he would certainly have been killed.

My fogbound search lasted an hour or more and yielded nothing. I could occasionally still hear the cowbell. I was hoarse from shouting and beginning to despair. In three hours' time, it would be dark. I needed to raise the alarm. If I was to get down to the porters at Camp One I would have to leave very soon, as

I reckoned it would take every bit of two hours and probably more, given the poor visibility, to get back down those two or three thousand feet. I would be relying on the map and my compass.

I made the tent as welcoming as possible in case Derek managed to find his way back to it after I'd gone and wrote him a note, explaining that I'd gone to get help. I was just zipping up the flysheet when the mist lifted and there he was, sixty or seventy yards away, banging away on his mess-tin, which sounded just like a cowbell.

"I thought I should let you know where I was, in case you were worried," he said. "Should have taken a whistle, but forgot. You certainly did an awful lot of shouting. Managed to fill the bottles, though."

I was just in time to grab the note and screw it up before Derek could have a chance to read it and to tick me off for panicking.

The clouds melted away and we were treated to a beautiful late afternoon, which Derek spent eyeing possible routes up the ridge that led to the summit. I tried not to think about what lay ahead. The ridge rose at an angle of forty-five degrees. It was a mass of pinnacles, gaps, arrêts and other mountain horrors, with plenty of snow. Derek reckoned it would be a doddle. Only another two or three thousand feet, with a path up it, trodden regularly by dainty ladies in saris. I wished more and more fervently that I was back at home in Delhi, getting ready for that evening's drinks party.

We had supper and turned in early – very early – as it got dark at half-past six and we couldn't risk wasting gas for lighting. There followed a very long night, during which the wind got up, Derek snored happily, the glacier creaked and rumbled and I developed a splitting headache. I kept dropping off to sleep, only to wake ten minutes later, over and over again. I felt very sick, with anxiety and with straightforward nausea. Perhaps the altitude – 15,000 feet or maybe a bit more – was getting at me.

When at last it grew light and I tottered out of the tent I was secretly ecstatic to see that we had almost certainly been saved by the weather. Kolahoi and most of its approach ridge had disappeared in thick cloud, as had the valley below us, which was filled with billowing cotton wool. We were in an intervening clear zone, but the wind was now little short of a gale.

"Bit dicey," said Derek. "Looks as though the monsoon's arrived early. Could be risky."

I hastened to agree, in a tone that I hoped conveyed prudence tinged with disappointment, though without too much of the latter in case Derek felt moved to accommodate my apparently dashed hopes.

We wrestled with the tent, ramming it into its bag before it blew down the cliff to the glacier, from which perhaps it might eventually emerge to puzzle some twenty-third-century archaeologist. In under two hours, we were back down with the porters, who didn't seem over-surprised to see us, ostensibly three days early, and we were comfortably back on board the *Lady of Shalott* in time for a *chota peg* or two before dinner. By this time the clouds had rolled away and the weather had resumed its perfect suitability for serious mountaineering. "Could have cracked the bugger after all," observed Derek, but fortunately there was not enough time left in our holiday to try again. We spent the remaining three days fishing (unsuccessfully – too much glare), swimming, water-skiing, eating, drinking, like normal Kashmir holidaymakers. The Robbinses gave me a lift back to Delhi in the Range Rover, where Catherine set about identifying my damn daisies.

A couple of weeks later, an uncharacteristically giggly Cynthia announced that Derek, poised beside her to pour placatory drinks, had a confession to make. He had made a few enquiries and discovered that we'd gone the wrong way. The dainty lady route to the top of Kolahoi lay right the other side of it, with no glaciers, precipices, or arrêts involved, approached up another valley unrelated to the Lidder. The four of us almost spilt our drinks laughing and Derek never breathed another word about damn daisies.

Chapter 21
Bhutan

After I had sold my scooter to the Royal Bhutanese Mission, my friend Mr Wangchuck became more and more interested in the possibility of a British aid programme in his country. He wanted our help to improve its schools so that a new generation of ambitious young Bhutanese would not be obliged to seek secondary education in other countries – in practice, as in his case, in India. I said I would see what we could do.

I asked my boss, the half of the economic and commercial counsellor who dealt with aid. This was Oliver Forster, a very nice and very wise man. He realised that quite a large part of my new-found enthusiasm for aid to Bhutan was that I was busting to go there, still at that time a virtually closed country, where very few British officials had ever been. This was because we had no diplomatic relations with it, even though we recognised it and also because the Indians regarded it as *chasse gardée* and might well make difficulties if they thought we were trying to cosy up to its government. Nevertheless, Oliver and Terence Garvey, the high commissioner, undertook to make a case to the ODM and in due course, the latter agreed to an exploratory visit by one of their officials, David Stanton, accompanied by me and by Philippa Drew, the second secretary in chancery.

Bhutan is small – about the size of Wales – and almost entirely mountainous, Himalayanly so, with only a narrow strip of *terai* (forested foothills in northern India) along its southern border. Getting there in the seventies was not entirely straightforward. In those days the country had no airport and very little modern infrastructure of any kind. What you had to do was first fly to Baghdogra, a semi-military airport in the Indian plains below Darjeeling, requiring a special permit, followed by several hours in a car to a border post a mile or so short of Phuntsholing, accompanied by a Bhutanese minder, who dealt with the border formalities. Phuntsholing was then little more than a large village, indistinguishable from the Indian ones which we had passed through on our way, but it was equipped with a comfortable rest-house where we spent the night. Most of the next day was spent on the narrow, twisting mountain road to Thimphu, the capital, which we reached late in the day. We were installed in the government rest-house, probably the only accommodation available for visiting foreigners. It was built in traditional Bhutanese style, slightly reminiscent of English Tudor buildings, with much timbering and small-paned windows. It was comfortable enough and provided good food, but it was draughty and chilly at night, which was unsurprising given Thimphu's 8,000-foot altitude.

The Bhutanese wanted us to help them make the secondary school in Thimphu as good as anything in Darjeeling, but did not seem particularly bothered about education anywhere else. We persuaded them that a single, inevitably elitist, school in the capital alone would not be in the country's best interests and made it a condition of any help we might give that educational opportunities should be developed throughout the country, with the Thimphu school as the focal point, under the direction of a British head teacher who would also advise on education nationally. Depending on how the initial stages went, we would consider providing more teachers, to work in other towns, including the frontier town Phuntsholing, the former capital Punakha and maybe Paro, 35 miles away and now the site of Bhutan's new and only international airport. These other teachers would be under the general direction of the headteacher in Thimphu.

Bhutan had become a kingdom in the early years of the twentieth century. The third king had died in mid-1972, only months before we first began to think about an aid programme, and had been succeeded by his sixteen-year-old son, Jigme Singye Wangchuck, who at the time had been at school in England. Buddhist tradition called for a long period of mourning, so it looked pretty certain that the young king would still be uncrowned during our visit the following year and consequently unlikely to be able to have much if anything to do with a visiting delegation; and so it proved. Nevertheless, I had been deputed to carry a royal gift of trout flies for His Majesty, a keen fly-fisherman, just in case he decided to receive us.

On the way over the pass to Paro, we had a puncture. The driver and our minder had more or less finished changing the wheel when a jeep stopped and a couple of young men got out and asked us, in English, if we needed any help.

We thanked them and said that everything seemed to be in order, whereupon they got back into their jeep and drove away. Our two Bhutanese companions seemed to be in a bit of a fluster, even though they had managed to change the wheel, so we asked them if anything was amiss. Not at all, they assured us, but that was His Majesty.

After this demonstration of democratic kingship, we decided that the flies should be got somehow to the King, and this was arranged. We heard that they had been gratefully received and, months later, that they had been put to good use.

Bhutan was more or less an Indian client state, a situation that dated back to the days of the Raj when British India had treated it as a princely state. It was nominally independent, but India ran its foreign affairs and three-quarters surrounded it geographically. Its northern border, much of it un-demarcated, ran along high Himalayan ridges, on the other side of which lay Tibet. India had fought a brief and unsatisfactory war on its north-eastern frontier with China only a decade earlier. Anything to do with its border with China, or with its Bhutanese proxy border, was sensitive, so we took great care to keep the Indians fully informed of what we were up to, both in Thimphu and in Delhi, and to begin with they seemed relaxed, even moderately supportive.

The return journey to Delhi again meant spending a night in Phuntsholing, which gave us an opportunity to call in on the secondary school, where we hoped in due course to base a couple of teachers. When we stopped at the border next morning we checked our passports, which contained no proof of our ever having entered Bhutan. It would have been good to have some kind of exit stamp, just for the fun of it. We put this consideration to our minder, who readily agreed and disappeared with the three passports back into what we assumed was the border guards' cabin. A few minutes later he re-emerged, clutching them open at the page where, in each of them, appeared the proud message *Received with thanks. J Patel and Sons, Purveyor of High-Class Provisions, Phuntsholing.* We wondered whether the Bhutanese border people, or perhaps Mr Patel, had got the idea from the film Passport to Pimlico, but reckoned that even the best Ealing comedies were, on balance, unlikely to have been shown in Phuntsholing.

A few months after our visit, the ODM recruited someone to fill the crucial central role of Headmaster or Principal of the school in Thimphu. This was John Tyson, a distinguished mountaineer, explorer and teacher who had already been selected for a similar role in Khatmandu which, in the event, he had not been able to take up. He was steeped in the ways of the mountain peoples of the Himalayan region, parts of which, in Nepal, he had explored and mapped for the first time. He was experienced in both teaching and educational administration. He had an enthusiastic and supportive wife. In short, he was ideal.

The Tysons stayed with us in Delhi, from where I accompanied them to Thimphu and, I hope, helped them get established. Together we called on the various functionaries with whom they would be working, including the Indian Resident and visited some of the chortens and dzongs (fortified monasteries), including of course the enormous Tashichho Dzong which was the main seat of government as well as a religious foundation – a sort of Buddhist Vatican, presided over by the Chief Lama of Bhutan. Bhutan had for centuries been a theocracy and to a certain extent still was, with supreme power shared between the King and the Chief Lama, an arrangement that the new King was destined gradually to dismantle until he turned the country into a more or less democratic constitutional monarchy in 2006, shortly after which he abdicated in favour of his son, job done.

It was during this visit that I was accompanied for part of the time by my old friend from Delhi, Mr Wangchuck. He had all the right ideas and insisted that I take a bit of time off for some trout fishing. I cannot remember if we caught anything, but it was during a fishing break that he assured me that the King was enjoying using the flies which I had brought for him the year before.

It turned out that John Tyson knew my mountaineering cousin Michael Ward, who had been a member of the successful 1953 Everest expedition. Michael was a surgeon, specialising in high altitude conditions, had paid many visits to Bhutan and was well acquainted with members of its royal family. He wrote me a number of helpful letters, warning me of potential protocol and sensitivity pitfalls, and he and John were in close touch. It was probably he who drew my attention to the unfortunate precedent of Michael Aris's time as tutor to the royal children, which it was said had ended prematurely following some inadvertent breach of royal or Buddhist protocol. This was the Michael Aris who later married Aung San Suu Kyi.

I visited Bhutan once more, shortly before the end of our Delhi posting in late 1975, to see how things were going and also to take up some urgently needed domestic supplies and equipment. I stayed with John Tyson and his American wife Phebe (sic – the American spelling presumably), by now well installed and already starting to recruit the extra teachers who would form part of our aid project. They were full of enthusiasm and all seemed to be going well. We called on the Indian Resident, who seemed relaxed. But only a few months after Catherine and I were back in Britain at the start of a home posting I heard that the Indians were raising difficulties and becoming obstructive. They ensured, for instance, that the Bhutanese refused to issue the Tysons with exit permits so that they were effectively prisoners in the country in which they were running an aid project. In due course, the project had to be abandoned, for no better reason than post-colonial spite on the part of the Indians, with the Tysons, left high and dry.

This regrettable denouement led also to the end of my links – admittedly never much more than tenuous – with Michael Ward, who took it into his head that I was responsible for the Tysons' plight and wrote to say so, in coolly unfriendly terms. It was no use my explaining to him that I had left India the previous year, since when I had been engaged in a completely different job in the FCO in London, or that it was the Indian government that had decided to wreck the project and with it John Tyson's career; it was still in Michael's view all my fault. I never heard from either him or the Tysons again.

Chapter 22
Delhi to Prague via Sydney
and Chatham House

After leaving Delhi, we spent four years back in England. But first, we had an opportunity to visit Australia, Catherine's home country in which she had not set foot for ten years. One of the local staff in the high commission, who was responsible for everyone's travel arrangements, was reputed to be able to work airline routeing miracles, so I asked him if he could send us home via Sydney, at minimal extra cost, which we would meet. He said he would see what he could do and seemed quite optimistic since, as he pointed out, Sydney was to the east of Delhi, while London lay to the west. I hadn't the faintest idea how this simple geographic consideration, with which I was in full agreement, could have any bearing on the issue, but I threw caution to the winds and asked him to go ahead with the booking.

A few days later the promised miracle had been worked. For an extra cost which we could afford we had a fistful of airline tickets which would entitle the five of us to return home via Sydney, where we would break our journey for a month, leaving Delhi on 29 November 1975. Catherine hadn't seen any of her family for ten years, apart from her mother who had visited us in Delhi over Christmas and New Year in 1972–3. I had never been to Australia. Nor, needless to say, had the children. We were very excited.

But then disaster struck. The high commissioner, Sir Michael Walker, who until that moment had never shown the slightest interest in me or my work, presumably because Aid was below the high commission salt – as was I, not having been to Eton, the alma mater of most of his chancery staff – wished to give us a farewell lunch. This was to be a couple of days into December, a date that was, according to his PA, non-negotiable. The PA, a sympathetic soul, had explained that we were booked to have left by then, but Sir M reckoned that we would simply have to reschedule and leave a few days later – and his word was law. He would be particularly pleased to invite some of my friends from the Polo Club to lunch. And then the penny dropped (discreetly confirmed by the PA). Sir M had only recently discovered that his lowly first sec economic was a member of the Polo Club, where he regularly rode and consorted with an assortment of (ex-)maharajahs, only a few of whom Sir M had met. So now was his opportunity to meet some of the others, an opportunity which he had only days to seize.

All international airfares were due to rise, heftily, on 1 December, which was why we had booked ourselves to leave before the end of November, and we would now not be able to afford the extra charge, which would rise commensurately.

"No problem," said my locally engaged colleague, "you will just have to start the journey from somewhere else, before the end of November, with a break in Delhi long enough to cover the high commissioner's lunch."

"How? And where from?"

"Oh, Agra should do nicely. I'll let you know."

After a few days spent wondering how I'd manage to get us all to Agra, to leave India after a four-year posting, only to reappear half an hour later back again in Delhi for a few days' stopover, where we might very well no longer have anywhere to lay our heads, I was presented with a fresh bundle of tickets. The top ones were valid for a flight from Delhi to Hong Kong and Sydney, departing 3 December, the day after the lunch.

"But what about the Agra to Delhi bit? We've still got to get down there and where are those tickets?"

"You've already done that bit, yesterday," said Jimmy, showing me five torn-off stubs at the top of the bundle.

"There wasn't any need to go physically to Agra."

"So how much extra do I owe?"

"Nothing. Agra is to the east of Delhi, so you are not being charged for the unavoidable doubling back to Delhi."

Once again it seemed to be a matter of East is East, entirely satisfactorily so.

The lunch went with a swing. The High Commissioner met all the maharajahs and when he bade us a final farewell he muttered something about how much he regretted not having had an opportunity to get to know us better before our departure. He'd actually had about two years; but never mind.

We had a wonderful holiday in Sydney. Catherine's mother treated us to a month in a hotel next to Centennial Park, with a huge Holden station wagon thrown in. Goodness knows how she could afford this, a divorcee on a very modest salary as a university lab assistant. But somehow she did. She fed us, organised expeditions, rounded up friends and relations and quickly became the children's way-out favourite Gran.

Back in the FCO, I was made one of the two assistant heads of financial relations department, in charge of the department's development assistance side. I had been put there as the people in Personnel reckoned that, after the best part of four years doing the aid job in Delhi, I was the nearest to a development assistance specialist that they had. Their thinking was logical, though I am not sure that it was entirely justified. But I bluffed my way through, discreetly helped by the FCO's chief economic adviser, Patsy Harvey. She became a great friend and an indispensable prop.

While I was in FRD I was told that I had been put on a list of possible candidates to replace the secretary of state's assistant private secretary, a plum job for a properly ambitious and clever chap – which I wasn't. I said I had already done my bit in a private office and had no great wish to repeat the process, not least because we would almost certainly have to move to London, as private office staff had always to be readily accessible. Moving would be financially ruinous and a great strain on our marriage. The personnel chap warned me that turning down such an opportunity would be recorded on my file (that dreaded object) and would forever be counted as a black mark against me. I meekly gave in to this unsporting threat and then did my best not to think any more about it. For a year or so I heard no more and really did forget about it.

Then one day, out of the blue, I was telephoned at my desk and told to report to the secretary of state's private office, to enable the private secretary and his soon-to-depart assistant to give me the once-over. The two of them were surprised that I had heard nothing for over a year, during which the shortlist had apparently been whittled down to two, and they were merely checking that I was a fit person to be subjected to the S of S's scrutiny, an ordeal that would take place within days.

This was very alarming news. I knew I wasn't up to the job and couldn't imagine how anyone had ever thought I might be. If I got it I would often be alone with the S of S, in Brussels or wherever, when he would encounter his various European opposite numbers who as like as not would address him in

French and it would be up to me not only to help with interpretation but also to take a note. My French was, at best, rudimentary. And there was more to it than that; I knew far less about the kind of political and diplomatic essentials – especially EEC ones – than an APS would need to know if he was not to make a fool of himself and be a sackable liability.

I was torn in two ways. My instinct was to confess my inadequacy and get myself ruled out, even though that would earn me an even blacker mark on my file for having allowed things to come to this pass. Or I could abandon myself to my fate, in the hope that the S of S would see through me and choose the other chap, in which case I would presumably escape the black mark. For, despite all my doubts, I was flattered to have been put on a shortlist of two for one of the most sought-after positions at my grade in the FCO.

I spent a few very worrying days. Catherine heard me out, over and over again, and without her support I would probably have had some kind of crisis.

I was told who the other candidate was. I didn't know him, but it was clear that he was in every way more suitable than me. He was doing a political job in an EEC post, entirely immersed in the sort of things that I knew so much too little about, and he was probably a competent linguist. Surely he would be chosen?

The S of S, Tony Crosland, saw me a few days later.

"You see," he said with a twinkle, indicating a fat file (presumably The File, the dreaded one) and a number of loose papers. "I already know all about you." He was unstuffy and friendly and I enjoyed our conversation, which lasted about half an hour.

I didn't get the job. Crosland said he couldn't decide and left the choice to Personnel. My head was relieved, but my heart was disappointed, though not for long. For, only a few weeks later, Tony Crosland was dead. He was succeeded by David Owen, a brilliant mind, but a graceless martinet and not a pleasure to work for.

In May 1978, I was promoted to counsellor and sent on sabbatical to Chatham House as the FCO research fellow. I was there during a phase of international relations known as the North-South Dialogue. My research project, they said, should relate in some way to economic development in general, or to the economy of a developing country. I had a rather generalised bee in my bonnet about India being in many ways a developed country (world-class science, nuclear programme, diversified industrial base, democratic government, etc.), but burdened by a grossly over-large and therefore impoverished, population – a notion that most of my interlocutors found simplistic and far-fetched. So I asked if I could devise a project that would demonstrate my thesis, and I was encouraged to go ahead with a series of seminars designed to illustrate India's ability to export technology, which I reckoned was a sign of developed industrial status. With the help of the Chatham House director and its director of studies, I got together a study group, including the ever-helpful Patsy Harvey and, as its chairman, Sir Terence Garvey, who had just retired from Moscow, where he had served as ambassador after handing over to Michael Walker as high commissioner in Delhi. Unlike his Delhi successor, Terence had taken a great interest in aid and Catherine had worked closely with Rosemary, his wife, in the Mobile Creches movement. The Garveys were our sort of people whereas, frankly, the Walkers weren't, and Terence made an ideal chairman of my group – sharp, no-nonsense and funny.

The group met once a month to discuss a paper. Chatham House practice was for each member to write one of the papers, but in the event, I wrote them all, apart from one on export credit which, thankfully, was put together by a kindly expert from some appropriate institution in the City. By writing most of the papers I was better able to steer the project's argument the way I wanted – perhaps not best research practice, but one that certainly suited me. And when, after an agreeable month's field research in India, the UAE, Kuwait and Saudi Arabia and I had drawn all the threads together and the director had asked me if I would like to turn them into a book, I was of course flattered and suddenly very busy – more so than I had been during the months of research. I had to rejig a fair amount of my material, which meant cajoling overworked secretaries, already assigned to new research projects, to do just a little more typing for me (this was before the days of word processors) and then to find someone somewhere in Whitehall to hammer out an entire typescript (top copy and two carbons), ready for editing and publishing. Both the FCO and the ODM refused to help, but the MOD, surprisingly, agreed to take the job on and completed it in under a week.

Three copies of a book even as short as mine in typescript are surprisingly heavy, so I put the two carbon-copy flimsies in one plastic bag and the heavier top copy in another and set off from the MOD back to the FCO on the other side of Whitehall, where I had arranged to leave my precious cargo for the night. I waited by the Cenotaph for a gap in the traffic and then made a dash for the pavement, where I arrived a few seconds later minus one of the bags, which was sitting in the middle of the road with a No 24 bus bearing down on it. I had dispiriting visions of an explosion of typescript all over Whitehall. This miraculously failed to materialise and I had just enough time to run back and retrieve the bag before the arrival of a speeding No 77. Both bag handles had broken.

While all this book production was going on the FCO administration were plotting to appoint their own diplomatic service person as the IBRD 'alternate' in Washington, a slot traditionally filled by someone from the ODM. I was to be the fall-guy, an exciting but extremely alarming prospect. There were two 'alternates', both nominally counsellors in the embassy, but in practice permanent delegates respectively to the IMF (a Treasury person) and the World Bank or IBRD (hitherto always and logically, someone from the ODM/ODA). The FCO lost this Whitehall battle so that, towards the end of my sabbatical, I suddenly became a spare body, available to fill any unplanned counsellor slot that might crop up. And one very soon did, in Prague, where the head of chancery had had to be withdrawn following a domestic tragedy. Thus it was pure happenstance that launched the East European part of my career and we were bundled off to Prague in short order, with little time for briefing and preparation and none for language training.

Two weeks after our arrival the ambassador went on four months' leave. He was about to retire and was anxious to use up all his untaken leave before his final departure date. This understandable ambition had been thwarted twice – first by Mrs Thatcher when she became prime minister and promptly suspended ambassadorial leave world-wide, and then by the tragedy that had required my predecessor to be withdrawn. So, in December 1979, after sixteen months spent living the calm and unhurried life of a scholar at Chatham House, I was suddenly chargé d'affaires in deeply communist Prague. I had never before served behind the Iron Curtain; I was newly promoted, innocent of all but a few words of the Czech language, and desperate to finish my book. It is hardly surprising that the embassy staff wondered what they had been landed with by way of a temporary boss, and it was a month or so before we all began to see eye to eye.

Finishing the book meant exchanges of detailed correspondence, via the diplomatic bag, with the Chatham House publications editor, a lady of whom all Chatham House writers were in justified awe. She improved my efforts hugely, but in doing so reduced the book's already slender proportions – and it had seemed enormous when lying as a defenceless typescript in the middle of Whitehall, threatened by an oncoming No 24 bus – to something little fatter than a pamphlet, hardly justifying its hardback format. She achieved this by throwing out all the adverbs and most of the adjectives, as well as the summaries at the end of each chapter – a cunning book-fattening wheeze passed on to me by an old Chatham House pro (now a knighted professor emeritus, not that his book-fattening skills can have had much to do with his later eminence). This blatant padding, however, which had added about twenty pages to my miserable 160, notes and index included, didn't fool the editor for an instant. Out it all went. And then, just when I had re-honed one of the remaining paragraphs to my satisfaction, back would come, a fortnight later, yet more questions and demands for citations or sources – demands that were not easily met now that I was cocooned seven hundred miles away in Eastern Europe, trying to do my new job and to learn at least a smattering of Czech. But eventually, all the loose ends were tied up and in 1982 the book was published by Christopher Hurst for the Royal Institute of International Affairs, aka Chatham House. Its snappy title – *India's Emergence as an Industrial Power: Middle Eastern Contracts* – can't have done much to enhance its sales, which I suspect were modest to the point of undetectability. But I never had to know the full, deflating details, as the copyright lay with the RIIA.

The book remained in print for an amazing twenty years, at the end of which Christopher Hurst rang to ask if I had any ideas about what he should do with the fifty or so copies that he still had in stock, ridiculously priced now at over £30. When I suggested chucking them in the recycling bin he said I could have half a dozen for a fiver and, presumably, took my advice for the rest of them.

Chapter 23
Prague

We drove out to Prague, where we were to be based from November 1979 to February 1983. Our new Cortina Estate was packed with clothing, books (including The Book, still in typescript) and other essential paraphernalia, without which we reckoned we would not be able to manage before the arrival of our heavy luggage. We were also towing a fourteen-foot sailing dinghy. This turned out to be even more of a nuisance than Catherine had warned me it would be, as I was incapable of reversing while it was hitched on. Reversing was unavoidable when I had taken a wrong turning, which invariably happened in the middle of busy towns at rush hour, where we would cause bad-tempered traffic jams while one of us unhitched the trailer and manhandled it across the road while the other turned the car around and manoeuvred it back to be reconnected. The Germans were more understanding on these occasions than the Belgians, particularly the inhabitants of Liège, who got particularly cross. And once we got to Prague we had to negotiate the final approach to the embassy, more of an alleyway than a street and equipped with a right-angle bend, which was also something of a challenge.

The ambassador in Prague lives over the shop, in the top two floors of the Thun Palace, above and surrounded by the embassy offices. We already knew Peter and Pat Male, the current incumbents, as we had been together in Delhi, where Peter had been the minister, the No 2. So, after we had gone through the now-familiar contortions of turning the car and the boat around and leaving them in a state in which they would not over-impede the workings of HM embassy, we went upstairs for a cup of tea, to be told that, once the important business of the staff Christmas party had been dealt with, Pat and Peter would be away till after Easter. As it was still November, with Christmas still more than a month away, I had assumed that I would have about four weeks in which to learn the ropes before being left in charge. But no, the Christmas party was to be held right at the beginning of December and the next day they would be off. I had barely a fortnight to get used to the idea of being the boss for the ensuing four months. I had been warned that I was to be thrown into the deep end. But surely not quite so soon.

After tea, we were handed over to a cheerful first secretary (appropriately nicknamed Tigger) who led us across Prague to the Vila Bělka, which was to be our home for the next three years. Tigger let us in, fumbled around for a light switch, as by now it was getting dark, explained that our housekeeper Miša had been borrowed by the cultural attaché to help at his farewell party (to which we could come if we wanted – we didn't), but that she would be in to meet us on Monday morning (this was Friday evening) and had left some bits and pieces to eat in the fridge, and then pushed off. We were alone in a huge and spooky house, somewhere in an unfamiliar city in an unfriendly East European communist country. This was the house in which the domestic tragedy that had led to my sudden appointment had taken place. We felt vulnerable and not very welcome.

Things perked up over the next month. The ambassador duly went on leave and the embassy staff began to cheer up. The children arrived for the Christmas holidays. There were parties and snow for cross-country skiing. Miša soon became a friend, cheerful and efficient and equipped with serviceable if idiosyncratic English. When Catherine bade her farewell and wished her a good weekend each Friday afternoon, she always replied, "I you too wish also," and when she reappeared on a Monday morning, she was wont to announce, by way of initial greeting, 'Blue Winter.' When it really was winter and we all might be blue with cold, we agreed and admired her economical and poetic mastery of our language, but found it harder to concur when, as she often did, she repeated this greeting in midsummer. It was nearly three years before the penny dropped. She was complaining about the wind. 'Blow Wind.'

Not only was I the counsellor and head of chancery, in modern parlance the DHM (deputy head of mission). I was now also the chargé d'affaires, from before Christmas till after Easter. This baptism of fire was cushioned by welcome perks, the best of which was an enormous Daimler limousine, jump seats and all, piloted by a tall, gloomy but dignified minder-cum-chauffeur called Josef, always faultlessly turned out. Once, not long into my stint as chargé, I was required to visit Prague's Technical University in order to present some books for its library. The Daimler drew alongside an imposing flight of steps leading up to the main entrance. Catherine and I remained in the back while Josef went up to look for our hosts and announce our arrival. We watched as he was greeted by a posse of the university's top brass and were just in time, having scrambled hastily after him, to hear him explaining that he was the chauffeur, while the chargé d'affaires was that scruffy little chap heading up behind him.

During our time in the Vila Bělka, which was in an inner suburb called Nusle, close to the Višehrad fortress, the Palace of Culture was built next door. Gottwaldova metro station, since renamed Višehrad, was at the end of our vegetable garden and from the top of the main tower (the Vila had two of them), we could see all over Prague. The embassy tennis court was in our garden.

Once built, the Palace of Culture loomed bulkily and menacingly above us. It had three immense metal flagpoles, with halliards that clanged incessantly against them. The building was surrounded by wide expanses of level paving – perfect for our children on their roller skates. It was also perfect for twelve-year-old Alexander's radio-controlled toy car, which he soon discovered shared a frequency with the Palace's remotely controlled doors. This meant that he could drive the car in and out of the empty building at will, with the great glass doors opening and closing at his command. The frequency was changed, however, for the grand opening occasion, a meeting of the Warsaw Pact, headed by Brezhnev, to consider whether to discipline *Solidarność* and Poland. And Alexander was kicked smartly out by a 'huge man, covered in medals'.

The Vila was large and eccentric. Its original core had been built in a restrained, almost demure, Regency Gothic style. But onto this had been added wings and a courtyard in a flamboyant mix of Dracula's Castle and Scottish Baronial. One of the wings was occupied by the embassy visa clerk. The house was owned (i.e. requisitioned) by *Sprava Slušeb* (Services Administration), the Ministry of Foreign Affairs agency that catered for the needs of foreign diplomats. It was assumed to be bugged, so we tried to avoid having conversations that might be of interest to the communist authorities. Their agent on the spot was a Mr Novak, a *Štatni Bespečnost* (State Security, i.e. Secret Police, or StB) driver who was also our *domovnik* (caretaker), assisted by his wife. They lived in a flat over our garage with their two teenage daughters. We once caught Mr Novak in our drawing-room, but he fled through the French windows before we could ask him if he was looking for something. We knew what his job was, he knew that we knew, and so we maintained normal polite relations.

154

We assumed that one of the Novaks let their office know whenever we went out because it was usually only a matter of minutes before we had picked up a tail, usually a Russian built Lada saloon equipped with a big whip aerial and crewed by two leather-jacketed men. These StB cars seemed to work in pairs, for no sooner had we apparently shed one than another would appear from a side-road and take up station forty or fifty metres behind us, only to be replaced by the first one after a few kilometres. We called the StB in all its manifestations 'Boris' and to this day if Catherine or I become aware of a car sticking to our tail we announce that we have picked up a Boris. Old habits die hard.

The outside fabric of the Vila Bělka was shabby and looked uncared-for, much like most of Prague, which seemed not to have seen a lick of paint since the communist takeover in 1948. Some of the stucco was cracked and peeling, again like most of Prague, much of which was permanently sheathed in scaffolding, put there as much to protect pedestrians from falling masonry as to assist in restoration.

As well as scaffolding, Prague – like other Czechoslovak cities – was decorated with large red and gold banners advertising the merits of socialism and exhorting the citizenry to greater exertion in pursuit of the communist nirvana and universal peace. Otherwise, the only advertising consisted of small posters announcing concerts and exhibitions.

The shops were small and uninviting. The *potraviny* (groceries) were often half-empty and the one near us invariably had a pile of dusty jars of gherkins as its only window display. There were two department stores, *Mír* (Peace, of course) and *Kotva* (Anchor, less obviously). The latter was supposed to be the smarter and more modern of the two, but we could discern little difference. Once Catherine dared to touch some of the merchandise – a blouse or a pullover – and was promptly slapped on the back of the hand by an assistant for daring to indulge in such decadent behaviour. Goods were to be looked at and perhaps bought but certainly not to be handled.

There were very few tourists and as a result, Prague was wonderfully and beautifully, empty. Catherine would often walk to the embassy. She remembers one occasion in mid-winter crossing the Charles Bridge when hers were the only footprints in the snow.

The embassy was equipped with a number of UK-based staff welfare facilities, including a shop and a social club. Certain other embassies were permitted to use the shop and the club was open to all non-communist diplomats, journalists and business people. (Interestingly, we counted Yugoslavs as non-communist.) It was generally thought to be the best of the various embassy clubs, better even than the US Marine House. It contained a bar and a lending library and once a week functioned as a cinema. It was run by a committee, with volunteer rosters for its various activities, which also included the embassy nursery school. The shop was as well-stocked as a decent British village shop and was managed by an embassy wife, though briefly and very successfully, by a local employee, till he was killed in a road accident that many believed to have been deliberately and cruelly engineered by the StB. Much of the stock was brought in from Weiden, over the border in West Germany, in the embassy lorry, driven by a member of the locally engaged ('LE') staff. One day we were telephoned by the driver to say that he had done the shopping and filled the lorry, which we would find safely locked up in a secure garage, but that he would not be returning as he had decided to try his chances in the West.

Embassy clubs and shops were the norms in all our 'Iron Curtain' posts. They fulfilled a necessary function in places where UK-based staff had very restricted access to local facilities, which were in any case poorly stocked or far below normal western standards.

Foreign diplomats, especially those from the West, were not just objects of suspicion, to be followed and monitored day in and day out. They were also very privileged. We enjoyed many of the same special facilities as the Party bosses, such as the best restaurants, permanently reserved (and presumably bugged) seats at concerts and the opera, use of the hard currency shop Tuzex, where one could buy western imported goods and Russian Lada cars. There were also a polyclinic and a social club reserved for foreign diplomats, although the use of this last facility was discouraged by our own security people, on the grounds that it provided the StB with copious opportunities to encourage compromising and therefore blackmailable behaviour. Western diplomats even had their own reserved slot at the Smíchov ice-rink where, every Sunday morning, one could see them, gravely skating round and round, deep in conversation.

Social contact between Czechs and western diplomats was discouraged, by both sides. It seemed to be assumed by the communist authorities that our main objective was subversion, from which they needed to protect their own people, while we were constantly on our guard against being set up in compromising situations, on the principle that someone with something to hide, such as an illegal currency transaction or a sexual peccadillo, could be blackmailed and turned. Our own rules were strict. Junior staff were not permitted to socialise with Czechs, including our own LE staff, without my permission (for as H of C I was in charge of security), and any approaches or breaches of the rules had to be reported as soon as possible, on the principle that something shared with the embassy 'confessor' (me) and therefore with our own personnel and security authorities at home, could not be used to blackmail the individual concerned. More senior staff, whose jobs necessitated some social contact, were required to report back to me after each occasion. As a result of these rules, I knew a great deal more about people's private lives than I cared to, and I found this part of my job tedious and distasteful.

As most Czechs steered well clear of western diplomats our socialising tended to be amongst ourselves. We entertained each other frequently and probably unnecessarily. Guest lists were repetitive, but food and drink and extra domestic help were cheap and we needed each other to unwind with. Quite often – and this applied particularly to the ambassador or the chargé d'affaires (I was chargé for nine of my thirty-six months) when there were visiting delegations – Czechs would be included in the guest lists. As often as not the person who showed up at the dinner or reception was not the one we had invited, but a 'representative'. Only on the major occasions, such as the Queen's Birthday Party, could we be reasonably confident that the actual invitees, or a reasonable proportion of them, would attend.

One curious side effect of the various security and currency regulations was the means by which we paid for extra domestic help, such as cooks and waiters. They were not interested in Czech Crowns. What they wanted were US Dollars. But foreign currency transactions were forbidden. Some diplomats ignored this rule and lived very cheaply as a result. But most of us, especially those representing the main western countries, were not prepared to break the rules (at the risk of compromise). So we paid sometimes in Tuzex Crowns (a kind of semi-hard currency negotiable only in Tuzex shops), but more often in 'units', a euphemism for bottles of Scotch whisky or cartons of 200 western cigarettes. A waiter for an evening would charge, say, three 'units', while a cook would ask for maybe five. When they went home at the end of the function they carried bulging bags which clinked. Our entertainment allowances were calculated by the FCO's overseas inspectors partly in 'units'!

When Catherine and I opened a locked storeroom in the Vila Bělka in the evening of our first arrival we were astonished to find it full of whisky, several cases of it. No-one had briefed us about 'units', so we assumed that our predecessors had had a major drink problem – an assumption that proved wide of the mark. This strange method of getting around the hard currency regulations was tolerated by the authorities and even encouraged. Perhaps that is how they obtained their Scotch? The country must have been awash with the stuff and we never discovered what happened to it.

Some Czechs either ignored the no-socialising rules or enjoyed some kind of licence. The former were mainly dissidents, while the latter were generally well-known artists or academics such as Petr Eben or Ota Janeček, whose international fame to a certain extent insulated them from the unpleasant attentions of the authorities. Not so of course for the dissidents, who if they were lucky were employed in menial jobs, but otherwise were unemployed and therefore at risk of being arrested and prosecuted for parasitism. As western diplomats, one of our primary tasks was to uphold and demonstrate our attachment to human rights, whether by offering discreet moral support to political and religious dissidents (by for instance attending or trying to attend VONS[1] and Charter 77[2] trials) or by making our views plain to the Ministry of Foreign Affairs and other parts of the government. Activity of this sort was invariably pronounced interference in internal affairs (a cardinal diplomatic sin), which of course is precisely what it was. The point, however, was that we, as representatives of liberal western democracies, regarded those particular internal affairs as beneath contempt.

One of the artists allowed a certain amount of licence was Jiři Ropek, an internationally renowned organist. Jiři was to be found every Sunday at St James's in the Old Town, which his presence and activity as organist helped maintain as a fully functioning church throughout the communist period. He was too well-known throughout the musical world for the authorities to risk adding St James's (Kostel Sv Jakuba) to the long list of churches 'closed for repairs'. Their leniency did not, however, extend to any noticeable provision for heating; the church was like an iceberg in winter, but well attended nevertheless by parishioners and by visitors lured by the prospect of a free recital at the end of mass. Once Jiři had established that I could read music, more or less, he deputed

---

[1] Committee for the Defence of the Unjustly Prosecuted.

[2] closely connected with VONS, but with a wider remit, for the defence of human rights and a larger membership

me as his occasional page-turner, a pretty alarming experience when trying to follow a dense score, such as Widor's Toccata, his showiest piece.

Jiří had a comfortable den-cum-practice room in what had presumably once been some kind of vestry. This was where he kept most of his sheet music and a piano and a harmonium, as well as a lifetime's accumulation of related bits and pieces. But, only a few weeks after the Velvet Revolution, with freshly revealed priests reappearing all over Czechoslovakia in an apparent ferment of religious revival, the full panoply of the Church moved back into Sv Jakuba and kicked Jiří out, as though he had been some kind of squatter rather than the brave soul who had kept it going through all the bad times.

This act of thoughtless ingratitude may have been symptomatic of a newly self-confident, even arrogant, Roman Catholicism after the collapse of communism, but it was in marked contrast with the bravery and self-sacrifice of many of its priests during the communist era, led by the great Cardinal František Tomášek. In order to be allowed to call on him, in about 1981, I had to seek the permission of a government body – permission that was not readily granted. At the time he was living under virtual house arrest in his Archbishop's Palace.

British and other western diplomats did not force themselves on the dissidents, as this could have endangered them. But we let it be known that we were at their disposal if they wished to associate with us, and many of them did. Getting to know these people, and giving them moral support, was one of the most rewarding aspects of our time in Prague. Catherine and I were aware of many of the activities of the 'Patočka University'[3] and we were shown *samizdat*.[4] When the pressures became intolerable for them, we supported dissidents – sometimes whole families – who wished to leave the ČSSR for a new life in the UK or elsewhere. This entailed long and usually unpleasant negotiations with the Czech government before, eventually, the people concerned were granted exit visas and we were able to grant them political asylum. But for some others who either did not wish to leave, or were prevented from doing so, we did our best to help, often unofficially and privately, because we were only human.

---

[3] seminars and lectures held in secret for the benefit of students prevented for political reasons from attending public universities. Some of the speakers were Western academics, including Roger Scruton, posing as tourists.

[4] banned or subversive literature, secretly published and disseminated, usually typed with many carbon copies.

We got to know Jiři Frodl and his family. Jiři, a former journalist and a member of both Charter 77 and VONS, was prevented from obtaining any kind of officially recognised employment. He kept body and soul together by helping out at the Reuters office, but in due course, he was forced out of that too and the family suffered severe hardship. Jiři was frequently called in by the police and threatened with prosecution for parasitism. It was only his increasingly poor health that kept him out of prison. We and other embassy colleagues helped with food and attempts at good cheer while negotiating with growing desperation to take the family into asylum in the UK. Jiři's illness was getting worse and we were determined to get him to Britain where he could receive the treatment that was systematically denied him in Prague. But he died before the papers came through and then the process had to be started all over again on behalf of his widow and two little girls, who were eventually allowed to leave and settle in England.

Jiři's funeral was held at a crematorium on the outskirts of Prague and it was, like all funerals at the time, strictly secular. It was well attended by friends and by fellow dissidents, including Vaclav Havel, who had just been released from prison for what proved to be a rather short spell of liberty. It was also well attended by policemen, both overt and secret, many of them busy photographing the mourners. Someone introduced me to Havel, whereupon a leather-jacketed thug shoved a camera in my face and, I suppose, took a photograph. The aggressive way he did this, in the middle of a funeral, was no doubt regarded as normal police behaviour by the dissidents, but it brought home to me in a few very unpleasant seconds the brutality and inhumanity of the regime.

Another of the security authorities' unpleasant practices was to harass junior western diplomatic staff. On the whole, they left senior staff alone (apart from the military, who were regularly given a hard time), but they seemed intent on breaking the morale of our secretaries and clerks. Maybe they thought they would be a soft touch. They seemed to take sadistic pleasure in upsetting young, single people, many of them on their first overseas posting. One of their favourite practices was to jump on car roofs, knowing no doubt that the car they were damaging was its owner's most prized possession. Another was to enter a flat in mid-winter and make it clear that someone had been in, by for instance leaving a window wide open for the snow to blow through, breaking a precious reminder of home such as a framed photograph of Mum, fouling the lavatory, or eating the two or three coveted bananas left over from the victim's last visit to Weiden (bananas were unobtainable in Prague) and tossing the skins on the floor. These creepy activities were meant to unnerve and it is hugely to the credit of our staff that they put up with them, almost cheerfully. And when, over and over again, I went in to protest to the MFA, I was always assured that they were the actions of a very small hooligan element that even a paradise like the ČSSR had been unable to eradicate.

Much of the above paints a sombre picture. But of course, it was not all doom and gloom. Despite the dreariness and the inhumanity, we enjoyed our three years in Prague – enormously. We lived in one of the most beautiful cities in Europe. My office in the embassy was the room reputed to have been assigned to Mozart by the Countess Thun (the Count was his patron) when she was chivvying him to get on and finish composing *Don Giovanni*. It was overlooked by the elegant spire of the church of St Nicholas, complete with its StB camera focussed on our embassy.

In personal terms, we were well insulated from the privations endured by the majority of the Czechoslovak population. We went to wonderful concerts and operas and saw around picturesque *zameks (châteaux)* and country towns and villages. Despite the restrictions, we got to know a number of Czechs, some of whom remain good friends to this day. We admired the stoicism and humour; Czech political jokes were unrivalled in Central and Eastern Europe. And we made the most of some of the sillier nonsenses of the Cold War, an example of which could be a good note on which to end this chapter.

I had not tried playing the viola since laying it aside in favour of political agitation, about Suez, during my first term at Oxford. Perhaps, now that I was living in one of the most musical places on earth, it would be worth having another go. I had long since lost track of my instrument, so, having bought a replacement, I set about finding a teacher. Eventually, through the good offices of Anglo-Czech friends, a teacher was discovered. She was a music student and she had to get permission from her conservatorium and her local Party and Konsomol (Party Youth) branches. Meanwhile, I had to get permission from my own authorities, not made any easier by the youth and attractiveness of the girl in question – a potential honey-trap. I was allowed to go ahead provided the lessons took place in my own house, with Catherine or a member of the UK staff present. The girl said that that was out of the question as she would never be permitted to enter, let alone work in, a western diplomat's house. Eventually, after more negotiation with the security people in London, I was allowed to take my lessons in her aunt's flat close to the embassy in Mala Strana, provided the aunt was present (to the latter's bewildered amusement). The girl wanted to be paid in hard currency. I offered Tuzex Crowns. She insisted on genuine hard currency, but said that it could be paid to her sister in Vienna. Our people checked out the sister and to my astonishment agreed. The lessons at last began, but one day the girl failed to turn up. A few weeks later she sent me a thank-you message from Vienna. I had unwittingly enabled her to defect! And that was the end of my attempt to relearn the viola.

In the early 1980s, we believed that nothing much would change, for decades or even generations. We talked a lot about détente, but I doubt whether we thought that it was much more than a pious hope. But towards the end of the decade, I presented my credentials to a hoary old dictator in Sofia and three months later he was in gaol, toppled by the upheavals that were spreading all over Eastern Europe, which none of us had foreseen.

In 1990, Catherine and I revisited a very different Prague, swarming with tourists, and we were far from the only people crossing Charles Bridge. We have been back again a couple of times, once staying in a flash new hotel just over the road from the Vila Bělka which, we were glad to see, had been done up and was gleaming in new paint.

Chapter 24
Iceland

At some stage, during our third year in Prague, the head of POD (personnel operations department) paid us a pastoral visit, during which he asked me what I hoped to do next when our time in Czechoslovakia came to an end. I said that we rather wanted a home posting, but he disabused me, on the grounds that we had already had a straight four years at home immediately before Prague. We should expect to do at least another three years overseas.

I had already been in charge for a total of seven or eight Prague months. After my initial alarm, I had acquired a taste for being the boss and was always a little down in the dumps when the real one returned from his latest absence. The thought of three more years as Number Two, or even further down the pecking order if we were sent to a large post, did not appeal. As a counsellor, I would be a head of department in London, but London had been ruled out. So I said I'd like to be considered as the head of a mini-mission.

Mini-missions were a relatively new idea. They were miniature embassies or high commissions, headed by someone of counsellor (DS4) grade, with only a couple of other UK-based staff. They sounded ideal. A minimum of administrative and representational flim-flam, but operating in places where HMG had decided we could not afford to be absent. A friend of mine had headed the first one, in Gabon, and had waxed enthusiastic. My Head of POD colleague said he would bear this ambition in mind but could make no promises.

A few months later, we were lounging on the beach on Chios, later a hell-hole for sad and wretched refugees, but in 1982 a basic and blissful Greek island where we were among the very few foreign tourists. Someone came rushing down from the shack that served as the beach's bar, shouting, "*Kyrie Thomas, telefonon.*" This was alarming. If someone had taken the trouble to track me down to this remote and unknown beach and then managed to get through on the phone, something awful must have happened. But, dimly through crackle and fizz, I could hear one of my colleagues in Prague saying that POD wanted to know if I was happy to be nominated ambassador to Iceland. This was not awful; it was wonderful and I was more than happy.

I bounded back to the family with the news. "That's fine," all four of them said, "please yourself. But we're not coming." And with that discouraging reaction they all turned over to roast another part of their anatomy.

But of course, they did come and we all loved Iceland. For the children, there was skiing, camping, swimming in hot springs, learning to drive on rough lava tracks in our Range Rover (quite a step up from a Cortina), fishing, naval visits, friends to stay (all busting to come) and total safety, so that they could visit friends or discos and walk back alone through Reykjavík at any time of the day or night without a care in the world, for us or for them. And for us, there was the whole amazing richness of Iceland's history, landscape and people, whose inbuilt reserve we gradually learned to penetrate (admittedly assisted by judicious administration of alcohol).

The day before we were due to fly to Iceland I was on the point of taking leave of my new London interlocutors in the FCO's WED (western European department) when the phone rang.

"It's Reykjavík," said the desk officer. "Hang on a bit, till I've heard what they've got to say."

Then, "Good lord. Really? Dear, oh dear. He's here now. I'll let him know." I was all agog.

"Your butler Jarvis has been arrested. He's apparently tried to murder his boyfriend in the residence basement and they're doing their best to mop up all the blood before you arrive tomorrow."

This news was sensational in every way. An attempted murder, bloodstains in the basement, desperate mopping up. Iceland was famous for its lack of crime and yet our new house, which we would be moving into in less than twenty-four hours' time, was the scene of something straight out of Agatha Christie (though she would probably have avoided the gay dimension). And I'd had no idea that we rated a butler, let alone one so P-G-Wodehousely named. But as things turned out, that proved the full extent of our butlered existence; we might have had one, if only he had not been so handy with a kitchen knife, but we met him just once, when he popped in to apologise for all the trouble he'd caused. He was serving a longish sentence but, this being Iceland, on a weekly boarder basis, so that he was free to wander around Reykjavík at the weekend to see his friends and catchup with the shopping.

In due course the scene of the crime became Alexander's bedroom. Our colleagues had done a terrific job with the blood, but some stains persisted – too faint to warrant a new carpet, as HM Treasury's bean counters have strict criteria for deployment in such circumstances, which is reassuring for us all as taxpayers. Alexander relished the stains, which he categorised as cool, even classy.

Without a butler (thank goodness) Catherine was obliged to fall back on part-time domestic help, up to a cumulative maximum of one and three-quarters of a person (the all-knowing Treasury bean counters again). At least these people did some work, while providing insights into the Icelandic way of doing things, whereas Jarvis would presumably have stood around looking supercilious and offering to fetch one a drink. Then one day we rescued two young English au pair girls who had run away from their abusive employers and they became our housekeepers, more like surrogate daughters than domestic helpers. They somehow together counted as only one and three-quarters of a human being – perhaps because they were only eighteen years old. Jane and Tracey were giggly and fun and we loved them dearly. Thirty years on and Jane is still in Iceland, married for a second time, with half a dozen children and two jobs, as a teacher and as a tour guide and still our friend.

Icelanders are famously brave and tough. They have had to be, to survive over the centuries in such unpromising surroundings. Soon after the war, a British trawler was wrecked in a winter storm at the foot of the thirteen hundred-foot Látrabjarg cliffs, at the extreme north-western tip of Iceland, which is also the westernmost point of Europe and not much further from Greenland than from Reykjavík. The locals, of whom there were very few, accustomed to dangling on ropes up and down the cliffs in search of seabird eggs, rescued all the crew, pausing nonchalantly halfway up the cliffs, which are Europe's highest and uniformly vertical, to give the British fishermen some hot soup out of a thermos flask to keep them going.

The leader of this life-saving team had in due course become the lighthouse keeper. He had received a British decoration for bravery and had been invited for many years to the annual Queen's Birthday Party in Reykjavík. But for some reason, his name had dropped off the list and he hadn't been invited for ten or more years. He was quite probably offended, justifiably, but far too well-mannered to raise the matter. His omission needed repairing and what better way than to go and apologise to him in person and see where the heroic rescue had taken place? Besides, we had not yet visited the West Fjords and this expedition would ensure that we travelled their full length.

The lighthouse keeper, now an old man, was delighted to receive us, in his house perched at the top of a terrifying cliff, miles and miles from any other habitation, somewhere out in the middle of the North Atlantic. He served us coffee and pancakes and showed us pictures and accounts of the rescue and his medal. I was struggling to pay appropriate attention and to register our appreciation in shamefully hopeless Icelandic, but I was distracted by what I thought I could see on a television set at the other end of the room. As soon as I decently could I went closer. And it was true. York Minster was burning down. This was certainly appalling. But witnessing it in real-time from one of the remotest places in Europe was also totally surreal, weirdly so, an impossible nightmare in broad daylight.

Our time in Iceland was punctuated by a series of these surprising and idiosyncratic events which in retrospect seem so unlikely that sometimes I wonder if they were only dreams. But they weren't; they were real enough.

There was the literary seminar, chaired by the president of the republic, at which the two leading participants were Margaret Drabble and Michael Holroyd. The president was a very erudite and glamorous lady called Vigdis Finnbogadóttir, who could speak at least twelve languages and, when we knew her, was brushing up her Hebrew, ready for a state visit to Israel. The seminar took place at Bessastaðir, the president's official residence, and was attended by Iceland's leading literati (and us, a bit less literate).

There was the present we received from our embassy landlord's wife when we stayed with the two of them in their wild summer retreat, an isolated log cabin with all mod cons perched on the edge of a rocky gorge through which roared the Laxá (Salmon River). The present was a copy of her translation of Njálssaga into Sanskrit, grandly printed and bound, a mere *jeu d'esprit* which had kept her amused during the previous winter. Sigrún Laxdal (Sigrún Salmon Valley) would have been surprised if we'd admitted to having spent our spare winter evenings just reading books and watching telly, rather than doing something a little more intellectually stretching. Her husband, our landlord, was Sturla Friðriksson, the scientist in charge of Surtsey, the world's newest island, then only twenty years old. They were a formidable couple.

Then there was the time when our three children did what Icelandic kids did each summer, which was to take over the grownups' jobs for a few weeks, the only way that a country with so small a population could keep functioning while the adults took a break. Thus, when you stopped at a country petrol pump in July or August or paid for your purchases at the supermarket till, you were served by a teenager. Phoebe worked in a fish factory; in a neat irony Alexander was a temporary member of the coastguard, chipping paint off the Þor (Thor), one of the two gunboats that had defeated our Royal Navy in the Cod Wars only a few years earlier; and Corinna, judged at fourteen too young for a genuinely adult job, worked as a gardener in Reykjavík's parks department. They all earned proper money; the two temporary adults went back to school with about a thousand pounds each, while Corinna had to make do with eight hundred.

There was Thursday evening when there was no television, so that the Icelandic Symphony Orchestra could hold its weekly concert without unfair competition. And, conversely, there were two occasions on other days each week when Icelanders, who were serious telephonaholics, would not have dreamed of ringing each other up. For the whole population was watching either 'Yes Minister' or 'Dallas', Vigdis, Sigrún and Sturla included.

Then there was the contrast between the harsh modern world of the Cold War, epitomised by the American manned NATO base at Keflavík and the land of myth and magic, peopled still by trolls and fairies and saga folk who lived on in the names of their farms and on the vellum of the sagas themselves, stored like the hallowed relics that they are in secure underground vaults.

"You may have your castles and your cathedrals, but we have our sagas," as President Vigdis used to say.

And what an astonishing body of mediaeval literature they are. My appetite was whetted when I studied Hrafnkelssaga as part of my degree course at Oxford, and three years' residence in the land of their creation brought me face to face with them again. In retirement, I tried to give audiences on cruise ships a flavour of them and a tidied-up version of one of these talks can serve as a saga chapter in this memoir, in juxtaposition with a couple of NATO base tales.

Chapter 25
Burns Supper

I am not Scottish, not even partially. Nor is Catherine. So neither of us had had much experience of Burns Suppers. But during our first few months in Reykjavík we learned that the Burns Supper at the NATO base at Keflavík was something special. We assumed that it was a largely American affair, given that the base was operated on behalf of the Alliance by the Americans, specifically the US Navy, but that Icelanders would also be involved, naturally enough. And we also assumed that, as fellow NATO members, we would be invited, along perhaps with our NATO diplomatic colleagues from the US, France, Denmark, West Germany and Norway. We even thought that, since Scotland was part of the United Kingdom and the Supper was in celebration of Scotland's national poet, we would have priority. Furthermore, RAF maritime patrol Nimrods operated regularly in and out of the Keflavík base, so that in a sense it was British as well as American.

Christmas and New Year came and went. But no invitation.

When we received an invitation a year later we were slightly fazed. Did they really want us? Had word of our disappointment the previous year somehow reached the ears of the admiral commanding the base and had he taken slightly demeaning pity on us? In other words, should we accept? For by this time we had discovered that none of my fellow NATO ambassadors had ever been invited, not even the American. But we were also aware that our predecessors, who were fully paid-up Scots, had been, as had a few – very few – Icelanders. So, chin up and be brave and we accepted.

Keflavík is about twenty-five miles from Reykjavík and the weather in Iceland in January can be challenging, especially at night. The invitation, for 7 pm, specified carriages at 1 a.m., so we were apprehensive about asking Rikki, the embassy's driver and resident sage, with a family to go home to in the evening, to take us. After all, we had a Range Rover of our own and one of us could resist the temptation to overdo the booze, even supposing that there would be any. For was not the US navy dry? But Rikki was having none of it. We would both, he assured us, be very drunk by the time we emerged in the small hours and it was his duty to ensure our safe return. He knew somewhere where he could spend the six-hour wait in comfort. He would probably doze. He would be all right. He insisted.

On our way to the officers' mess, or wardroom, or whatever it was called, we had to pass an apron where were drawn up serried ranks of Lockheed Orions, the US navy's standard maritime patrol aircraft. We were glad to see that there was also a Nimrod, which meant that we would probably enjoy the company of a few fellow Brits. And I thought I could discern a few more, out on the dark edge of the airfield beyond the Orions. But surely not; my eyes must have been deceiving me, as I knew that no more than one Nimrod at a time ever spent a night away from home in Scotland.

Rikki deposited us and immediately we were swept up in official US navy hospitality, with Catherine on the arm of a super polite young ensign, all *Yes Ma'am, No Ma'am, This way Ma'am,* and me meekly following another, into an ante-room, where coats were removed and drinks were offered – soft only, as I had suspected. There were uniforms and kilts and glittery ladies and suddenly a bagpiper, behind whom we processed into an enormous dining hall. As we were marched round to our allotted places I gradually began to realise that many of the uniforms were air force blue, RAF blue to be precise.

Catherine was shown to her seat, on the admiral's right, with me – thank goodness – to her right. (So we were the guests of honour: oh dear.) In front of each place stood a full litre bottle of Famous Grouse and a carafe of water. The admiral invited the Queen's RAF chaplain to say grace, which he did in a suitably pawky, Burnsish way, and we were off. Gradually over the next five or six hours, amid the speeches and sketches and increasing alcoholic fuzz, we learned that half the RAF's top brass were present, having flown over from Lossiemouth in a flotilla of Nimrods, bearing enough Grouse, neeps and haggis to fuel a Scottish army, and that this important exercise happened every January in pursuit of greater allied coordination in the North Atlantic. The Russians meanwhile, Burns-lovers to a man, sportingly undertook by tacit understanding not to play any alarming games on the one night a year when most of NATO's North Atlantic air surveillance capability was otherwise engaged.

The order of events, including the ritual stabbing of the haggis and numerous witty recitations, appeared on printed menu cards by each place. Slowly we worked our way through them, till the prospect of Rikki, the car and home to bed began to appear feasible, if still only remotely. But then, through my befuddled head, came unwelcome news, relayed to me from the admiral via Catherine. The British ambassador would wind proceedings up with an (unscheduled) address.

Goodness knows what I said and I don't suppose it mattered as my audience were a long way past caring or even listening.

The admiral pronounced the evening at an end and we were ushered out by our ensigns, both apparently still stone-cold sober. So maybe the US navy – or at any rate part of it – was still reassuringly dry? Rikki was there, happy to see that his predictions had proved correct, and an hour later we were home in bed, nursing hangovers earned in the service of the Crown.

We were not invited again. Perhaps my closing speech had not come up to scratch. Or maybe it was because our friend the admiral had by then been relieved of his command, not for holding a gargantuan party, but for giving his dentist a friendly pinch on the bottom. The dentist, a US naval officer, was female and in those days, some US admirals of Italian descent still thought it reasonable to pat or pinch a girls' bottom, after she had pulled their tooth out. But this was not how the Pentagon, or the dentist, saw things. The replacement admiral was a very different kind of chap, certainly not the sort who pinched dentists' bottoms and we never got to know him very well. He may even have discontinued the traditional Keflavík Burns Supper. We shall never know. It would have died anyway, as the one we attended took place only four or five years before the end of the Cold War and the Keflavík NATO base is now only a distant memory.

Chapter 26
Satan Comes to Iceland

We were halfway through a briefing deep in the bowels of the NATO base at Keflavík. The visiting minister was learning all about the numbers of Soviet submarines passing through the Greenland Gap when there was an interruption. A civil airliner was about to make an emergency landing with a bomb on board, or so it was said. (Keflavík functioned both as Reykjavík's international airport and as NATO's eyes and ears in the North Atlantic.) The plane was British, a BA jumbo en route to Los Angeles. Our US navy hosts looked at us accusingly, as though we had arranged this uncalled-for interruption to the smooth running of the base, and brought the briefing to a speedy conclusion.

We moved into the admiral's office for what was to prove a protracted stay. The plane had meanwhile landed and come to an inconvenient halt across the taxiway leading to Keflavík's two hardened hangers that contained who knows what agents of Armageddon. The passengers, we learned – mainly blue-rinsed Californian matrons on their way home from a convention – were now milling about in Keflavík's modest arrivals hall, minus their shoes and most of their belongings, having slid down the escape chutes. There were more than three hundred of them and they were not happy. Nor was their captain. This information and plenty more like it was relayed to us by a harassed lieutenant USN who had drawn the short straw as that day's officer liaising with the civil authorities across the way.

The stricken plane was British. Its passengers were mainly American. They were on Icelandic soil and presumably under Icelandic jurisdiction. But Keflavík was a NATO base, operated by the US navy. According to a note found in one of the plane's lavatories, a Libyan agency had planted a bomb on board – and this was only weeks after the St James's Square outrage when a sniper in the

Libyan embassy had shot and killed a young policewoman on duty outside on the pavement. No-one could take any risks.

The passengers wanted to go home to California, but there were no other aircraft available to take them on their way. The Icelanders wanted their airport terminal – their only international one – cleared so that normal business could resume. The admiral wanted that darned civil aircraft out of the way of his hardened hangers, if not off his base altogether. But bomb hunters were in short supply on the base, or indeed anywhere in Iceland. In fact, there were none. There were a couple of sniffer dogs, said the Icelandic head of airport security, but they only did drugs, not explosives.

The minister offered to summon the UK Bomb Squad. His offer was gratefully accepted and messages were relayed via NATO channels. By now it was mid-afternoon and we had eaten a sandwich lunch. Goodness knows what the passengers and crew had found to eat in a terminal equipped with only a small snack bar. Since it was clear that we were in for a long haul the Icelandic authorities had started to move the passengers into Reykjavík, 25 miles away, where some of them were found hotel accommodation. The rest were dotted around south-west Iceland, in hostels and farmhouses, for there were nowhere near enough vacancies in the capital, equipped in those days with only four, quite modest, hotels. A replacement plane arrived that night, to take them on their way, but by then everyone was tucked up in bed, some of them seventy or eighty miles away.

My memories of the hours between lunch and our eventual departure at two in the morning are of frustration, bad temper and crossed wires. Early in the piece, I learned that there were only four telephone lines out of the base, all of them – or so it seemed – permanently engaged. They were my only means of telling Catherine and my colleagues in the embassy what was going on and why I had not appeared hours earlier with our important guest. At some stage, the head of the Icelandic foreign service rang to ask what I thought I was up to importing a sniffer dog into Iceland. Didn't I know that Iceland was rabies-free and that the dog would have to go into six months' quarantine? I reminded him that the UK was also free of rabies. But rules were rules and permission was only granted when the admiral had given his word that every single dog on the base – some hundreds – would be rounded up and kept indoors until the visiting sniffer dog had left for home.

Later that night yet another jumbo arrived, containing BA's own security squad. They were told that their services were not required, as the stricken plane was in a restricted military area and would be dealt with by NATO experts, who were by then on their way from the UK in a lumbering Hercules. They were not pleased.

Eventually, the Bomb Squad arrived, headed by their most important member, an enormous black Alsatian called Satan. Within a few minutes, he was leading his RAF handler into the plane, from which they emerged a quarter of an hour later.

"No bomb," said Satan, before returning to Brize Norton with his human colleagues, where he was promptly arrested and put into six months' quarantine. Now it was the RAF's turn not to be pleased.

The British tabloids, which we saw a few days later, were full of pictures of a dejected-looking Satan and his distressed handler, with headlines like *What a way to treat a hero!* and *Jankers for hero Satan*. Suddenly, the Bomb Squad was one expensively trained dog down, and all for a false alarm in another country.

But later we heard on the grapevine that Satan had been discreetly rechristened Beelzebub, before being reposted to Northern Ireland.

BA tried to recover the costs of this fiasco from Her Majesty's Government. This meant that the Department of Trade and Industry wanted to know why the idiotic ambassador in Reykjavík had blocked BA's normal security procedures and instead insisted on summoning the RAF Bomb Squad. The omens for the future of my career did not look good. But once I had been given a chance to explain that these decisions had been made by a visiting minister, I was forgiven, with a deep sigh on the part of the superintending undersecretary at the FCO. I never heard whether BA got their money back, or indeed whether the DTI and the FCO managed to persuade the Ministry of Defence to rein their minister in.

Chapter 27
Closed for Sunshine

Sunshine was a scarce commodity in Iceland during our time there. But when it made one of its rare appearances the locals, especially the female ones, made full use of it, positioning themselves in strategic spots and engaging in Pre-Raphaelitic contortions so that all their countenances were tilted at the same angle towards the magic rays, like satellite dishes on a row of houses, to ensure maximum exposure. This behaviour, mildly sybaritic, occurred on any sunny day, not just weekends and holidays. It was as though people just took the law into their own hands, downed tools and made for the great outdoors.

But they hadn't taken the law into their own hands. They were enjoying an eminently sensible, even legal, right to enjoy a spot of good weather. Shops, offices, government departments, all would be closed for sunshine. I reported this custom to our parent FCO department, who readily agreed that the embassy should abide by it. After all, not to do so could seem discourteous in our host country's eyes and discriminatory from the point of view of our locally engaged staff.

One bright and sunny morning, when I had just sent a telegram to the FCO reporting that Iceland was closed for sunshine and that the embassy would be following suit, the telephone rang. Ingvi Ingvarsson was on the line, to point out that it was a beautiful day and that he thought we should go fishing – sea fishing, not fly-fishing on a river, for which the weather was unsuitable. His wife, Hólmfríður, had prepared a picnic, so could we meet in half an hour at his boat?

Ingvi was the head of the Icelandic foreign service, by our standards a tiny organisation, but a formidably effective one, and I was only too happy to accede to this *démarche*. We had known each other since NATO days and it was good to discover on arrival in Iceland that the MFA there was in the hands of an old friend. We had not, however, then seen very much of each other because, like all

Icelandic diplomats, Ingvi was obliged to multi-task. Not only was he the PUS; he was simultaneously accredited as non-resident ambassador to half a dozen countries, each of which he had to visit at least once a year. So this invitation, out of the blue (almost literally), was doubly welcome. Not only would I have an opportunity to learn a bit about sea fishing, but I would also have a real chance of bringing our acquaintanceship up-to-date.

Ingvi had brought along the MFA's doorkeeper-cum-security officer who, it soon turned out, was his closest office friend and his special fishing buddy, a happy demonstration of one of Iceland's most attractive features, its total classlessness. The two of them were already aboard and as soon as I had joined them we set off into the middle of Reykjavík Bay, where we joined a whale which, so I was assured, was only there because it had found plenty of fish, which we would now help it catch. Whales seen close up – say twenty or thirty feet away – are alarmingly colossal, especially if viewed from a small cabin cruiser less than half their length. This one, black and sleek, was about the size of a double-decker bus and it kept shooting up to the surface where it would squirt foul-smelling air and spray from a hole between where its ears should have been had it had any, before suddenly standing on its head and vanishing, with a whack of its enormous tail. Sensing that I was more than a little alarmed – scared rigid in fact – my companions assured me that whales rarely overturned boats and that, besides, we had plenty of life jackets aboard. After about half an hour, the whale disappeared, fortunately without telling any of its friends and relations about all the lovely fish, which we were then left on our own to haul out of the depths as fast as we could re-bait our multi-hooked lines.

When I thought we had caught more than enough fish, mainly haddock, but with some cod and a few saithe, we stopped for lunch. The sun was still out, Esja, Reykjavík's guardian mountain, loomed to the north, snow-capped, while Reykjavík itself stretched out along the shore to the south, glittering and multi-coloured. The picnic was delicious, apart from the obligatory *hákarl* (rotten shark) and it was washed down with the aptly named and sleep-inducing, *svartadauði* (black death – Icelandic poteen). But post-prandial snoozing was not on the agenda, even though the boat was equipped with bunks. It was back to work with the lines, hauling up yet more fish.

Eventually, Ingvi called it a day and we returned to port and a division of the spoils. I said I'd be happy to take a few haddock and even some cod if it could be spared. Ingvi decreed that we should each take home one-third of the catch, which amounted to 68 haddock, half a dozen cod and a couple of saithe each. This was an alarming prospect. What on earth would I do with so much fish? Where would I put it? What would Catherine say?

Rikki was on the dockside. Sensibly, he had brought the embassy's ancient and decrepit Range Rover, which already reeked of oil, petrol and horse manure, so a bit of essence of fish wouldn't matter too much. We loaded our seventy-six sizeable fish into the back and headed for home.

As expected and as was hardly surprising, Catherine was not best pleased. It was already quite late in the evening, but still broad, summer daylight, so she made us some sandwiches and said she'd be off to bed. It would be up to me to gut the fish and stick it in one of our enormous chest freezers, even if it took me all night. The ever-helpful Rikki insisted on staying on to help. As he had been a professional fisherman before joining the embassy staff, he knew what he was doing and gutted at lightning speed. I eventually got to bed at about 3 a.m. – once again in full daylight, after the one-hour sunset-cum-sunrise that passed for night in June.

Sportingly, the other members of the embassy staff, as well as Rikki, each relieved us of some of the haddock and cod, so that in the end we were left with manageable amounts. I cannot remember what we did with the saithe, which is disgusting. Perhaps Snorri Tómasson, our faithful *Íslenzk fjállhundur,* had it as a special treat.

Chapter 28
Sagas

After I retired from the diplomatic service, I tried to share some of the magic of the sagas with audiences on a variety of cruise ships and then later with fellow members of the Winchelsea Literary Society. This is what I said to them, beginning with a taster extract. (All the extracts are original translations kindly provided by Sir Christopher Ball.)

'One summer Earl Thorfinn went raiding in the Hebrides and various parts of Scotland. He himself lay at anchor off Galloway where Scotland borders on England, but he sent some of his troops south to raid the English coast, as the people had driven all their livestock out of his reach. When the English realised that the Vikings had arrived, they gathered together, made a counter-attack, recovered all that had been stolen and killed every able-bodied man among them, apart from a few whom they sent back to tell Thorfinn that this was how they discouraged the Vikings from their raids and looting. The message was put in distinctly abusive terms.'

'This extract from Orkneyinga Saga is a good illustration of all sorts of things saga-ish. It is concise, written in spare prose. It reveals that the saga-writer, who was Icelandic, was well aware of how the Vikings were viewed in the non-Norse, non-Viking world. It also almost casually shows us how the Vikings spent their summer holidays, for they were as fond of cruising as we are, though in longships rather than P&O (or Saga) liners and for a spot of raiding rather than sight-seeing. It is humorous: "The message was put in distinctly abusive terms." And it is historical, as many of the sagas are. For this saga, the Orkneyinga Saga, recounts the history of several generations of the Earls of Orkney from the tenth to the thirteenth century, with some fictitious leavening. And, while it is concerned with the Norwegian Earls who ruled Orkney and in this extract was recounting the adventures of one of them who lived in the eleventh century, when he and his associates were most definitely still Vikings, it was written by an Icelander, in Iceland, towards the end of the thirteenth century, when Viking behaviour had died out.

'"Vík" means "bay"/ Vikings were literally "Bay People", a curiously anodyne term for a whole race of aggressive Scandinavian sea-farers and traders. It was when they took to terrorising the inhabitants of the British Isles that the term Viking acquired its piratical connotation. However, if Vikings stayed on somewhere that they had raided or explored, such as North East England or Iceland, they were by definition after a generation or two no longer Viking, but simply immigrants, conquerors or colonisers. So King Canute was not a Viking, any more than were the "Rus" princes who ruled Kiev and later, Moscow, and thus helped lay the foundations of the Russian state. ("Rus" was a reference to the hair colouring – red – of Rurik and his fellow Swedish Vikings who settled first in Novgorod and later all along the waterway route to Miklagarđur, "Great City" or Constantinople.) No-one really knows why these people originally called themselves Bay-People; perhaps as sea-farers, who were likely to live near their ships in sheltered bays, they wished to distinguish themselves from habitual inlanders such as farmers. The word "vík" is preserved in coastal place names wherever their language held sway, as in Narvik, Wick in Caithness, Wicklow, Harwich, Reykjavík, etc.

'But, first of all, what is a saga? What does the word mean? In modern English usage, it generally implies a long, rambling, quite possibly tedious, account of a series of events, or even misfortunes. However, the literal translation of the word "saga" is 'something said": in other words, a tale – which is something told – or less precisely a story. The word is related to "say" in English and is cognate with "saw", in the sense of a saying, a 'wise saw". This etymology was long felt to point to an oral origin; most scholars used to believe that the sagas were later transcriptions of old stories recounted from memory during the long, dark winter months; and there were plenty of those in mediaeval Iceland – dark winter months, I mean! But it is now accepted that most of the ones that survive, particularly the great "classics", are original compositions – in other words, mediaeval historical novels and histories. Of course, they draw on folk memory, as I shall explain shortly.

'I won't go far into the reasons why scholarly opinion has shifted (largely because I'm not up to speed in this regard), but here are a few pointers. First, we do actually know who wrote some of both the sagas and other, connected works of mediaeval Icelandic literature, such as the Íslendingabók (a kind of Icelandic Domesday Book, written by one Ari the Learned) and Snorri Sturlason's Heimskringla, which is a complete history of Norway, written by Iceland's greatest scholar, in the thirteenth century, as well as a number of others. (Snorri, by the way, lived from 1178 to 1241.) Second, there are plenty of references in contemporary Icelandic literature, including the sagas themselves, to saga writing and writers, as well as to what was already becoming a popular national pastime, *sagaskemmtun* ("saga-entertainment" – the reading aloud of written sagas). Third, scholars have identified more and more internal and cross-references and give-away anachronisms. Critical analysis of the ways in which these anachronisms appear shows that they are part of an original, written account and cannot be transcriptions of recitations. And besides, all sagas were written in prose and prose is much more difficult to memorise than verse.

'There are hundreds of sagas, mediaeval narrative compositions, long and short. They were written in Iceland, mostly in the thirteenth century. There are three main types: first, the so-called 'family' sagas, second, the "kings" sagas and third, the legendary or heroic sagas. I know nothing about the third category, which are generally described as fantastic adventure stories about legendary heroes and I have never read any of the ones about kings – kings of Norway (there were never any Icelandic kings) – most of which form Snorri Sturlason's Heimskringla. Snorri's other works, including especially the "Prose Edda" and quite probably Egil's Saga, form the basis of our knowledge of Norse and Germanic myth and of Old Norse poetry writing and poems, but that is another diversion which I shall studiously avoid, as again it would lead me into dangerously unknown territory. (The "Poetic Edda", incidentally, are a collection of poems, possibly predating the settlement of Iceland, also recounting Germanic myths.) I shall stick to "family" sagas, which incidentally are often also historical, and above all to what they have meant to me.

'If you live in Iceland, as we did for three wonderful years in the 1980s, it is impossible to be unaware of the sagas. They are all around you, both as artefacts, wonderful manuscripts preserved in a kind of underground Fort Knox in the centre of Reykjavík, as archaeological remains and as a spirit or feeling that informs almost everything that happens or is thought about in that astonishing little country. Even though the sagas were written in the twelfth and thirteenth centuries, i.e. rather more than a hundred years before Chaucer, they can still be read with comparative ease by any modern Icelandic schoolchild, so conservative is Icelandic, a language that has changed less in the last eight hundred years than English has since the time of Shakespeare. Masses of present-day place names are in fact saga-names. They are a permanent record of the names of the people who settled there – their addresses in fact – in the ninth and tenth centuries – the age of settlement and the age of the sagas. And even the descriptive names, such as Reykjavík, or "Reekie/Smoky Bay", from the wisps of steam issuing from the many hot springs there, are the names that the original settlers gave them, as recorded in Ari's Íslendingabók.

'Ari's Íslendingabók is short and pretty dry, though nothing like as bureaucratic a work as our Domesday Book, which is really more of a directory drawn up for taxation purposes. The Íslendingabók contains some information about the settlers it lists and even a few anecdotes. But it is in the much fuller, and at times rather more fanciful, Landmannabók, or Book of Settlements – almost certainly also written by Ari – that we find the information on which the saga writers drew. For most of the family, sagas are about actual people and are based in part on actual events. But, like modern historical novels – Hilary Mantel's perhaps, but possibly even more so – they are imaginative literary works. As one would expect, given that there are about forty "classic" sagas still extant – for many more have been lost – they vary greatly, in length, quality and nature. Some of the earliest are very short – just a few pages – while the greatest and grandest, like Njál's Saga and Laxdæla Saga, are three hundred or more pages long in their standard Penguin Classics English translation format.

'Iceland was first settled in 874, when Ingólfur Arnason, on the run from King Harald Fairhair of Norway, found where his high seat pillars had washed ashore and, obedient to customs ordained by his Norse gods, set himself up as a góði, a mixture of a priest, a farmer and a chieftain, in Smoky Bay, or Reykjavík. If one was a Viking looking for somewhere to go ashore and settle in the heroic Viking and saga age, one threw one's high seat pillars overboard and then searched the shore to find where they had ended up. High seat pillars were the decorated props which supported a chieftain's high seat in his hall. They had totemic significance and any chieftain worth his salt and considering moving house took them with him in his longship. It took Ingólfur several weeks to find his pillars and it is by pure coincidence that, seven hundred or so years after his arrival, a fishing village on the site of his farm grew into the town that is now Iceland's capital. But it is a very happy coincidence, serendipity even.

'Iceland's population grew rapidly in the hundred or so years after Ingólfur's arrival. Word spread in Norway and in places where Norwegian Vikings had settled, such as Ireland and the Orkneys and Shetland, that there was good land to be had in Iceland, for anyone with the gumption to go there. "Iceland" was the misleading nick-name given to the place a few years before Ingólfur's arrival by another Norwegian wanderer, who had seen that one of the North-West Fjords was choked with the summer sea ice that often to this day drifts down from the Arctic. But the nickname stuck and by the beginning of the eleventh century, there were about forty thousand Icelanders. These were the people whose exploits, real and imaginary, are recounted in the sagas. By the late thirteenth century, when the sagas were written, the population had plateaued at around sixty thousand, an amazingly small number to have produced so much of mediaeval Europe's greatest literature.

'How could this have happened? How could somewhere with a population of, say, Folkestone, at a time when hardly anyone could read or write, have produced so much, and such wonderful, literature?

'Well, for one thing, most people in Iceland *could* read and write. For Iceland was different from anywhere else in Europe, or probably anywhere else in the world. It was a kind of republic, free of the malign rule of kings, largely free even of the priestly grip on education exercised by the mediaeval church in the rest of western Europe. At the time of the settlement, it was pagan, though a few of the settlers, who had come via a generation or two in Ireland or the Hebrides, were Christian (and quietly tolerated). Full conversion came, after due consideration in the Althing (the annual General Assembly or Parliament) in the year 999. Many of the *gódar* (the plural of *gódi*) switched seamlessly from pagan to Christian priesthood, loosely overseen by an imported bishop or two, but the church never acquired the grip over general life in Iceland that was the standard pattern in the rest of Europe.

'There were no villages, let alone towns, in mediaeval Iceland. There was plenty of good empty land to choose from and the settlers grabbed as much as they fancied, which was usually far more than they needed, which in turn meant that the earliest estates were big enough to be divided over and over again, for the benefit of later generations and further settlers. The climate was better than it was to become later, or even than it is now, so that it was possible to grow cereal crops as well as to rear animals. So Iceland was a land of scattered farms, many of which had their own little church, where one of the original *gódar* had settled. Thus there were no parish churches and at first only one diocese and cathedral (at Skálholt in the south), with fifty or so years later a second one at Hólar in the north. Since there were no parish churches there were no parish priests. Instead there developed a system whereby fully trained and ordained priests paid occasional visits to bolster the amateurish arrangements in the farmhouse churches. To this day Iceland is dotted with tiny, lonely churches, often miles from anywhere, marking the spot where once there was a saga-age farm owned by a *góði*-cum-priest, or later by a farmer-priest who was not necessarily a *góði*.

'There were originally thirty-six *góðar*, three for each of the country's twelve districts, though eventually twelve more were added. They were chieftains, a bit like the heads of Scottish clans and their power and prestige were measured by the number and effectiveness of their followers. They each presided over their local 'Thing' or assembly, and together they constituted the membership of the Althing, which was established in 930 and met every midsummer at Thingvellir (Assembly Plains) for a couple of weeks, to settle disputes and to modify or add to the laws, which were recited by the Law Speaker over a three-year cycle, one third per year. He was one of the *góðar*, the only one to receive any remuneration, and was elected to his position. The laws derived from Norwegian law, with one vital omission, for they contained no provision for a monarchy. This amazing oral format and transmission were mirrored by the way the folk memories, which were eventually to be written up as sagas and particularly the history of the settlement, were preserved. The laws were not committed to writing till 1117–18, to be followed soon after by the Íslendingabók, the Landmannabók and then the Eddas and the sagas.

'The annual Althing had no executive or fiscal powers, which were unnecessary in the quasi-democracy of the 'commonwealth' period, which came to an end in the late thirteenth century when the *góðar* voluntarily renounced their powers in favour of the Norwegian crown. It was a legislative and judicial body. It was also a gigantic party, when the *góðar* and their followers, from all over the country, met to trade, arrange marriages and fosterings (a peculiarly Icelandic custom which still persists), pick and hopefully settle, quarrels (either by legally agreed but unenforceable compensation, or exile, or often, unfortunately, by blood feud), but above all to gossip, catch up with the news and discuss the stories that became the stuff of the sagas.

'Some of these stories, the ones about the first settlers, were scooped up in the Landmannabók, later to be greatly elaborated and added to in the sagas themselves. And I shall explain in a minute or two how they came to be written, disseminated and preserved. But I think it is time to read you an extract or two, as they are great literary works and they should be given a chance to speak for themselves.

'Many consider Njál's Saga the greatest. It is a massive work, in three parts. Like most of the major sagas it is a complex tale of family relationships, loves, hates, murders and vengeful blood feuds. But within this unpromising sounding material lies a noble epic about two great men, Njál himself and his friend and protégé Gunnar. Njál is a farmer who lives on Iceland's south coast, not far from the now infamous Eyjafjallajökull, the glacier-covered volcano that disrupted air travel all over the northern hemisphere a few years ago, on the actual lower western slopes of which lives Gunnar, a few miles inland. At the climax of a complicated feud, which lasted fifty years, the wise and prophetic Njál is burnt alive with his family in his home.

'The main characters in the sagas are always introduced to the reader in a paragraph or two of physical and psychological description. This is how we met Njál.

'Njál was wealthy and handsome, but he had one peculiarity, in that he could not grow a beard. He was so skilled in law that no-one was considered his equal. He was a wise and prescient man. His advice was sound and benevolent and always turned out well for those who followed it. He was a gentleman of great integrity; he remembered the past and discerned the future and solved the problems of any man who came to him for help.

'His wife was called Bergthóra. She was an exceptional and courageous woman, but rather harsh natured.

'Nevertheless, Njál was unable to control the events that eventually led to his horrific end, because they were preordained, as all events in sagas were. He had the wrong kind of luck, or at any rate a shortage of the sort that might have steered him past the dangers that lay ahead. Luck plays a vital part in the lives of the saga folk, for it too is preordained.

'Great importance is also attached to place and geography. The saga folk are strongly attached to their homes, fatally so in some cases, such as that of Gunnar, Njál's friend. Later in the saga, after a complicated series of lawsuits, feuds and killings, in which Gunnar is involved and for some of which he and his ally

Kolkskeggur are both implicated, they are sentenced to a three-year outlawry. Outlawry in practice meant exile, as an outlaw had no legal protection or redress in his own country. In this extract we see the newly outlawed Gunnar setting off from his beloved farm Hlíðarendi.

'Early next morning, he made ready to ride to the ship and told all his people that he was going abroad forever. Everyone was saddened at the news, but hoped that someday he would return. When he was ready to leave he embraced them all one by one. The whole household came out to see him off. With a thrust of his halberd, he vaulted into the saddle and rode away with Kolkskeggur.

'They rode down towards the River Markafljót. Just then Gunnar's horse stumbled and he leapt from the saddle. He happened to glance up towards his home and the slopes of Hlíðarendi.

'How lovely the slopes are,' he said, 'lovelier than they have ever seemed to me before, golden cornfields and new-mown hay. I am going back home and I will not go away.'

'This change of mind set in train a series of violent and tragic consequences.

'The other two great sagas are Egil's and Laxdæla. Njál's Saga and Laxdæla Saga are connected, with the former, as it were, branching out from the middle of the latter, where there is an ominous reference to the sinister thief's eyes of a tall, beautiful child, Hallgerður Long-Legs, who is destined in Njál's Saga to take Gunnar as her third husband. Her various machinations and her enmity towards Njál's wife Bergthóra, who we have just heard a minute or two ago was rather harsh natured despite being exceptional and courageous, added to the fatal mix of relationships leading eventually to the burning of Njál.

'Laxdæla (Salmon Valley) Saga is probably the most popular of the big three, for at its heart lies a romantic tragedy about the beautiful and imperious Guðrún who, married against her will to her lover's best friend, forces her reluctant husband to kill her former lover and thus forfeit his own life. The feuds and murders that take place over the saga's 150-year span are fuelled by love, jealousy and revenge, and Guðrún herself is generally considered one of the great tragic romantic heroines of world literature. Intriguingly too, the saga encompasses most of Iceland's early history, from the settlement, through the establishment of the Althing and the switch to Christianity, to the birth of Gudrún's grandson Ari the Learned, the writer of the Íslendingabok and probably the Landmannabok. So the saga takes us almost up to its writer's own time, when all the sagas were written and the commonwealth came to an end. This saga is the perfect example of the Hilary Mantel type historical novel, or faction.

'Egil's Saga is the story of the life of Egil Skallagrimsson, a brutal tenth-century farmer and warrior who was also, contrarily, one of mediaeval Iceland's greatest poets. His saga is where we find his poems. And, as I have already mentioned, many scholars now think that it was written by his descendant Snorri Sturlason.

'Now to the writing and dissemination. How were these many and in some cases long and complex works written down and published before the invention of printing?

'Before the arrival of Christianity and the Church Icelanders were largely illiterate. A few people, presumably *godar*, knew how to write, using the runic alphabet inherited from their Germanic ancestors, but there is no evidence that anything other than the odd notice or inventory was ever attempted. But with the new religion came a few foreign priests, mainly English and German, including the first two bishops, who were both English. And with them came writing, with the English alphabet, i.e. the Latin alphabet plus thorn (þ) and eth (ð), which the Icelanders wisely retained, while we allowed ourselves to be bullied by the Normans into dropping (though in this text I am eschewing thorn except when really necessary). These foreign priests also brought books and manuscripts – in Latin.

'Latin never really caught on, apart from in the precincts of Skalhólt and Hólar cathedrals, where it was used for a shortish period for the reproduction of standard religious material and by a few writers, including Saemundur the Learned (1056 – 1133), Iceland's first historian. He was educated either in Franconia or Paris and in due course inherited his father's chieftainship, which meant that he was also a priest. He never became a bishop, but he was a power behind the religious scenes and he persuaded the Althing to adopt commonwealth Iceland's only tax, a church tithe. Nothing of Saemundur survives apart from his reputation and, probably exaggerated, association with much of Iceland's early literature, particularly the Poetic Edda. But it is probably precisely because he wrote in Latin that nothing survives. For, almost from the word go, most written material was in the vernacular. It had to be, because of the nature of Iceland's Church – national, not international, scattered, with farmhouse churches manned by the *godar* and other leading farmers, who doubled as amateur priests. These people knew no Latin and were none too keen to learn any. So religious and therefore secular, material was disseminated in Icelandic. And disseminated is the *mot juste*, as every one of the larger farms had its own little church. To be able to function, someone in each of them had to learn to read and write and it was not many years before Iceland became Europe's first literate society – and probably the world's. This happened in the twelfth and thirteenth centuries, when in England not even the King could write (which is why King John sealed, rather than signed, Magna Carta).

'Literacy and composition developed simultaneously. Sagas were written, Eddas were both recorded and written and copying became a major winter-time activity, always – and even long after the arrival of paper and printing – on vellum. Most bull calves were slaughtered soon after birth for their skin, the vellum that became books. Every farmhouse had a good supply of books, necessary for the *sagaskemmtun* (saga-entertainment) evenings which became the national pastime, for many centuries. These books were read and read, usually but not always out loud, and worn out and recopied. As a result, there are many variants in the surviving editions. Not until comparatively modern times were printed, paper editions produced, almost all of them in Denmark.

'By the twelfth century there were a few monasteries in Iceland and some of the saga manuscripts and other books were produced in them – in Icelandic and for the most part on secular subjects. For Icelandic monks felt as unbeholden to Latin as Icelandic farmer-priests.

'Eventually, Iceland became little more than an obscure and impoverished Danish colony, as Norway, of which Iceland had become an appendage in the late thirteenth century, had also long since lost its independence, to Denmark (and much later to Sweden). The Danes were indifferent and even cruel colonial masters and for centuries showed little inclination to study Iceland's rich cultural history. But all that changed once the Renaissance had, belatedly, stirred up an interest in old manuscripts and their subjects, and there was soon keen competition to acquire them, by force if necessary. The major part of the entire corpus of the best editions, most of them handwritten on vellum and some of them mediaeval, ended up in the Royal Library in Copenhagen, where a distressing number of them were destroyed in the Great Fire of 1728. Fortunately, one of the two Royal Commissioners charged with the cataloguing both of Iceland itself (a census) and the custody of the Icelandic manuscripts, the great Icelandic scholar Arni Magnusson, managed to save the most important of them, and in later years quite a few copies of the ones that had been destroyed surfaced in other collections. Most of these were inferior copies of copies of copies, but they were better than nothing.

'Iceland regained its independence in a series of incremental stages, culminating in 1944 while Denmark, which was under German occupation, was in no condition to demur. One of the first things that the newly independent – or once again independent – Icelandic government did was to demand its sagas back. At first, the Danes refused even to consider returning them. But then, in an amazing act of reconciliation and generosity, they relented and gradually, manuscript by precious manuscript, they were nearly all sent back to Iceland, where they now repose in the Arnamagnaean Institute. How unlike the British Museum and the Elgin Marbles!

'Perhaps the best known of all the classic sagas is also one of the shortest. It is a perfect, tragic novella, called Hrafnkel's Saga. In its Penguin Classics English version it is only 35 pages long, which makes it uniquely accessible for impatient, modern, non-Icelandic readers. It is also the perfect text for students, and I confess that it is the only one that I ever attempted to read in the original Old Norse when I was preparing for my degree all those years ago. But I was so gripped and smitten by it, and so surprised by the modernity of so much of its descriptive and psychological content, that I developed an interest in Iceland that has lasted ever since, and which to my delight my bosses in the Diplomatic Service pandered to when they posted us there.

'Hrafnkel was an early settler, a sheep farmer in the east of the country. He was a pagan and he was a *freysgódi*, or Priest of Frey. Frey and his twin sister Freyja (hence our Friday) were the gods of fertility and abundance. Hrafnkel was so devoted to Frey that he gave him a half share in his favourite horse, a stallion which he named Freyfaxi (Frey-mane). And he forbad anyone from riding the stallion without his permission, on pain of death. One day thirty of Hrafnkel's sheep went missing. The newly appointed shepherd, one Einar, fearful for his job, spent all day looking for them, without success. He realised that he hadn't a hope of finding them before dark on foot, so he tried to catch one of his master's many horses. All of them galloped away, apart from Freyfaxi. He knew he was taking a big risk, but he saw no other way, so he rode the forbidden horse, found the sheep and hoped that Hrafnkel would never know. But Freyfaxi, lathered and filthy, went to the farmhouse door and whinnied. Hrafnkel was outraged and immediately killed poor Einar. The scene was set for a tragedy which I will not recount, for I suggest those of you unfamiliar with it read it for yourselves. It is a marvellous story. It would make a wonderful film.

'I will, however, read you just one short extract, to illustrate what I mean by the saga's remarkable descriptiveness. It is about the route across Fljótsdal Moor. After describing one boggy patch the sagaist moves on to another.

'They came to another swamp, called Oxmire. It's very grassy and has a good many soft patches, which make it almost impassable. This bog is about as wide as the previous one but much softer so that travellers have to dismount. That is why old Hallfred used to take the upper path, even though it was longer; in his opinion, these two swamps were almost total barriers.'

'This was written in about 1300, yet it could have been written by Wainwright about somewhere in the Lake District in 1950. Those bogs are still there and the description still fits.

'I come finally to the two short Vínland Sagas, Grænlendinga Saga and Eirík's Saga, Eirík being the chap we call Eric the Red, who settled Greenland in the late tenth century. Neither of these sagas enjoys quite the literary qualities which distinguish the three "greats" and Hrafnkell's. But they are packed with "history", much of which was taken until recently with a generous pinch of salt. It is from them that we derive our knowledge of the Norse discovery of America at the very end of the tenth century.

'Like Ingólfur Arnason a hundred years earlier, Eirík was an outlaw who needed somewhere safe to live. He had heard rumours of land to the west of Iceland from sailors who had been driven off course, and sure enough they proved true. He found good pasture in what we now know is the south-west of a very large island and he named the territory, which appeared to be uninhabited, Greenland, even though he could see that much of it was covered in glaciers. He did this as an early exercise in spin in order to attract more settlers. This ruse succeeded and within a generation two settlement areas had developed, with a total population of perhaps five thousand.

'Over the next few years more land was sighted to the west and south by one Bjarni Herjólfsson, so Eirík's son Leif Eiríksson went on a series of voyages of exploration, partly in the hope of finding timber, which up to then had all to be imported from Norway, via Iceland. He landed, in succession, on Helluland ("Slab Land", probably northern Labrador, which does feature areas of flat, treeless, slabby land), then Markland ("Forest Land", southern Labrador and Newfoundland) and finally Vínland ("Vine Land", New England). All this and a good deal more is described in the two sagas. The descriptions fit, in that wild grapevines do grow in New England, as far north as Maine, and salmon, which also feature in the stories, do run, as far south as the Hudson. But there was little else in the way of hard evidence to back the accounts in the sagas, which were consequently regarded by many people – especially Spaniards and Italians keen to maintain Columbus's reputation as the first European to set foot in the Americas – as fanciful fairy tales.

'But then in the 1960s, the remains of a large mediaeval Icelandic style manor farm were discovered at a place called Anse Les Meadows (from Anse Les Meduses, or Jellyfish Bay) by the sea in north-west Newfoundland. And the rest, as they might say, really is history.

'The truth of the two Vínland Sagas is confirmed in other ways, with one of which I shall bring this talk to an end.

'Christianity arrived in Iceland in 999 and very shortly afterwards in Greenland. Eirík stuck to his old religion, but his wife Thjódhild embraced the new one and announced that she wanted to build a church. Eirík permitted this, provided the church was out of sight of the farmhouse, Brattahlíd, which he had built on the shores of his own eponymous Eiríksfjord. Brattahlíd was excavated in 1932, but no trace of Thjódhild's church was found, so that story was also discounted. But in 1962, a few yards further away and true enough out of sight from Brattahlíd, the foundations of a tiny mediaeval church, sixteen feet by eight, were discovered and duly excavated. A replica church now stands next to the archaeological site.

'Eirík's farm and his wife's church, are still there, in a hamlet now called Kagssiarssuk, just where the sagas said – a thousand years on and five hundred years after Iceland's Greenlandic colony ceased to exist, in the New World, hundreds and hundreds of miles from Iceland and Norway. Catherine and I have been there. I found those little ruins and the tiny reconstructed church, in that distant, lonely place, very moving.'

Chapter 29
Inspector

We flew home from Iceland over the 1986 August Bank Holiday and on the next day I reported for duty as an overseas inspector. I had hoped that I would become a head of department, but there were no suitable vacancies, whereas there was an urgent requirement for a new inspector.

The four inspectors each rated as a head of department. They had a roving existence, living out of a suitcase and making themselves unpopular with the posts that they inspected, where it seemed that their main job was to find financial and efficiency savings – in other words, to cut jobs. I was not looking forward to the job, but there was a carrot. I was told that, provided I kept my nose clean, I could look forward to rapid promotion to DS3 (minister or under-secretary equivalent). And this is more or less how things turned out, as I was told only two years later that I'd be the next ambassador in Sofia.

We were now living in North London. Catherine and the children had rebelled against the prospect of returning from Reykjavík to live, as they put it, miles from anywhere in a muddy field, so we had sold Barrow to our tenants and bought a three-storey terrace house in Tufnell Park. It was a good house, but in a pretty grotty district, a point underlined by the policeman who called to authorise the importation from Iceland of my (never used) shotgun. I was already hundreds of miles away busy making myself unloved in whichever post I was inspecting and Catherine was fed to the teeth with the Customs' disapproval of the gun, which was holding up the release of our heavy luggage from Reykjavík.

"They can keep the bloody thing as far as I care."

"Oh, I don't know about that," said the kindly bobby, "I'd hang on to it if I were you, living in a street like this."

The inspectorate operated on a school term timetable, so I was away for twelve or thirteen weeks, three times a year, and each departure felt just as school-like, with packing and gloom and home-sickness for the first few days. The only time Catherine and I had been apart for more than a few days was once when she visited her mother in Australia, yet now I was doing the only job in the diplomatic service which routinely separated officers from their spouses, and neither of us cared for this novel experience one little bit. Catherine joined me for two or three weeks while I was inspecting posts in Turkey and Greece and that made a huge difference, but it was also hugely expensive as the system didn't provide for accompanied inspectors, so we had to pay for her fares and subsistence ourselves. As we couldn't afford to repeat the experiment, I soldiered on unaccompanied for the next five terms while she redecorated the whole of our new house on her own.

In an official, bureaucratic sense I wasn't unaccompanied, as each of the four inspectorate teams consisted of a roving threesome made up of the inspector, the assistant inspector (a first secretary) and a PA. If the members of this tight little family got on together even reasonably well life for them was bearable, but if as sometimes happened they didn't, things could be pretty hellish. On the whole, the three of us rubbed along fairly easily, which was fortunate as we were in each other's pockets every waking hour for three months at a stretch. I do, however, remember being at first surprised and then privily irritated when the PA and the two assistants (the extra one was taking over from the other) sang along to the 'musak' every evening at dinner in the hotel, beating time with their cutlery, which they rattled against their plates and glasses by way of extra percussion. To add insult to injury, the assistants were invariably dressed in shiny shell suits and trainers, because they were off duty, in insensitive disregard of all the other diners, natives of whatever country we were in, who were in their best clothes, as befitted people out for a special treat. I dropped hints about the locals' sartorial smartness, in contrast to the sloppiness of the average Brit abroad, but my efforts were in vain, as my colleagues fully concurred, outwardly at least, while no doubt sharing pitying thoughts about their toffee-nosed counsellor boss in his boring sports jacket and flannels.

But the job was a good one, absorbing and educational, as it gave us a complete insight into the workings of the diplomatic service in posts all over the world, with plentiful opportunities to correct or improve our colleagues' living conditions and work practices. It was our own living conditions, for months on end and in hotel after hotel, that were so unenjoyable.

But there were lighter moments now and again, as for instance when, at dinner in a hotel in Lusaka, I ordered mangetout peas to accompany my roast chicken. The waiter looked puzzled. What was it that I wanted? I pointed to mangetout on the menu.

"Ah," he said, with a huge smile as he very kindly corrected my pronunciation. "You mean man-get-out."

And then another time, we had just finished inspecting the Luanda embassy, where for once we had been able to recommend a fairly hefty increase in the allowances in recognition of serious local shortages and the alarming state of affairs with which our doughty colleagues were coping. Angola was in the midst of a vicious civil war, the effects of which were never far even from the parts of town where foreign diplomats lived and operated. On the morning when we were interviewing junior staff, one of the PAs was late for her session as she had slipped in a pool of blood right outside her flat's front door, where the concierge had not yet had time to mop up after the previous night's, fairly routine, murder. Later that day, while we were holding our standard wives' welfare meeting (this was before the days of spouses, partners and so on), we were alarmed to hear small arms gunfire close by and suggested that we should adjourn and perhaps take cover.

"Not to worry," said the imperturbable wives, "the army chief of staff lives next-door-but-one and someone's probably trying to bump him off. Whoever it is won't be interested in us." So we carried on.

We packed up and said our goodbyes. The admin officer accompanied us to the airport, where we were due to catch the daily flight to Kinshasa, our next port of call. We presented our tickets to the check-in clerk who explained that the flight had been cancelled. When we asked to be booked onto the next one the clerk was unhelpfully vague. The flight hadn't operated for a couple of months and no-one knew when the next one would be – maybe in a month's time, maybe never. This was bad news for us, as we were due to start the Kinshasa and Brazzaville inspection on Monday and it was now late Friday afternoon. It was also bad news for the admin officer, who thought that he had got shot of us and should perhaps have known that our flight was a mere figment of some travel company's imagination. Kinshasa was not all that far away, but impossible to reach by road owing to the war.

The wretched AO took us back to the hotel and was about to vanish as fast as possible when we were told that the restaurant was closed as it had run out of

192

food, whereupon he invited us to share a few scraps with the embassy staff that evening. The few scraps turned out to be a Thank-God-The-Inspectors-Have-Gone alfresco banquet. The tables were piled high with delicious viands, including lobsters, fish, meat of every kind, fresh vegetables and fruit, clearly all locally procured, and plenty to drink. We had been comprehensively hoodwinked, but we looked the other way and everyone had a very good evening. We reckoned that anyone putting up with life in Luanda in 1987 deserved the odd blow-out, and never mind if we had set allowances that the Treasury would probably have regarded as unnecessarily generous. Besides, many of the vegetables had been grown in the kitchen garden that the ambassador's wife had established and cared for, for the benefit of everyone in the embassy.

The next day we had another go at getting to Kinshasa, with a greater chance of success, this time via Paris and Brussels, rather a long way round that would take the whole weekend and would assuredly cost a small fortune. But before we could sink into the luxury of the UTA Paris-bound flight there remained the small matter of negotiating the Angolan airport formalities. My colleagues sailed through and then waited seemingly forever for their boss who had failed to emerge. I had excited the interest of an impressively armed official who directed me into a small windowless room where he told me to open that bag. I pointed out that he had no right to see inside a diplomatic bag, for which I had all the necessary documentation, as he could see.

"Open," he said. I cited the Vienna Convention.

"Open," he said and emphasised his directive with a sharp jab in the ribs with the muzzle of his Kalashnikov. I got out my courier's passport. He jabbed harder and I could see that he had his finger on the trigger. He surely couldn't really shoot me, could he? Wouldn't the bang arouse a certain amount of curiosity? And wouldn't he get into trouble? But would any of these considerations apply in Angola, in the middle of a civil war?

I tried a different tactic.

"Money?" The finger came off the trigger, which I confess was a bit of a relief.

"Dollars," he said, beginning to look quite cheerful. "I'm afraid I've only got pounds. Would five be OK?" He smiled broadly, took the fiver, shook me by the hand, patted me matily on the back and wished me a safe journey.

We made it to Kinshasa ready for a 9 a.m. start on Monday.

Chapter 30
The Changes in Bulgaria

Late in 1990, Zhelyu Zhelev beckoned me over to have a word. We were at a reception at the American embassy. Zhelev was the newly elected, non-communist president, Bulgaria's first-ever democratically elected head of state. A communist majority had been narrowly re-elected to parliament that summer, but now they were calling themselves socialists and beginning to lose both their grip on power and their ideological ardour. So we had an anti-communist head of state presiding over a government formed by former or half-hearted communists, all anxious to ingratiate themselves with the West.

Zhelev was due to visit Britain in a few weeks' time. We had won the race to be the first western country to welcome him for an official visit and thus demonstrate our status as Bulgaria's new best friend. We were going to roll out the red carpet. Zhelev was to be accompanied by several ministers and by his wife. There would be lunch at the Palace, a reception at Mansion House, talks followed by lunch at 10 Downing Street, even a visit by helicopter to Dorset to visit the grave of Georgi Markov, the Bulgarian dissident and émigré who had been murdered by someone using a poisoned umbrella on a London street in 1978. This was to be the next best thing to a state visit and was to last five days.

There was, however, a problem. Immediately after his election as president Zhelev had dismissed most of Bulgaria's ambassadors, including Zhukov in London, a former member of the Politburo and therefore no longer suitable as the representative of a state that had thrown off communism. To replace Zhukov Zhelev had selected Philip Dimitrov, a lawyer and anti-communist Union of Democratic Forces (UDF) MP. We had been busy getting to know Dimitrov and his doctor wife Elena, helping brief them for their new life in London, when there was a leadership crisis in the UDF and he suddenly became its leader and therefore leader of the de facto opposition. Now what? No ambassador in London and only weeks to go till the visit.

"I've found an ambassador," said Zhelev, having steered me into a corner. "Johnny Stancioff." I suggested that Johnny (Ivan) might not be quite suitable since he was, as far as I knew, British – or Scottish, to be more precise. It was after all in his capacity as a member of the Scottish Conservative Party that he had asked me if he could use our diplomatic bag as a secure means of sending material to the UDF for use in the previous summer's election (and I had pointed out that this was against the rules, as no doubt he well knew).

"No, he's not," Zhelev replied, "he's American," as though that clinched it. I said that that was hardly any better. What we needed was a Bulgarian.

A few days later, I heard that Johnny had found his old Bulgarian passport, issued in 1938, complete with a photograph of his nine-year-old self, which the authorities had accepted as proof of his citizenship by birth. By the time Zhelev's visit took place the Stancioffs were installed in the London embassy and were thus able to play their part, even though Johnny had not yet presented his credentials. Catherine and I were included in the junketings, as members of Dr and Mrs Zhelev's suite, which meant that we spent five very splendid nights in Claridges and joined in all the engagements, including lunch with the Queen.

Johnny presented his credentials a few weeks after the Zhelev visit. His grandfather had been the Bulgarian minister in London in the 1920s (in the days mostly of legations, headed by ministers, rather than ambassador-led embassies). He still owned his grandfather's diplomatic uniform, which he was determined to wear for his own presentation in 1991, even though it was a bit too small. A skilful tailor let it out a bit. One of the tailor's other clients happened to be the Duke of Edinburgh's ADC, who must have spilt the beans, for the Queen, on receiving Johnny's letters of credence, gave him a knowing smile and congratulated him on the good fit of his uniform.

This all happened more than a year after the appearance of the first signs of what became known as 'The Changes'. When we arrived in Sofia in May 1989 Bulgaria was still a loyal Soviet satellite, so loyal indeed that it was not required to host a Red Army garrison and almost indistinguishable from the USSR's own constituent republics. There were rumblings of discontent in other parts of Eastern Europe, especially the GDR and Poland, but nothing much seemed to be happening in Bulgaria, which is perhaps why I, a generalist equipped with relevant experience gained from only one previous Iron Curtain posting (Prague, ten years earlier), had been deemed suitable enough to be sent there as ambassador. The president, a hoary old dictator called Todor Zhivkov, kept me waiting several weeks before I could present my credentials, and when he finally did receive me, treated me (and Catherine, who thank goodness was with me to soften the experience and help me remember what the old goat had said) to a half-hour harangue on the beastliness of the British. This departure from standard initial courtesies could perhaps have been a sign of incipient insecurity. Or maybe it was really how he and many other Bulgarians felt about us. Anglo-Bulgarian relations, after all, had rarely been much better than correct. Bulgaria had managed to be on the wrong side in both world wars, and no British politicians had ever shown much interest in it, with the single shining exception of Gladstone. But only five months after the presentation Zhivkov was deposed and spent the rest of his life under house arrest.

Soon after our arrival in Sofia, I asked the embassy staff what arrangements were in place for contact with political dissidents. None, I was told, partly because there were no dissidents to speak of and even if there where it was not 'our policy' to make contact with them. I pointed out that it had been very much our policy ten years earlier in Prague to keep in touch with any dissidents who wanted to be in touch with us. How else would we know, in so closed and repressive a society, what was really going on, and how to make clear to those who stood up to the regime that we were on their side? I added that I found it hard to believe that there no real dissidents in Bulgaria and said that I would like to meet any who wished to meet me. Of course, there should be no question of seeking these people out, if they existed, as to do so might endanger them. But we should let it be known that henceforth the British embassy would be happy to meet people of all political persuasions, for or against the regime. And, to my relief, most of the staff seemed to agree with me.

There was a snag. As the embassy had not had any appreciable contact with dissidents, how were we to identify them and let them know that we would be happy to hear from any who wished to be in contact? Fortunately, so I was told, there were a couple of British expatriates living in Sofia who might possibly be able to help us. Denise Searle and Mike Power were the editors of an English language news magazine aimed at visitors and English-speaking foreign residents. It was non-political, in other words totally compliant, but better than nothing. Mike and Denise must have had strong communist sympathies to have been able to land such a job. They were, however, friendly enough and were rumoured to disapprove of some of the regime's more hard-line policies, including its determination to obliterate the identity of its ethnic Turkish population in a form of ethnic cleansing, though that expression had not yet come into vogue. It was also said that they were in contact with locals who sympathised with their disapproval, potentially political dissidents. After discreet enquiries, it turned out that this was indeed the case. Mike and Denise knew lots of dissidents and they agreed to act as go-betweens.

A few days later, fourteen people trooped into my room in the chancery. Their names had been taken by the police post outside, but no attempt had been made to stop them entering. I asked each of them to say who they were and what they represented. A number were from Ecoglasnost, ostensibly a body that drew attention to environmental concerns and in doing so frequently courted official disfavour. We had heard of it but had not until then quite realised that an apparently apolitical exterior concealed a well-organised core of anti-communist dissidence. A couple were from Podkrepa (Support), whose leader Konstantin Trenchev was at the time incarcerated as a political prisoner. Loosely modelled on the Polish Solidarność, Podkrepa was an illegal umbrella organisation linking anti-communist trade unionists. Up to that moment, we had not heard its name, or not enough to take it seriously, though we were aware of Trenchev's existence and imprisonment, about which I was under general instructions to show official concern – as I was about all political prisoners.

The leader of Ecoglasnost was Petur Beron, a direct descendant of the great nineteenth-century scientist of the same name who was generally regarded as the founding father of modern, post-Ottoman Bulgaria. Most of those present seemed to regard the present-day Beron as their de facto leader, and indeed it was his dismissal the following year from the leadership of the UDF that led to his replacement by Philip Dimitrov and Johnny Stancioff's subsequent re-Bulgarisation in time to serve as ambassador in London.

Later another fourteen people trooped in. One of them said very little, but I gathered that he was called Zhelyu Zhelev, a Sofia University philosopher who had spent several years in internal exile for writing a subversive book, cunningly entitled *Fascism*, which drew parallels between fascism and communism. Zhelev was at that stage the chairman of the equally cunningly named Club for the Support of Glasnost and Perestroika, proscribed even though, obedient to the Kremlin's commands, Bulgaria was officially following a policy of perestroika and glasnost. This was just a year before he was elected president.

Bulgarians are good linguists and most of my twenty-eight visitors could speak English. Some members of the embassy staff had pretty good Bulgarian, though at that stage the third/second secretary language specialist post, which had existed in the past, had yet to be reinstated. I was only at the beginning of my attempts to learn and therefore linguistically useless, so at these first two meetings, we all had to manage without professional interpretation. Later, once the regime was no longer making any serious attempt to prevent contact of this sort, we brought in the embassy's locally engaged ('LE') translator, Marta Nikolova. Marta was our senior LE and like all the LEs, she had been foisted on us by the Ministry of Foreign Affairs and was therefore assumed to be working for them rather than us. This was standard practice pre-1989 in 'Iron Curtain' posts. We had to be careful what we said in the presence of our LEs and use their services with discretion. Many of them managed in due course from 1990 on to convince us that they were on the side of the emerging democratic forces and one or two even resigned in order to go and work for the UDF. However, we could never be quite sure about Marta. She was a powerful character, a hard worker and an excellent translator/interpreter. She also had excellent contacts. But the other LEs seemed to be frightened of her. We were told that her embassy job was a front, that she was a fairly senior member of the secret police and Party commissar in charge of all our LEs. This could all have been nonsense, fuelled by jealousies. But on the other hand, it could have been not too far from the truth, as that was the way things often worked in pre-1989 Eastern Europe.

But as The Changes advanced so we were able more and more to disregard old suspicions. So what if Marta had originally been a dangerous member of the other side, now that its component factions had largely either disintegrated or switched alignment? Marta certainly threw herself into what must have seemed to her a radically new role, suggesting people to meet, pushing me to the front of demonstrations and parliamentary meetings, introducing me to politicians, suggesting initiatives. Judging from the nature and quality of her contacts I found it difficult to believe that she was some kind of double agent, as they all without exception proved to be what she said they were. As a result, we were one of the best informed western embassies, with some of the best contacts. Certainly, my fellow ambassadors envied me my luck to have such a useful member of staff and I often caught them consulting her on the quiet – and why not.

It was with a heavy heart that I eventually told Marta that she had been declared redundant as the result of a London-based review of LE staff in Eastern

Europe. She was distraught, at what she, I am sure, genuinely regarded as a stab in the back and gross ingratitude. And she was right. The redundancy and the review were fictions, devised to pander to the fears – more likely jealousies – of other members of the LE staff, and also plain dislike on the part of many of the UK-based staff. I had resisted moves in this direction for as long as I could. But, after a period away on leave, I found that the scene had been set – letters were written and rumours created – and I caved in, ignominiously.

In next to no time a new post had been created, with a very slightly different job description, and an admirable person got the new job. But she was not a patch on Marta, who was exceptional.

1989 was a year of political ferment all over Eastern Europe. Disaffected East Germans had spread into other fraternal countries, with a number holed up in the West German embassies in Prague and elsewhere, where they were safe from the attentions of fraternal police. There were even a few trying to reach the West German embassy in Sofia, one of whom frightened the wits out of me late one night. I was reading the paper, with just one reading light on and everyone else already in bed, with my back to a French window leading out to the garden terrace, which was in darkness. Something tapped on the window and I looked round to see a man apparently trying to break in. As soon as I got up to investigate he fled. It was only later that I realised he must have been an East German seeking sanctuary with my West German colleague, whose house also had a French window at the back leading on to a garden terrace, and that he had come to the wrong one. My German colleague had a number of uninvited guests who arrived in this way at the time, whose existence and whereabouts had to be concealed from the Bulgarian authorities. But soon everything changed when the Hungarians opened the border into Austria, the pent-up pressure was released and the other East European regimes lost much of their earlier determination to restrict the movement of their subjects.

Meanwhile the Bulgarian regime continued its ethnic cleansing of the country's main minorities unabated. Something like ten to fifteen percent of the Bulgarian population was either Pomak (ethnic Bulgarians who had adopted Turkish ways and religion during the Ottoman period) or ethnically Turkish, mainly the latter. There was also a sizeable Roma minority, most of whom were also Muslim. For reasons best known to himself, but presumably as a distraction from the mess that the regime was making of the economy and people's living standards, Zhivkov had determined to remove these minorities from the demographic composition of the Bulgarian population. As even he could not very well liquidate or expel them – there were after all maybe one and a half million of them – he had resorted to a cruel mass campaign of identity suppression. By the time we arrived in Sofia, this was well underway. All Turkish names had had to be Bulgarised, mosques were closed and in many cases demolished, Muslim graves were vandalised and desecrated and it was a crime to speak Turkish or to wear Turkish style dress. For example, the acknowledged leader of the ethnic Turkish community, Ahmed Dogan, had had to rename himself Medi Doganov and was in any case in prison, as were the trade unionist Trenchev and Father Hristofer Subev, a turbulent Christian Orthodox priest who had made a public point of supporting the right of Muslims in Bulgaria to practise their own religion.

Along with other western ambassadors, I was under instructions to make it clear that we did not approve of this abuse of human rights, and was expected to raise it whenever I visited the Ministry of Foreign Affairs. But the Bulgarians had a ready answer. There was no such thing as a Bulgarian ethnic Turk. All Bulgarians were Bulgarian, so what were we complaining about? And the same went for so-called Pomaks and Roma. Have some more rakia. And maybe another cup of the Ministry's excellent Bulgarian coffee? (Remarkably similar to the Turkish variety, I would sometimes suggest, though this attempt at humour was rarely, if ever, acknowledged.) It was no good my pointing out, as I usually did, that in all the censuses up to the last one these minorities had been clearly listed and enumerated. I should not bother myself with out of date inaccuracies of that sort. Look instead at the latest census: no mention of any ethnic minorities.

The official with whom I conducted these sterile exchanges, Lyubomir Gotsev, was officially the under-secretary equivalent in charge of relations with western countries, but we believed him to be a general in the state security apparatus, a belief that was confirmed when he was unmasked once the communist regime had collapsed. My predecessor had apparently been in the habit of lunching with Gotsev every few weeks, to keep in touch with Bulgarian official thinking on this and that in a social, civilised way, and my deputy head of mission was keen that I should continue this practice. But I could not bring myself to do so. As far as I was concerned, Gotsev was a nasty piece of work with whom I had no wish to share tittle-tattle. I was wrong to be so fastidious, of course, for diplomats have to swallow their personal prejudices if they are to be effective. But luckily for me, Gotsev eventually became a has-been, before reinventing himself a few years later as a socialist MP and business 'oligarch', though not before I had had a few run-ins with him.

During the late summer and early autumn of 1989, the regime's campaign against the ethnic Turks came to a head, with a stand-off between it and the Turkish government. Ethnic Turks were allegedly being rounded up in so-called 'lagers' ready for 'voluntary' departure or enforced expulsion across the border into Turkey. All this was going on in the south-eastern corner of the country, where most of the ethnic Turks lived, which was officially out of bounds to western diplomats, but we drove down nevertheless, to get a better idea of what was happening. The police, overt and secret, were too busy harassing their own citizens to be able to keep a proper watch on us, so most of us got into the forbidden zone and were able to confirm that large numbers of people had been cooped up in ramshackle camps in the countryside before making their way, on foot, in donkey carts, cars and trucks overflowing with goods and chattels, to the border crossing at Svilengrad on the main road to Edirne and Istanbul. The roads and the crossing were jammed with traffic and pedestrians, all going the same way and all in shock and distress. In the course of three or four weeks over 300,000 Bulgarians who were ethnically Turkish left their country, most of them under duress – about 4% of the total Bulgarian population. This was said to have been the biggest single human displacement in Europe since the second world war. It passed almost unnoticed in the western media, which was preoccupied with events further west, in and around East Germany. The Bulgarian media, still entirely state-controlled, explained that all these people – without specifying how many there were – had gone to Turkey on holiday.

Soon after the ethnic Turks had been conveniently shooed out of the country, Bulgaria staged an 'Eco-Forum', an international conference on ecological concerns, under the auspices of the Conference on Security and Cooperation in Europe (CSCE, later renamed OSCE, for Organisation), in an attempt to burnish its credentials as a modern forward-looking state. Governments and NGOs from around the world were invited and all the apparatus of a major international conference was set up in Sofia's Palace of Culture, a massive modernist edifice set about with communist statuary in a park a mile or so from the city centre. The Forum was opened by Zhivkov and it soon transpired that the host state was represented only by its government, with not a Bulgarian NGO to be seen. We had assumed, naively perhaps, that at least Ecoglasnost would be taking part. But enquiries by western delegations met with bland assertions variously that no such organisation existed or that, if it did, it had not asked for accreditation. As we knew that these assertions were untrue we all walked out, explaining that we could not participate unless Bulgarian NGOs were allowed the same degree of access as NGOs from other countries, with particular reference to Ecoglasnost. The conference ground to a halt barely an hour after it had started, but a few hours later we were told that an administrative error had been corrected and a Bulgarian NGO would participate after all. So Ecoglasnost was admitted and the conference resumed its deliberations.

With the Eco-Forum finally underway and its participation assured, Ecoglasnost felt confident enough to stage a small demonstration in a park next to all the main public and Party buildings in the middle of the city, mainly to protest about the environmental consequences of a projected dam in the Rila Mountains. Unmindful of the likely PR consequences for a government hosting an international conference on the future of the environment, the authorities broke up the demonstration, arrested some of the ringleaders and carted most of the participants a few miles out of town where they were tipped out and left to find their way home as best they could.

News of what had happened spread quickly. The demonstration had taken place while the ambassadors of the NATO states were holding one of their regular meetings and we heard what had been going on when we emerged from the Turkish embassy, outside which were parked our various official cars, each flying its national flag – a small mark of western solidarity laid on for the benefit of the Sofiote citizenry after every NATO and EU monthly meeting.

I told Simeon, my driver, that I'd like to go home via Crystal Park, where the demonstration had taken place. Simeon was reluctant, suggesting that the road had probably been blocked and that it would be better to go straight back to the residence. As with the rest of our locally engaged staff, Simeon's loyalties lay partly with the Bulgarian authorities who had supplied him, in his case the Interior Ministry, as he was my personal protection officer, in more senses than one, and he could well have been told to try to keep me away from the scene. But I insisted. There were no roadblocks, and a few minutes later our very British looking Jaguar, flying a small union jack emblazoned with the royal arms, drove slowly past all that was left of the demonstration – a couple of overturned market stalls, two or three policemen and a straggle of bystanders, one of whom I recognised as Petur Beron, the leader of Ecoglasnost. It seemed only natural to stop the car and get out to greet him. We shook hands, and as we did so the bystanders applauded, watched by the policemen.

Over a hurried lunch, Catherine and I caught up with each other's news. She had heard that there was to be a march down a nearby street, which she would watch while I nipped into the chancery to report as much as I knew to London before visiting the Palace of Culture to exchange notes with our Eco-Forum delegation, which was led by a senior FCO official, Sir Anthony Williams, who was our ambassador to the CSCE. In the event Catherine allowed herself, willingly, to be swept along into a protest meeting, where she noticed that she was not the only westerner present when she caught the eye of my French colleague.

The conference had again been adjourned, to register the concern of the western delegations at the treatment meted out to members of Bulgaria's leading environmental NGO (in truth probably Bulgaria's only tolerated NGO of any persuasion), an NGO moreover that was part of the Bulgarian representation at the conference. There was a good deal of to-ing and fro-ing and eventually, some kind of face-saving formula was agreed to enable the proceedings to be resumed. While this was going on I heard that I had been summoned urgently to the Ministry of Foreign Affairs for a meeting with Mr Gotsev.

Bulgarian is an explosive tongue, mainly because, unusually for a Slavonic language, it employs definite articles, which are post-positional and consist mainly of the letter *t*. Thus 'bridge' is 'most', while 'the bridge' is 'mostut', 'mother' is 'maika', while 'the mother' is 'maikata', 'dog' is 'kuche', while 'the dog' is 'kucheto' and so on through the three genders and two numbers. This linguistic quirk gives an angry Bulgar plenty of opportunity to sound like a busy machine gun, emitting a steady shower of spittle in the process. Meetings with Gotsev were normally conducted in English, which he spoke almost perfectly, but on this occasion, presumably to emphasise the gravity of the occasion, he spoke in Bulgarian, with an interpreter. The three of us were seated around a small coffee table and I soon learned the full force of near-hysterical spoken Bulgarian, in both its acoustic and wetting potential, as Gotsev shouted at me from a distance of about a foot for what seemed an age but was probably only four or five minutes. The gist of what he had to say was that I was interfering in Bulgaria's internal affairs to an intolerable degree and that the MFA was minded to declare me persona non grata unless I mended my ways. After wiping my face clear of some of Gotsev's spittle with the demonstratively large white handkerchief that fortunately I had in my pocket, I said that shaking hands with the head of an NGO which was accredited to a CSCE conference attended by both our governments didn't strike me as interference, but undertook to report the minister's remarks to my authorities, and took my leave.

Gotsev's reaction was bad news. Expulsion of an ambassador was tantamount to breaking relations and I doubted whether the FCO would thank me for having precipitated such a dire state of affairs. In fact, I was pretty sure that they would be fed to the teeth and would at best consign me to some dreary job at home, organising queen's messenger schedules perhaps, or running the Tuvalu desk and at my previous rank (for I was still on probation as a Grade 3), or at worst propel me into early retirement. Like most people posted abroad at the end of a spell at home, I had been bumping along on empty, on an overdraft and seriously extended credit cards, a dismal state of financial affairs from which I was only just beginning to emerge. And of course, I had no wish to complicate the UK's foreign relations, though this loftier consideration was, I confess, greatly outweighed by my baser personal worries.

I sought out Anthony Williams at the Palace of Culture and told him how worried I was. He clearly thought I was a wimp and he was probably right. He suggested that we should have a robust telephone conversation, during which we would discuss the Bulgarians' many failings and the likely consequences – mainly financial, as they were heavily in debt to western institutions including British banks – if they were to carry out any of their threats. The Residence telephone was well and truly bugged, so we were sure that our conversation would be monitored and that Gotsev would get a transcript in next to no time. And sure enough, a few days later I encountered him in the margins of the conference. He was smarmily all sweetness and light. There was no way of knowing whether he had decided to let the matter drop as a result of the telephone conversation or whether – all bark and no bite – he had been bluffing.

On 11th November, I was half-listening to the BBC World Service 8 a.m. news. I was shaving and I almost cut myself. Zhivkov had been deposed! And where was I? On a short break in Istanbul. In the wrong country. Not in post. Away from the action. The stuff of ambassadorial nightmares. Why couldn't whoever had given Zhivkov the push have waited a couple more days? Would there be mayhem? Would the border remain open?

But all remained calm. It transpired that Zhivkov had been persuaded to resign by a cabal of Politburo members who had had enough of his patent inability to arrest the country's economic decline and rampant corruption and his apparent determination to stir up internal unrest, which was bringing Bulgaria into ever greater international disfavour. One of the leaders of this palace coup was Petur Mladenov, who as foreign minister had seemed moderately broad-minded. Another was the foreign trade minister Andrei Lukanov, a smooth KGB-trained 'Euro-Communist'. Mladenov took over as interim president.

Quite by chance, the PUS (permanent undersecretary, Head of the diplomatic service and very much my boss) was booked to arrive in Sofia on a regular pastoral visit to the embassy only a couple of days after Zhivkov's ouster. This was an amazing stroke of luck, which we massaged to look as though we had planned it on the spur of the moment so as to register British approval of this latest turn of events. So I was able to accompany one of the UK's most senior officials on a call on Petur Mladenov on the very first day that he was open to diplomatic business. It transpired that Sir Patrick (later Lord) Wright was not only the first western dignitary to pay an official call on Mladenov in his new role; he was the first from any foreign country. This apparently slick British manoeuvre drew much envious comment from my western colleagues.

Again quite by chance, a couple of years later, Patrick, newly retired and doing us a favour by advising the MFA on how to run its affairs in an accountable and democratic manner, as part of our Know How Fund programme, was staying with us. It was getting late and we were enjoying a gossip over a nightcap when the telephone rang. Philip Dimitrov had been asked by President Zhelev to form a government, as the UDF had just won the second post-communist general election, ousting the Bulgarian Socialist (formerly Communist) Party. Could he stop by, straight away, as he had some pressing matters to discuss concerning the make-up of his new administration – with many apologies of course for the lack of notice and the lateness of the hour? I told Philip that he was always welcome, at whatever time of day or night, and then did some urgent telephoning of my own, to muster some support. I have half-forgotten now who came. Certainly Les Buchanan, my deputy, maybe Nicholas King, the defence attaché and maybe also Christine Laidlaw and Sarah Lampert, the commercial first and chancery third secretaries respectively, four very doughty friends and colleagues.

Philip duly turned up, accompanied by a couple of UDF colleagues, Stefan Tafrov and Solomon Passy and explained that he wanted to be sure that the British government would have no serious concerns about any of the people he proposed to include in his administration. This was such an extraordinary request that we found it difficult to conceal our amazement, but we put on what we hoped were calm business-like expressions and went carefully through the list that Philip had brought with him. There was no-one on it to whom we could have had the slightest objection, so of course we said so, and then we all drank to the success of Bulgaria's new government, the first truly democratic one in its history.

After our guests had left, Patrick said that he'd seen some pretty amazing things in his time, but never had he witnessed a foreign prime minister checking out his proposed administration with the British ambassador, nor had he ever expected to. It certainly was a long way out of the usual way of doing things and it proved to typify the state of Anglo-Bulgarian relations for the next year or two. What a sad contrast to the state of relations from 2014 on, when the British government began to make toadying to the Daily Mail and UKIP tendencies by demonising the Bulgarians (and Romanians) a plank of their EU, immigration and eventually Brexit policies.

A great deal had happened between these two serendipitous Patrick Wright events, as 'The Changes' gathered momentum and took effect. We were soon assured in November 1989 that Zhivkov's ouster had amounted to no more than a reshuffle. Bulgaria was still a one-party communist state with a command economy, a member of the Warsaw Pact and of Comecon. But the genie was out of the bottle. It was not long before a swarm of new political parties began to develop, posters and pamphlets began to appear, some of them eventually morphing into newssheets and, later, newspapers. All this activity was still technically illegal, but the authorities lost the will to clamp down on it, and when the Romanian revolution broke out over Christmas, only five or six weeks after Zhivkov was toppled, Bulgarian television crews, still in theory Party controlled, were in Timisoara and Bucharest beaming back reports couched in unashamedly non-communist and anti-Ceausescu terms.

Political prisoners were quietly released, including Dogan, Trenchev and Subev. The government's anti-Turkish rhetoric was toned down and as the policy of ethnic cleansing slowly fizzled out most of the people who had fled to Turkey began to trickle home again. Dogan formed a political party (the Movement for – ethnic Turkish – Rights and Freedoms), Podkrepa's illegality was forgotten and Subev harnessed the power of a renascent Bulgarian Orthodox Church, with massive and often very moving demonstrations. The greatest of these took place after dark in the great open space surrounding the Alexander Nevski Cathedral.

Our children were at home for the university Christmas vacation, so we went along as a family group. Word had got around that everyone was to bring a candle. There must have been tens of thousands present, in near darkness. Subev was a powerful orator and we all did his bidding. At one stage everyone turned to face east, in a gesture of Christian solidarity and then, for the peroration, we were instructed to light our candles. The square was suddenly filled with flickering candlelight, as a powerful and moving symbol of a reawakening enlightenment, and the great bass bell of Alexander Nevski, silenced for half a century, boomed out. The demonstration ended with everyone belting out Bulgaria's ancient patriotic hymn, *Mnogo e Leta*. Then we all went home, in silence, without even a hint of violence. It is difficult to convey how moving this was. It was as though the nation had at last returned home after a long and painful exile.

Anti-government and anti-BCP (Bulgarian Communist Party) demonstrations took place almost daily. Alexander caught the mood when he asked: "Dad, where's the Demo of the Day?" and one evening he reappeared, full of how he and 'the lads', Bulgarian students he had fallen in with, had climbed the statue of (Russian) Tsar Alexander II *Osvoboditel* (Liberator) in front of Parliament and cut the communist symbol out of the Bulgarian flag that was flying above it. This really was interference, provocatively so, about which Gotsev would have good reason to complain had he known who all the perpetrators were. Alexander assured me that he would try not to get quite so involved in future.

There was very little violence. A few barricades were set up and the odd bus set on fire, but this sort of thing seemed more for show than for real. A few people were injured and there were two or three deaths, probably the result of accidents rather than of intentional force. This largely peaceful course of events was in marked contrast to what was going on over the Danube in Romania, and just before Christmas we were told that first the Canadian and then the British embassies were to be evacuated from Bucharest to Sofia, as the situation had become too dangerous for them to remain in Romania. There was no Canadian mission in Sofia, so were deputed to help, as good Commonwealth partners. The weather was vile and many of the Sofia staff had flu. But we had security, food, power and fuel, commodities in very short supply in Bucharest. My deputy at the time, Mike Frost, took charge of the rescue party. He first met the Canadians at the frontier on the cynically named Freedom Bridge over the Danube near

Rousse, a couple of hundred kilometres away, provided them with enough petrol and food to get to Sofia, and then the next day repeated the exercise for our own, rather larger, contingent, some of whom, especially the ambassador's family, were pretty shaken up. Mike and many of his team felt rotten and full of flu and were up most of the night, two nights running, doling out supplies and driving up and down a couple of hundred kilometres of road to ensure that there were no stragglers or others in need of assistance.

The ambassador's wife and daughter had been holed up in the cellar of the Bucharest residence, hiding from a sniper who had set up shop upstairs, targeted by a tank in the street. Meanwhile, the ambassador had been in the embassy chancery in another part of the city, unable to communicate with his family and unaware of the danger they were in. Somehow they were reunited, unharmed. But the residence was wrecked.

All the refugees from Bucharest were installed in the Sofia Sheraton before flying home to Canada and the UK. The hotel management did a wonderful job and everyone was processed, fed and rested in an almost party atmosphere of relief. And it really was a party for the ambassador's daughter, whose 21st birthday fell that day. The hotel's champagne was on the house.

We were able to find seats on planes for everyone, but even though Christmas Day was not officially a public holiday in communist Bulgaria, Air Balkan's accounts department was firmly closed and the tickets could not be issued unless they were paid for. The ticket office told us that they had no means of billing the embassy's account and that we would have to wait two or three days for the finance department to reopen. This was not deliberate obstruction, just plain old-fashioned, maddening inefficiency. Fortunately, I had a 'Gold' American Express card, which I was now able to put to the test. It paid the necessary twenty-five-odd thousand pounds (about half my annual salary) without batting a celluloid eyelid and everyone got on their way. A couple of months later, after Amex had begun threatening me with dire retribution, not to mention crippling interest payments, the FCO's finance department eventually conceded defeat and paid up. They had found my means of paying staff fares unorthodox and most definitely unauthorised. They too had been closed on Christmas Day, unsurprisingly, but had assured me a few days later that, of course, my Amex account would be credited immediately, an assurance that they then promptly forgot. Perhaps they had to carry the unexpected expense over into a new accounting period. Whatever the reason, I endured an unsettling few weeks, with repeated explanations to finance dept and entreaties to Amex.

During the first few months of 1990, the BCP reinvented itself as the BSP (Bulgarian Socialist Party) and the various opposition groups morphed into political parties, newly legalised. A number of opposition newspapers sprang up, notably, *Democratsia*, all of them chronically short of newsprint, a problem that did not seem to affect the BCP paper *Rabotnichesko Delo* (Worker's Deed), renamed *Duma* (Word) once it became the mouthpiece of the new BSP. In the winter of 1990–91, when almost everything was in short supply during the switch to a market economy, Robert Maxwell, the British MP and publishing tycoon, who had access to limitless supplies of Canadian newsprint, offered some at mates' rates to *Duma*, the only paper which still had reasonably assured supplies, but none to the struggling opposition papers, which had none. I suggested to him that this was not only unfair but that it could well mean that he cut off his nose to spite his face, as it was only a matter of time before the anti-communist/socialist parties would have the upper hand and might well decide to reward him for such partisan and discriminatory behaviour by severing his privileged access to Bulgaria's printing industry, which was his main interest in the country. To my surprise and relief, this argument seemed to carry weight and he spread the offer to the whole press, with allocations in proportion to circulation. To give Maxwell his due, this emergency supply of newsprint, together with a load of essential pharmaceutical and medical supplies, helped save Bulgaria's bacon at a very difficult time. It was certainly a good deal more helpful than most of his other forays.

Bulgaria's first truly democratic elections took place in June 1990. The BSP won, but only narrowly and Zhelev won a seat for the UDF. This election paved the way in August for a Grand National Assembly (a constitutional survival dating back to the Bulgarians' nineteenth-century struggle to free themselves from the 'Turkish Yoke') to create a new constitution and elect a president. A new constitution, which provided for the direct election of the president, was finally adopted in July the following year and in January 1992 Zhelev won the first of the new style presidential elections. He then served a full five-year term.

The 1990 general election was very thoroughly monitored by teams of international election observers, including several from the UK. Our monitoring effort was organised by a team of British returning officers. Volunteers – mostly from the embassy, but also including a sprinkling from our small expatriate community of teachers and business people – were divided into groups of three or four, some of them led by the experts from home and all of us benefitting from a crash training course organised by them a day or two earlier. LE staff, most of whom did little to conceal their excitement at the prospect of a genuine poll, were included, mainly as interpreters. Catherine and I formed a team with Rosina, my language teacher and Simeon our driver, who took delight in arriving suddenly and dramatically at our allocated polling stations in his beloved Jaguar, sometimes in a carefully choreographed shower of gravel. If this was democracy western style, he was all for it. We did our best to curb a bit of his enthusiasm, which must have seemed arrogant. Nevertheless, it was undeniably fun to be so clearly in the driving seat for a day, in a country whose government had till recently made its poor opinion of all things western very clear. Rosina enjoyed every minute of it.

When the UDF and their allies lost they let themselves down in a display of sour grapes, alleging fraud, irregularities etc, when in fact the consensus of the international observers was that the election had in the main been conducted freely and fairly. The UDF's membership was mainly urban, sophisticated, radical and youthful and was almost certainly outnumbered by the rural, cautious, conservative middle-aged and elderly, who would have been easily persuaded by the BSP to stick with the old BCP certainties. It is easy to write this years later, with the benefit of plenty of hindsight, and I realise that at the time I sympathised with the UDF, thinking that we must all have been hoodwinked into believing that the election had been stolen by concealed irregularities. There was a good deal of naivete about at the time, on the part both of the anti-communists and the 'West'. Give democracy a chance and everything will come right in the twinkling of an eye – which was very far from the way things turned out.

The UDF – the Blues – had been deceived by the size and enthusiasm of their final rallies in Sofia and elsewhere, but particularly in Sofia, where theirs easily outshone that of the Reds. And certainly we in the embassy and our dozen or so acting returning officers, had never thought we would ever see such an enormous crowd, which we were told numbered more than a million people. None of us had the slightest idea of how to calculate crowd sizes. All we knew was that the Blues filled Boulevard *Tsar Osvoboditel*, from the Eagle Bridge in the centre of the city almost to the airport four or five kilometres away. This is a six-lane highway with, for a kilometre or so at its city-centre end, broad tree-lined grass verges in the manner of a somewhat shambolic Champs Elysées. To fill all that up must have taken an awful lot of people, and certainly far more than the competing Red crowd that stretched back from the Eagle Bridge in the opposite direction. The Reds, used to half a century of regimentation, would have turned out only if they really had to, while being fully prepared to vote for their side the following day even if they had managed to avoid standing around for hours on end in a rally. Whereas for the Blues the prospect of an anti-BCP/BSP rally was an exciting novelty.

The ruling BSP – in other words, the government – provided all the sound equipment and so on for the Reds. We had assumed that the Blues would have to manage with amateurish, improvised kit. But not a bit of it. Fraternal Greek centre and right-wing parties lent a massive amount of apparatus, so that half Sofia rang to the Blues' catchy anthem 'Forty-five years is enough', punctuated by impassioned speechifying. One of the speakers proved to be Sol Polansky, my US colleague. This was quite a surprise, completely against all the rules, and could well have proved counter-productive. I can well imagine what the UDF, and Sol himself for that matter, would have said if the Soviet ambassador had spoken for the Reds at their rally next door. But at the time Sol was received rapturously by the Blue crowd.

Soon after the election, we went on home leave, only fifteen or so months after arriving in post. Normally, we would have been expected to wait at least eighteen months, but we had two special reasons for wanting to get home early, one domestic and the other diplomatic. The former was my parents' diamond wedding, due on 19th July, and the latter was an invitation to dinner at Claridges from ex-King Simeon. We chose to drive back to England and, with a good deal of help from overnight car-carrying trains, made the dinner in the nick of time. Buckingham Palace had advised us that it would be wrong to address the King and Queen as Their Majesties, or even Royal Highnesses, so we managed to avoid calling them anything, which they clearly did not hold against us as they both proved charming and friendly hosts. This was just as well, as to our surprise we were seated next to them as guests of honour. The King had had to supply his own Bulgarian wine, much to his feigned chagrin, and the evening was punctuated by numerous toasts to Bulgaria, freedom, democracy and so on. There must have been at least two dozen guests, the cream of the Bulgarian émigré community, including Johnny and Alexandra Stancioff and Johnny's cousin Dimi Panitza, the European Managing Editor of The Readers Digest and his French wife Yvonne. Dimi was later to go on to set up homes for Bulgarian street children and to help found the American University at Blagoevgrad. Johnny, once he had managed to wrest ownership of his family's house on the Black Sea back from the Bulgarian navy, was to turn it into the renowned day centre Karin Dom for cognitively and physically disabled children, named after his much-loved late sister who had triumphed over cerebral palsy with the help of the quality of skilled care obtainable in the United States which he felt should be the birth-right of disabled children in Bulgaria. He could as easily have developed the property, perched on a low cliff in an idyllic coastal situation, into a money-making enterprise, a hotel perhaps, or a casino. But he chose instead, at great cost, to follow a more humanitarian path.

While we were away, things heated up in Bulgaria, especially in Sofia, where student-led protest became a daily affair. Mladenov, the prime minister, was caught on a UDF video apparently asking someone, with whom he was watching a demonstration from a balcony, "shouldn't we send in the tenks?" This did for him and he stepped down in early July, to be replaced by Andre Lukanov. Lukanov was the West's – especially western business's – favourite Bulgarian communist, a smooth-talking and plausible cosmopolitan, but he was not much loved by his own compatriots. The left thought he was too chummy with western businessmen and politicians, including Robert Maxwell, while the right could not forget his Moscow upbringing and his Soviet connections, especially with the KGB. I always found him good company, but had to remember to try extra hard not to let my guard down, as behind the apparent easy-going charm lay a razor-sharp and possibly still hostile mind. The poor chap was destined to be gunned down in 1996 at the door of his flat by an unknown assassin.

One form of protest was the 'City of Freedom', consisting of dozens of tents set up in the centre of Sofia and occupied round the clock by anti-government students. Some of it was still there when we got back from leave. But we missed the main excitement, which took place during the night of our return while we were sound asleep after our long drive across Europe – assisted once again by a couple of car-carrying trains – when the protestors broke into the Party House (BCP/BSP headquarters and one of the most imposing buildings in the city centre), ransacked it and set it alight. Most of the embassy staff watched from the side-lines, but they elected not to wake us, no doubt from the highest of motives. I was fed to the teeth to have missed out.

The protests continued well into the autumn, still led by the students but gradually spreading to workers in the media and hospitals and clinics. Lukanov gave up at the end of November and handed over to a caretaker 'technocratic' government led by Dimitur Popov, pending fresh elections. This was the government that presided over the switch to a market economy, a period characterised by severe shortages, hoarding and a currency collapse. There was nothing in the shops. The dreary, fly-blown supermarket across the road from the embassy, never over-enticing even at the best of times, contained nothing but bare shelves for two or three months, as did all the other shops that we came across. Queues for bread got longer and longer, power cuts became the norm and it was clear that there was genuine hardship. Most city-dwelling Bulgarians had rural connections – a granny in a cooperative farm or a friend with a scrap of land – from whom they could scrounge, and a certain amount of produce continued to find its way into the markets, so somehow people scraped through the winter.

This state of affairs had a perversely beneficial effect for the embassy's UK-based staff, as it coincided with the arrival of the FCO overseas inspectors charged with a management and allowances audit. Their final report, 'written by guttering candlelight in a freezing Chancery', painted an alarming picture and our overseas allowances were duly and satisfactorily bumped up.

It was during this grim winter that the great Zhelev visit to London took place, and the Bulgarian visitors were made uncomfortably aware of the plentiful supplies in British shops. Arrangements had been made by one of the Queen's ladies in waiting to take Maria Zheleva to a supermarket where she could have for free whatever she could cram into a large trolley to take back to Bulgaria, presumably in return for a publicity photograph. Maria was tempted by this offer, which she thought she could turn to good account by acquiring largish quantities of a few basics for a number of people at home she knew to be in pretty desperate need of help. But her husband would have none of it. She could certainly go ahead with the shopping, but she would pay for it like anyone else, for he had no wish to risk his, or Bulgaria's, reputation with such an exercise, which could easily be misrepresented by his political enemies and which anyway he thought would be wrong.

With a new government in power and the Know How Fund now extended to Bulgaria, our relationship with the country and its institutions widened and deepened. Programmes were set up in a number of fields, including local government (headed by the leader of our election monitors), labour and employment (with job centres – a novel idea in a country used to a command economy, where job choices were pre-ordained) and environmental issues. Ways were found to boost the scope of our special concern, the care of disabled children. We worked under the aegis of the Thomson Foundation to help Bulgarian journalists and the media in general become proactive and independent-minded – unthinkable in a communist state.

Within the embassy's own competence, we started programmes aimed at civilianising and making more accountable the defence and interior ministries. The defence attaché spent more and more of his time in the Ministry of Defence, to which he had a pass and in which he had his own office space. As part of this education process the head of what until very recently we had referred to as the secret police, the *Durzhavna Sigurnost* (State Security, or DS), together with half a dozen of his most senior officers, came to lunch, before setting off for a fortnight's exposure to western ways and training methods in England. As social occasions go, this was a pretty sticky affair, and surreal. These stiff but polite men, exchanging toasts to eternal Anglo-Bulgarian friendship and cooperation, were after all the very same ones who had spent most of their careers making dissidents' lives miserable, as well as harassing western diplomats and other foreign residents. The general – they all had military ranks – solemnly presented me with an Interior Ministry officer's ceremonial dagger as a memento of our cosy get-together.

We were, of course, aware before 'The Changes' got underway that we were all bugged, in our homes and in our offices, and under constant surveillance, by our locally engaged (LE) staff, by DS heavies and by electronic means of various sorts. The surveillance fizzled out very quickly and it was not long before we were able to be confident about our relationships with the LEs. Socialising with Bulgarians, hitherto permissible only for senior staff and within strict boundaries, soon became the norm. We were able to establish that the various bugs that we had identified had been deactivated, but one gadget – a concealed directional camera trained at times on the chancery entrance and at others on one or other of the residence front gates – was still functioning. We knew this to be so because our technical officer was able to see what it was seeing, through one of his gadgets that picked up the camera's 'tempest radiation'. The camera was hidden behind a grimy net curtain in an upstairs window above the supermarket across the road. We were puzzled and just a bit disconcerted. Why hadn't the camera been removed, or at least switched off, now that everything else of that sort had been scrapped?

An opportunity to find the answer came when we had the new minister of the interior to dinner. He was a former judge, seemed moderately apolitical and certainly well disposed. And, happily enough, it was he who brought the conversation round to bugging and how it had all stopped, thank goodness. But, I asked, what about the camera across the road? Why was it still there? Ah-ha, he replied, fancy your having spotted it. We could rest assured that it had been switched off some weeks ago. I explained that, on the contrary, it was still working and that the superior nature of our kit had long enabled us to pick up its transmissions. The minister said that he had given orders for the camera to be deactivated and that someone must have either forgotten to do this or had deliberately disobeyed his instructions. He would investigate.

The next morning, he rang me up. "Any better?" he asked. I said I'd find out and ring him back. I rushed up to our security boffin's eyrie and asked him to check. Sure enough, the camera had been switched off, to the boffin's distress, as he had enjoyed tuning in to see what it was looking at. I rang the minister back. Much better, I assured him. And a few days later we saw that the gadget had been removed.

New notes and coins were issued, with the Lev pegged to the Deutschmark, and goods reappeared in the shops, but at much-increased prices in real terms. Agriculture withered, with pathetic little private enterprise attempts to manage with whatever equipment had been filched from the now largely defunct or moribund cooperative farms. Commercial advertising gradually replaced communist propaganda banners, at first concentrating bizarrely on Marlboro cigarettes. Small private enterprise shops and restaurants sprang up, many of them in garages beneath blocks of flats. An unpleasing class of petty crooks or mafiosi developed, many of them armed. Their main field of activity appeared to be in stolen cars, with Mercedes the car of choice for anyone attempting to set up in business. Constantine, our hitherto totally dependable butler, son of Simeon his predecessor and grandson of the legation's first butler in 1914, suddenly upped and left, to try his hand as a 'businessman', complete with elderly Merc, trading in the Central Market. Economic change was certainly in the air.

When it became clear that there would soon be a second general election, we decided that it was time to try to learn more about the new political parties, particularly the ones loosely banded together as the UDF, by calling on their leaders or organising committees. We had perforce to concentrate on a relatively small selection from the ninety or so parties that we knew of, but we were careful to include the BSP and the Agrarian Party (a BCP/BSP front which had functioned during the communist era as a not very convincing indication of the regime's pluralist credentials), to demonstrate our political neutrality, even though we already knew all about them. We did not restrict ourselves to the parties' head offices in Sofia, but made a point of seeking out provincial branches, as well as mayors in some of the main cities. Catherine and I did some of this political tourism, accompanied by Sarah Lampert, the chancery second secretary linguist, who interpreted when necessary. At other times she accompanied Les Buchanan, the head of chancery. Between us we met a reasonable cross-section of the political activists dotted around the country and we were always given a friendly and hospitable reception, even by the BSP and Agrarians. We were plied with questions about the workings of British political parties and democracy in general, which we did our best to answer.

Informal relationships also changed, vastly for the better. Bulgarians turned out to be open-hearted, welcoming and hospitable, and in what seemed next to no time we were making friends with plenty of them. A walk in the countryside or through a village almost always included one or more encounters with people who were eager to know all about us and where we came from. Catherine exchanged knitting techniques with cheerful crones gossiping in village streets, nuns and monks invited us into their monasteries and plied us with yoghurt and rakia, fellow skiers stood us beers in the amateurish looking bars that were springing up around the ski-lifts. We spent a weekend at Nesebur, a picturesque old port, crammed with ancient churches and windmills, staying in a B and B, something unthinkable for westerners only a few months earlier. The proprietors insisted on inviting us to dinner, after which they serenaded us, at point-blank range across the dining table, with voice and guitar, a heart-warming if deafening experience.

We went on a seaside holiday with a family – Ivo and Regina Indzhev and their three children – at Ivo's old-style trade union holiday camp at Shkorpilovtsi, something else that would have been totally unthinkable only a couple of years earlier. Ivo was the head of the Bulgarian Telegraph Agency, and the BTA summer camp consisted of chalets and a central block containing a canteen and games rooms, all surrounded by sand dunes. We queued for our moderately disgusting canteen food twice a day, but did for ourselves for breakfast in our chalet, and spent the day lazing on the beach and splashing around with the children in the sea. It was a good, old-fashioned seaside holiday, little different from those enjoyed during the communist era by thousands of Bulgarians as a matter of course – provided they had kept their noses clean and done as they were told.

We got to know the Indzhevs well and spent many evenings with them in their Mladost (Youth) flat, one of thousands, all much the same, in the dreary, jerry-built, hortatively named blocks of flats that surrounded Sofia and most other towns and cities in the former Soviet bloc. Like most of their neighbours, Ivo and Regina had glassed-in their balcony to give themselves more living space. But even so, there was not enough bedroom space to go round and someone, usually Mum and Dad, had to sleep in the living room – a standard arrangement. (Childless couples were generally allocated single room studio apartments.) These blocks were mostly eight to ten storeys high and the lift was quite often out of order. But the Indzhevs enjoyed a wonderful view of Vitosha, the crouching lion-shaped mountain that rises straight out of Sofia's southern suburbs, and their hospitality was generous and fun – a welcome contrast to so much of the formal variety to which we were constantly subjected (and which perforce we had to dish out ourselves).

Ivo had learned his English by listening to and imitating Beatles songs on – frowned-on and frequently jammed – western radio. He was half Czech, on his mother's side, and Regina was German, from the GDR. He had spent a number of years as the BTA correspondent in Beirut, where he had been able to mix with westerners and, presumably, honed his anti-communist views. So the Indzhevs were a bit too cosmopolitan to count as a typical Bulgarian family, but they had played the system skilfully, keeping their real opinions well hidden from Party busybodies, so that not only did Ivo have an important job but the children were able to attend one of the best schools in the country, with places reserved largely for the offspring of Party bigwigs and fraternal diplomats.

We had first met Ivo during the early stages of The Changes, when he struck us as a friendly, open-minded and well-informed journalist, in marked contrast to most of the other local hacks we'd come across, though we didn't at that stage know him at all well. But when our daughter Phoebe and her boyfriend Kim Mordaunt, a student at Australia's national film academy, arrived at Christmas 1990 to stay for the Australian long vacation and Kim told us at that he wanted to make a documentary on The Changes as his final diploma exercise, Catherine reckoned that Ivo could well prove a useful contact and arranged for them to meet. Her hunch was spot on. Ivo and Kim got on well and Kim was soon introduced to a mass of people, all eager to help. It was as a result of all this networking that Catherine and I first got to know Ivo and Regina properly.

Making the film brought Kim into contact with an even wider spread of people, ranging from Maria Zheleva, the president's wife, to folk singers, former political dissidents, artists, journalists, poets – including the vice-president Blaga Dimitrova – actors, musicians, politicians, all sorts, most of whom eventually featured in the completed film. He met many of them through us or Ivo, but plenty more materialised out of the blue, having heard what was afoot, and so the range of contacts and cast-list snowballed. In the end it was a matter of Kim's introducing people to us as much as the other way round. We had arranged what we assumed would be a standard interview with the head of the BTA, little thinking that this meeting would grow into friendship with the whole Indzhev family, as at that stage we had known Ivo merely as an occasional official contact. We benefitted similarly from a number of Kim's other contacts.

Maria Zheleva was a documentary film-maker, and on her recommendation Kim was able to use an editing suite at Sofia's main film studios for free, provided he did so in the middle of the night when it was not otherwise required. So, while he stayed with us off and on for a number of weeks while he made the film, we did not see very much of him, as he tended to be asleep when we were awake. Eventually, we prevailed on him to accompany us on a trip to Ohrid in Macedonia (now Northern Macedonia), the Canterbury or Rome of the Macedonian and Bulgarian Orthodox churches, beautifully set on the shores of its lake facing across to Albania, full of wonderful mediaeval buildings and with restaurants featuring the arctic char for which the lake is famous. Kim slept most of the way there, but managed to wake up enough to enjoy Ohrid's buildings and view and the char.

'Forty-five Years Is Enough' was shown to an invited audience in a cinema and then, more publicly, on Bulgarian and Australian television. Inevitably it stirred up controversy in Bulgaria, with some old diehards maintaining that they had been traduced and not been given a fair hearing. But, for most of the people who saw it, it was a clear and moving account of an immense upheaval in Bulgarian history, and all the more remarkable for having been made by a student from the other side of the world with no previous experience of or exposure to communism or to Balkan or any other non-Australian form of politics.

As the political social and economic situations gradually settled into their new norms, various skeletons began to emerge from a variety of cupboards. The one that concerned us most was the appalling state of the *detsky domove* (children's homes) and the thirty-five thousand or more disabled, unwanted or politically inconvenient – mainly Roma – children who were hidden away in them. This became the main focus of our welfare concern and we got fairly deeply involved, so it is the subject of a separate chapter. While NGOs, foreign aid programmes and international agencies have paid a great deal of attention to this unpleasant legacy of decades of a cruel and uncaring system, quite a lot of it persisted, as various articles and television programmes, from Britain and other countries, have continued to demonstrate – to the irritated embarrassment of the Bulgarian authorities.

On a more cheerful note, cultural life and exchanges blossomed. The British Council, represented during the communist years by a single cultural attaché on the embassy staff, was able to re-establish its independence and activities, with a splendid new library and programme. The BBC opened a shop and English language teaching centre, and a steady stream of British academics, writers, musicians, artists of all varieties, flowed in. This was definitely a fun side of diplomatic life, and we were privileged to be able to entertain and accommodate many of these people, including Malcolm Bradbury, Julian Barnes, Margaret Drabble, Michael Holroyd, George Newson, John Amis, Susannah Walton, Steven Runciman and many others.

With Malcolm Bradbury, we became marooned in a hotel in a snow-bound Veliko Turnovo where he was the star turn at a residential literary seminar, reminiscent of something in one of his campus novels. Julian Barnes was in Sofia to mark the translation into Bulgarian of his novel *Flaubert's Parrot* (*Papalagut na Flober*); Michael Holroyd and Margaret Drabble (biographer husband and novelist wife) were with us off and on for a week while they lectured and held seminars in universities around the country; George Newson attended the premiere of his double violin concerto, commissioned by the Arts Council and dedicated to the Bulgarian violinists, Angel Stankov and Yosef Rodionov, who played it with the Sofia Philharmonic; John Amis and Susannah Walton led a group to perform her late husband William's *Façade* at the Rousse Festival; Steven Runciman attended a ceremony to mark at long last both the Bulgarian translation of his *History of the First Bulgarian Empire*, which he had written in 1934, and the conferment of a very overdue honorary doctorate by Sofia

University. He stayed with us for several days, carrying out an exhausting programme, speaking mainly in Bulgarian, which he had not used since 1940, and insisting on walking everywhere. Each evening, when he got back to us after whatever he had been up to that day, he would say, "Thank goodness I don't have to go on being polite for a bit!" then flop down on a sofa and accept a large restorative armagnac before bed. He was over 90.

Meanwhile, there was an equally steady stream in the opposite direction to London, where the Bulgarian embassy under Johnny and Alexandra Stancioff soon became known as a hive of stimulating arts events, spread throughout the land by Johnny's amazingly energetic and effective cultural attaché, Aglika Markova. Johnny and I often worked in tandem, swapping ideas for political and cultural exchanges. This bypassing of official channels undoubtedly speeded things up, but it irritated the FCO and maybe also the Bulgarian MFA, as they were not in the loop until we launched our jointly concocted suggestions on them. Much depended on the state of Johnny's personal rapport or otherwise with particular FCO officials. He got on well with one head of department and therefore kept him broadly informed of what we were up to. But this chap was succeeded by someone whom he didn't take to and therefore largely ignored – a recipe for irritation, which eventually rubbed off on me and my relations with both him and the undersecretary to whom he reported.

Sofia also became the destination of plentiful quantities of ministers, senior officials, trade unionists, MPs, business and finance people and so on. The general pattern was that we arranged their programmes, put them up in the residence, fed and watered them and laid on at least one meal or reception in their honour, so as to enable them to meet their opposite numbers in congenial company and surroundings. I accompanied many of these visitors on their calls, with specialised help from other members of the staff, while Catherine organised whatever was planned for the evening – reception, buffet supper or formal dinner. We could cope comfortably with a hundred or so at receptions (many more for the annual Queen's Birthday Party, but less comfortably, unless we were lucky with the weather which enabled it to spread out into the garden), around fifty for buffets and twenty-six for formal dinners. As the pressure on our entertainment budget increased we switched more and more to buffets, with people seated at round tables knocked up quickly by the embassy carpenter.

In our busiest year, 1991–92, we entertained over five thousand people, more than half of them to a meal. Fortunately, we had a good and hard-working cook,

Jenny. Her range was not very wide, but it included all the kinds of things that could readily be expanded for suddenly increased numbers and which, crucially, needn't cost too much. She used mainly local ingredients, except when, during the lean winter of 1990–91, there hardly were any – which meant that Catherine had to shop in Greece (a three-hour drive away) or sometimes Yugoslavia. The embassy had its own shop, located in our basement, mainly for home comforts and basic essentials, but it was stocked really for the needs of the UK-based families, so we tried not to use it to cater for official entertaining.

When Constantine, the butler, left us to become a businessman, we were at our busiest. It was the butler's job to manage the domestic staff, procure food and wine, recruit additional help for big parties and help the cook buy food in the market – all under Catherine's direction and budgeting, while the two of us did the necessary accounting for the *frais de représentation,* as a British ambassador's entertainment allowance was rather grandly called. We were lucky to find an excellent replacement for Constantine in the person of Veska, who had been the head stewardess on one of the Danube cruise boats and was used to managing a largish staff (and speaking to passengers in a variety of languages). Each morning she and Jenny met Catherine to plan the day's menus and the general requirements for the next week or ten days.

This kind of thing, which amounted to running a small but specialised high-class hotel, was expected of a head of mission's wife. It was hard and responsible work, with no training and entirely unpaid. Things, I'm glad to say, are different now, with training and pay. The FCO certainly drove a hard bargain and got more than their money's worth in our time – particularly from Catherine who, as she sometimes pointed out at moments of frustration, was not even British. While most of our official houseguests were appreciative and polite, a few were most definitely not. I remember the froideur that descended on the dining room when Catherine came down for breakfast one morning. Her bright 'Good morning' was totally ignored by the visitors, all happily chomping away on their bacon and eggs. They included an FCO minister of state, a Tory grandee who should have known better. So she repeated her greeting, adding, "I live here, you know."

These niggles were far outweighed by the plus side. We lived in exciting times in Bulgaria and Eastern Europe in general. We got to know many interesting people and made many Bulgarian friends. We had a huge and wonderful house in which to live and to operate, set in a fascinating if not particularly touristy city. We were very lucky to have excellent colleagues in the embassy and in the diplomatic corps and domestic staff on whom we could rely, more like family than servants. We were also lucky to have helpful back-up in London, always ready to consider sympathetically requests for extra funds for yet more official entertaining. And we had the privilege of living in one of the most beautiful corners of Europe. Bulgaria was certainly run down, but great swathes of it consisted of unspoiled mountains, forests and rolling agricultural land, dotted with pretty villages and more than four hundred monasteries, nearly all of which had something special about them, such as frescoes or carvings. The communist regime had done its best to spoil some of this, surrounding towns and larger villages with dreary identikit blocks of flats and polluting, crumbly factories and cooperative farms. But there was simply too much of Bulgaria for them to ruin everything and, to give them their due, they had made genuine and effective efforts to conserve a lot of their architectural heritage in places like Rila, Troyan, Lovech, Veliko Turnovo and Plovdiv.

The communists had reorganised agricultural production into large cooperative farms. Much of this had worked reasonably well, with viticulture as a particular success story. Wine had been produced for thousands of years in ancient Thrace and throughout the Bulgarian and Ottoman periods, but it was not until the government sought French technical cooperation in the sixties and seventies that large-scale production of internationally marketable wine took off. As quality improved so the market shifted, away from the Soviet Union to Western Europe, particularly Britain, where for a while in the late eighties and early nineties a certain Bulgarian variety was the single best-selling red wine – disparaged as Bulgarian plonk but decidedly drinkable and very good value. But in the years following the collapse of the communist regime the cooperatives withered and died, with very little work being done in 1990, 91 and 92. Assets were stripped, just as they were in industry, and then a law for the restitution of private property came into force, which to begin with added to the decline of agriculture, as people scrambled to reclaim what had once been their family land – most of it in tiny, scattered holdings. The vineyards were the first to suffer. Wine is still being produced, but far less of it is now internationally marketable than during the closing years of the communist era.

The new democratic government's honeymoon period did not last very long and all too soon the various factions and parties which made up the UDF started quarrelling and falling out with each other and with the largely ethnic Turkish liberal party, the Movement for Rights and Freedoms (MRF), with which it was in coalition. The government was dissolved in late 1992, to be replaced by an appointed technocratic team put together mainly by the BSP but led by an MRF economist called Lyuben Berov. Berov had been an economic adviser to President Zhelev and his heart was in the right place. But he was no politician, lacking even a scintilla of charisma.

During the Berov era, the secretary of state, Douglas Hurd, paid an official visit. The Bulgarians laid on an official dinner in Hurd's honour, the tedium of which began to play on his patience. Guests were placed at a number of smallish tables dotted about a vast banqueting hall, a relic of Zhivkov's grandiose architectural arrangements, and conversation was dwindling. I was placed at a table some distance from Berov and the guest of honour. At some stage, after what seemed innumerable courses and toasts, I was approached by a desperate assistant private secretary who whispered in my ear, none too quietly, to ask how in God's name we could break things up before the S of S died of boredom. I could only suggest a bout of diplomatic indigestion. Whether this tactic was deployed I never knew, but to everyone's relief – including I am sure poor Berov's – the dinner was suddenly at an end and we were able to escape back to the residence for a quiet nightcap. Douglas and Judy Hurd were easy and delightful guests, not at all like the ones who had once incurred Catherine's displeasure at breakfast.

Douglas Hurd's main objective was to encourage the Bulgarians to stick firmly to the UN Sanctions against Yugoslavia, which had been imposed in April 1992 in response to the Bosnian war, by for instance preventing smuggling across the border and money laundering, and by ensuring that the border and access to Serbia up the Danube were kept effectively sealed. The Bulgarians were complaining that their economy was being almost as badly damaged by the sanctions as the Yugoslavs', since the main route for their exports to Western Europe, the E5 road from Istanbul to Belgrade and beyond, was closed, as were the railway line and the Danube, with its freight barges. Their economy was already desperately fragile, having only just a couple of months earlier made the abrupt and hazardous modal switch from communist command to western market. And they were appealing for help.

The Bulgarians were voicing their appeals and complaints mainly in the UN in New York, and one day I received a lofty telegram from the UK mission there urging me to tell them to stop whingeing and use a bit of common sense. All their lorries had to do was to turn right to bypass Serbia by going through

Romania. I pointed out in my reply that there was a slight snag in this otherwise excellent piece of gratuitous advice: a mile-wide river called the Danube, which formed the Bulgarian-Romanian frontier, crossed by a single bridge which was at the 'wrong', i.e. eastern, end of the country, the approach to which was blocked by a thirty-mile-long queue of trucks emanating from Turkey and the Middle East, also forced to avoid Serbia. On the day I sent my reply the waiting time in the queue was seventeen days. I heard no more from UKMIS NY.

British diplomatic postings in my time generally lasted no longer than three or, occasionally, four years. We were lucky to have been left in Sofia by the FCO for more than five, during a time of momentous events and great change, a time which by then had indeed already come to be known as The Changes. We left in the summer of 1994, sadly, but enriched by what we had witnessed and shared with the Bulgarians.

Chapter 31
Disabled Children

One day in 1991, Dimi Panitza burst into the residence and tipped a bunch of photographs on to the piano in the drawing room.

"Have a look at these," he said, addressing Catherine. "Please help us to do something about this horrible business."

The photographs were horrific. They were of filthy, emaciated, naked children, most of them apparently disabled. Dimi said that they were the inhabitants of one of the mysterious *detski domove,* which we knew were dotted about the country, but which we, as foreigners – western foreigners – had never been allowed to enter. Dimi had somehow managed to get into one near Vidin and the photographs were the result of his visit. By this time the outside world was well aware of the state of the so-called orphanages in Romania, but we had no idea that the same sort of horrors existed in Bulgaria.

Catherine said that of course, we would try to help, and a few days later she and two or three embassy colleagues set off for Vidin. As far as I remember they were Toni Granchareva, Marta Nikolova and Sarah Lampert – together with Stanka Zheleva, who was President Zhelev's daughter and a good friend of Sarah's. Stanka pulled the right strings and the ladies were admitted. The condition of the children was just as alarming as Dimi's photographs, but the visitors were careful not to criticise, even when they were told by the director of the home that there was nothing that could be done for the kids as they were beyond hope, just idiots. Instead, Catherine and her colleagues sympathised with the director's moans about a lack of resources and said they would see what they could do to help.

Over the next few weeks, the ladies visited three other homes, in Mezdra, Stara Zagora and Vidrare. Conditions were pretty frightful there too, but the attitude of the directing staff and carers varied, from genuine concern to

225

indifference, bred, we suspected from ignorance. We assumed that Bulgarians were by nature no crueller than Brits, but realised that forty-five years of dictatorship had led to an attitude of 'the less seen the better'. Children with disabilities, especially genetic cognitive disabilities, were just one more problem that the state could do without, so they were hidden away in so-called orphanages, often in remote rural areas, where they were given minimal care by largely untrained village women on very low pay. Many of the children had been developmentally normal when they were put in care; their problem had simply been that they were unwanted, or racially – i.e. Roma – inconvenient, and over time they had lapsed into apparent mental disability, having lived every minute of their lives with other children who were genuinely disabled. The directors had had some specialised training, most of it discredited in modern, western terms, and some of them were assisted by a resident medical doctor, fresh out of medical school and dying to escape back to city life. We sensed that most of the directors resented what they thought of as their lowly status in professional terms. There were around 35,000 disabled children in residential care in Bulgaria, the highest number per capita anywhere in Europe, more even, we believed, than in Romania.

We had already built up a small amount of experience in helping residential institutions for disabled children through a small Friends of Bulgaria programme in aid of the two schools for the blind, in Varna and Sofia. Our son Alexander had just finished university and did a sponsored bicycle ride, with an LSE friend, from the Bulgarian embassy in London to the British embassy in Sofia and between them, they managed to raise over £15,000 in sponsorship with which the Friends purchased much needed braille printers for use in the two schools. So we had something of a track record with the various responsible ministries in Sofia, who were happy for us to put together a small aid programme targeted at the four children's homes.

We too were very short of resources as, while the Know How Fund (KHF) had already been set up, it had not at that stage been extended to Bulgaria. All we had were two standard instruments available to all embassies in developing or newly emerging countries, the Heads of Mission Gifts Fund (HMGF) and the Small Projects Fund. We managed to eke enough out of these relatively modest sources to help improve the lot of the children and, almost as a by-product, increase the staffs' self-respect and consequent humanity. For, we calculated, if a foreign embassy regarded their institutions as worthy of attention, then surely they themselves had jobs that were worthwhile and worth developing in professional and caring terms. In this respect, we were much inspired and helped by the example of the Stara Zagora director, an amazing person and complete exception from the norm. She needed no moral encouragement from us, but welcomed us as allies in her crusade to improve standards, and joined in enthusiastically, accepting whatever material assistance we could provide to help her turn her establishment into a national template of good practice – a sort of public sector equivalent of Johnny Stancioff's marvellous voluntary sector Karin Dom at Varna. And eventually all four directors worked hard to improve the standards of care in their respective homes. Vidrare was the most dilapidated, and it was heartening to see the growing enthusiasm of its director and the transformation for the better, in moral and material terms, that she was able to bring about.

In this way, we were able to provide for example a new central heating system for the Mezdra home and new kitchens and dining facilities for Vidrare. We were also able to provide all four homes with cars, by means of a simple wheeze whereby the HMGF paid a Lev or two more than the highest bid received by public sealed bids for our superannuated, but still reliable, staff cars. This seeming financial sleight of hand satisfied the FCO's finance department and HM Treasury.

The residence came into its own as the site of a seminar on the care of disabled children, to which we invited a number of directors of homes, including of course 'our' four, officials from the sponsoring ministries, experts and counterparts from the UK, and above all the Bulgarian media, especially TV. We deliberately made the occasion as glitzy as possible, in an attempt to show the Bulgarian government and public opinion that child care – especially disabled child care – was not a Cinderella affair, that above all it did not need to be carried out in secretive residential establishments, that it mattered and that there were all sorts of ways in which it could be provided, most of them non-residential and in the community. We were trying to give the people who worked in the sector a chance to develop their own feeling of self-worth and to demonstrate to the Bulgarian world at large that they were vital and important members of society. In this we were trying very hard to avoid what had happened in Romania, where the orphanages and the people who ran them had been vilified by the western press, thus running the risk of hardening entrenched attitudes and making things even worse for the children.

I don't know how much success we had. At least we had done something to bring the subject into the open, and in due course the KHF arrived in Bulgaria, and with it increased resources, including expert assistance. Our little amateur programme developed into a sector of our wider KHF programme and in turn was incorporated into something far bigger under the EU's PHARE umbrella. We tried not to appear superior or sanctimonious and we did our best to build on the goodwill and good practices that already existed. A number of embassy staff and families got involved, locally engaged and UK-based, and in general it was fun.

I have happy memories of days out at Vidrare, the nearest of our client homes and in many ways the one in most need of help, seeing the children's faces light up (especially when Simeon gave them rides in the Jaguar) and sharing in the staffs' pride in their revived and much-improved institution. Catherine and her friends even managed to explain and help set up a Vidrare version of an English village fund-raising fete, with stalls selling local produce and games for the children. We waited with bated breath to see if anyone would turn up, but they did, in relative droves, and quite a respectable amount of money was raised – by the home itself and from a voluntary sector that only a few years earlier would have been derided as a western frippery.

This account first appeared as part of a blog set up by the Sofia embassy in 2014 to mark the centenary of the residence. Catherine and I hoped that perhaps the four directors would read it, especially Maria and Nellie, of Stara Zagora and Vidrare, together with the members of the 1990s embassy locally engaged staff, who so cheerfully worked beyond the call of official duty with the rest of us to encourage new and more humane ways of helping Bulgaria's disabled children.

Chapter 32
A Day Out with Robert Maxwell

We were to meet at the VVIP lounge early the next morning. (Plain VIP wasn't good enough for Cap'n Bob.)

"Don't be late," he ordered. "I won't wait for you."

On that note, I took my leave from Villa No. 6, the mansion in Sofia's secretive Politburo estate permanently allocated to Maxwell in case he should drop by, which he quite frequently did.

Bulgaria provided Maxwell with cheap printing facilities, which he used mainly for his Pergamum Press books. The local nabobs, communist and immediately post-communist, regarded him with awe as some kind of hallowed intermediary between East and West, a reputation which he was happy to cultivate. With me, he was always full of his latest encounter with Gorbachev or Yeltsin, the fruits of which he would be passing on to Margaret (Thatcher) or John (Major) the moment he got home, so eager were they to debrief him. I didn't know how much to believe of all this, but took care to nod gravely and to assure him of the permanent availability of the good offices of the embassy – an assurance of which I later discovered he and his entourage had made profitable use in the margins of a reception which he'd persuaded me to lay on for him during what proved to be his last visit. They had made dozens of international phone calls, with no by-your-leave and of course no offer of reimbursement. International calls from Bulgaria were pretty pricey in those days.

But back to the outing.

Next morning, there we all were, punctual to the minute – apart from Maxwell himself, who was half an hour late. There were four or five local heavies (some of them allegedly deputy ministers of this and that) and a clutch of the great man's courtiers – on this occasion, as far as I remember, Joe Haines, Helen Liddell, Bernard Donoughue and a Frenchman with an Italian name

(Anselmini) who seemed to be in charge of the petty cash. I learned later that he was the boss of Maxwell's London and Bishopsgate Bank, various mutations of which we would all hear more about in the missing pensions funds scandal after the old rogue's death.

We trooped out to the planes. Most of the heavies, plus maybe one or two of the courtiers, were consigned to an elderly and suspect looking Bulgarian YAK executive jet. The rest of us followed Maxwell into his own sumptuous Learjet and off we went, bound for Burgas on the Black Sea coast. Zhivkov, the long-serving dictator and Maxwell's one-time dearest friend, about whom he had written a sycophantic biography which famously began, "Tell me, Comrade Zhivkov, how it is that the people of Bulgaria love you like their own father?" was now in jail and consequently no longer in much need of the various lodges and palaces dotted around the country, his so-called 'residences'. The new government was thinking of selling them and Maxwell thought he could use one of the seaside ones, along with its nearby annexe for senior Party apparatchiks, as a cross between private holiday home and bargain-basement film location for jet-set scenes in potboilers churned out for his various cable television networks – provided its harbour was big enough for his yacht.

At that moment, we were passing over the Arbanasi residence, two or three miles out of Veliko Turnovo, Bulgaria's mediaeval capital, possibly a good location for pulp costume dramas. I pointed it out and Maxwell more or less snapped it up on sight, with a curt command to one of his myrmidons to make a note of it.

The seaside complex was situated twenty or thirty miles out of Burgas, in a pine forest surrounded by barbed wire and sentry towers. We looked first at the annexe, a rotting concrete edifice with about fifty modest rooms, all with long-defunct mod cons and an opaque view of pine trees.

"This'll do for the actors," said Maxwell.

The residence itself was about a quarter of a mile away, facing on to a secluded beach and small harbour. It had been properly maintained and consisted of several enormous and tasteless rooms, a massive terrace overlooking the sea and the harbour that might or might not be big enough for the *Lady Ghislaine,* Maxwell's yacht named after his daughter, and a sports-complex grand enough for most dictators, with a fifty-metre indoor/outdoor pool. One of the accompanying deputy ministers explained that the whole pool building would roll away at the touch of a button if it were in working order, leaving the pool as an outdoor lido.

Maxwell was particularly taken with the grand chromed and multi-mirrored barber's saloon which adjoined the master bedroom – presumably where Zhivkov had had his morning shave on the two or three occasions when he was reputed to have actually used the place. And he approved of the terrace, where we had an excellent picnic lunch and rather too much to drink. Warmed perhaps by the wine, he suddenly asked whether there was anything I'd like from him. The courtiers had warned me that this might be coming, so I had prepared my request, which was for budgetary support for the Nottingham University archaeological dig at Nicopolis ad Istrum, an ongoing Anglo-Bulgarian enterprise which was perennially short of funds.

"How much?"

"Twenty-five thousand should do the trick."

"My dear Ambassador, a mere bagatelle. Tell your archaeologist friend to see my secretary in London and everything will be arranged," a forecast which later proved perfectly accurate, in that what proved to have been arranged was the bleak news that there would be no money as Mr Maxwell had changed his mind.

When we got back to the airport at Burgas, Maxwell offered us all dinner in Vienna. When I said that I really ought to be getting back to Sofia, as I had no authority to leave my post, Maxwell said that that was too bad and that he was sorry but he didn't have time to drop me off on the way. It was Vienna or staying put in Burgas, two hundred miles from Sofia – take it or leave it. I said that I would stay put and pointed to my official car, parked a little way away. I had become used to Maxwell's little foibles, one of which was a bully's pleasure in putting other people to maximum inconvenience, so I had made sure that the car would follow me down to Burgas, just in case.

Nothing came of this foray into the Bulgarian real estate scene, much to the dismay of the Bulgarian government, which, like the Nottingham University Archaeology Faculty, was seriously short of funds. Nobody was very surprised; this was just typical Maxwell behaviour, promising the earth and delivering very little. But it was always worth a try, because just every now and then he did come up with the goods, as indeed he had done with emergency supplies of newsprint for the Bulgarian press the previous winter.

No-one seemed too upset when the news came of his death, in mysterious circumstances, while cruising in the Atlantic in the yacht which might or might not have fitted into the harbour near Burgas.

Chapter 33
An Imaginary Love Affair

Sometime during 1992 or 1993 I was shown copies of inter-departmental Whitehall minuting, the gist of which was that I was enjoying an affair with the Bulgarian prime minister. Since both the PM and I were men, this was deemed a poor show, if not worse. The minuting had been copied by someone in the FCO to one of the embassy staff, suggesting that he might wish to show it to me as I might be amused. I was, as were the other members of chancery who saw it. In fact, general hilarity ensued.

The prime minister, Philip Dimitrov, was not really my type. First, he was the wrong sex. Second, both he and I were happily married – both of us to women. Third, while we got on well together, he was very busy running Bulgaria's government, the first non-communist one for the best part of half a century, and I doubt whether he would have had the time for extra-marital affairs with anyone, let alone the (same-sex) British ambassador. Fourth, Mr Dimitrov had but recently succeeded in luring his new wife from someone else, to whom only a few months earlier she had been married, so it seemed a little premature, and unlikely, that he would be embarking on yet another liaison.

Someone in the department in London had scribbled, "Blimey! Whatever next? Mr Thomas might be amused to see, so please copy to him," or words to that effect. And I was amused. But also puzzled. How on earth had such a strange story arisen? I waded through the whole lot – three or four pages of it. It went something like this.

Someone in British Aerospace had written to the undersecretary in the DTI to warn him that the ambassador in Sofia was far too close to the Bulgarian prime minister, 'a notorious homosexual'. The undersecretary had chosen to pass this important piece of multiple misinformation to his opposite number in the Foreign and Commonwealth Office, who had, in turn, passed it down to the geographical department that dealt with the Sofia embassy. And the department, no doubt rocking with laughter, had copied it to us.

It was clear from the tone of the minuting that the DTI undersecretary had not dismissed the story out of hand. Maybe he half hoped that it was true. He had been in his job for a number of years, during which he had himself become pretty close to senior members of Bulgaria's former, communist, regime – men who, beneath a veneer of civilised Euro-communist behaviour, including lavish attention paid to visiting Western businessmen and officials, had nevertheless continued to play their part in the management of a fairly ruthless dictatorship. He had continued to pin his colours to their mast well after the fall of the old dictator Zhivkov, right up to the moment when, after a couple of elections, they were out on their ear and he found himself friendless and contactless in the new, democratic Bulgaria. This was not for want of warnings and attempted guidance by us in Sofia, largely ignored or pooh-poohed, so maybe he was feeling a little silly and therefore more inclined to accept salacious gossip at face value than he would normally have been.

But how on earth could British Aerospace have acquired or concocted this story, and if the latter, why? I racked my brains. There was one possible catalyst. A year or so earlier BAe had mounted a sales pitch in Bulgaria of their BAe 146 airliner. Nothing had come of this as Balkan, the Bulgarian national airline, were stony broke. But during the demonstration flight, I had got talking to one of the visiting BAe executives and, perhaps unwisely, had asked him about the "Supergun" story then doing the rounds in various newspapers, as an offshoot, or possibly precursor, of the Matrix Churchill affair. The so-called Supergun had, as far as I remember, been developed in the UK and, because it was capable of lobbing nuclear-tipped shells sixty or seventy miles, had been subject to a general embargo. This had been circumvented by some wily operators intent on exporting the weapon to a nefarious destination, probably Iraq. Their method was to ship it in bits, disguised to look like parts of an oil pipeline, and Bulgaria had been rumoured to have been in on the act as an entrepot, assisted, so it was said, by shady people who had at one stage worked for BAe.

The executive had not reacted well to my enquiry and I sensed that I might have touched on a raw nerve, so I had changed the subject. But maybe, just maybe, this man had gone on to concoct the story about me and the PM, who had also been a passenger on the demonstration flight and whom it was clear I knew well, as a mad way of getting me off his back?

I thought no more about this until, some months later, I was in London and was called in by the personnel people for a regular assessment. The official whose job it was to conduct this was someone I had known for years, and the interview seemed to be going unexceptionally, till suddenly a copy of the DTI minute was shoved under my nose and I was asked to comment. I treated it as a piece of idiotic nonsense, but my colleague said that it had to be treated seriously as it had been referred to the FCO by another Whitehall department. I pointed out that I was heterosexual, as to the best of my knowledge was the PM, who had indeed reinforced his reputation in this regard by pinching someone else's wife, to whom he was now married, that homosexuality was in any case no longer a crime or anything to be ashamed of in all but the most antediluvian regimes (which did not include the UK or the new, democratic Bulgaria) and that it was surely part of my job to get to know Philip Dimitrov well. I was proud to have been able to do this, to such an extent that, when he was putting together his government after he had won the election in 1992 and thus at last defeated the dregs of the old communist regime, he had come round to the residence one evening to ensure, over a glass of whisky, that we, HMG, would not have any worries about the people he proposed including in his cabinet. This astonishing event had been witnessed by the recently retired PUS (permanent undersecretary – head of the diplomatic service), who happened to be staying with us at the time and who had said afterwards that he had never known of any other foreign leader checking out his proposed new government with the British ambassador. And yet here was I, apparently being ticked off for being far too close to the prime minister!

My colleague said that a note recording my comment would be left on the file. And that was that. I would have preferred the whole thing to have been shredded, as it deserved, but apparently, that would have been against the rules.

Chapter 34
Eastern Caribbean

We left Sofia in July 1994 and in October that year arrived in Bridgetown, Barbados, where I was destined to serve out my time in the diplomatic service as high commissioner, Eastern Caribbean. This meant that I was accredited to a string of island mini-states: Antigua and Barbuda, St Kitts and Nevis, Dominica, St Lucia, St Vincent and the Grenadines, and Grenada and to Barbados, east of the string, where we lived.

The main high commission offices were half a mile or so from our cosily named house, Ben Mar (for its original owners, Ben and Marge, not a Scottish Highlands peak), in a purpose-built block which we shared with a DfID development division, or Devdiv. There were four subsidiary offices, in Antigua, St Lucia, St Vincent and Grenada, each headed by a first secretary with the ungainly title of resident acting high commissioner, or RAHC. They were 'acting' because whenever I set foot on their patch I was technically in charge, as high commissioner proper. This was a clumsy and ugly sounding arrangement which must have irritated the poor old RAHCs as much as it no doubt confused the authorities to whom they were accredited. But it met all the relevant international legal requirements.

The Queen was head of state in six of these places, which were therefore classed as 'realms', each presided over in HM's absence (which was 99.99% of the time) by a governor-general, who was in most cases a former local politician. The exception was Dominica, which was a republic within the Commonwealth, headed by a non-executive president and by a redoubtable prime minister, Dame Eugenia Charles. Because Dominica was a republic Dame Eugenia's DBE was honorary, but woe betide anyone foolhardy enough to mention or try to employ this nicety. She was Dame Eugenia and that was that, as clearly indicated on the street sign of Dame Eugenia Boulevard, the main drag in Dominica's capital, Roseau.

BHC Bridgetown was a bit of a mish-mash, with people from various branches of HMG ostensibly on my staff, even though in many cases some or all of their duties lay in territories to which I was not accredited, such as British dependent territories, French DOMS, Dutch overseas territories and many of the independent countries in and around the Caribbean, including even Venezuela. These people were a mix of military (RN and RM), Customs and Excise, an anti-money laundering man from the Treasury, and sundry security people, all doing their best to help the various Caribbean governments cope with the subversive and destabilising efforts of the drugs barons. There was also a secretariat dealing with the dependent territories, headed by an FCO counsellor. Then there was the Devdiv downstairs, not on my staff from our point of view, but most definitely part of my mission from that of the government of the host country, Barbados. As far as they were concerned I was the chap responsible for the presence and good behaviour of about fifty Brits, all enjoying diplomatic immunity, and for the employment and welfare of about sixty Bajan locally engaged staff, at least half of whom were on the Devdiv's books. This curious state of affairs could well have led to turf wars and all manner of disputes (and occasionally did), but on the whole we all rubbed along well enough together. Fortunately for me, the two Devdiv heads with whom I coincided had sensible, conciliatory natures. Had they been prickly life could have become a little tense.

The overseas inspectors paid us a visit during our last year. They said they were impressed by the complexity of the management side of my job, which they had not been led to expect and truth to tell had not over bothered me. So impressed were they that they bumped my grading up a notch or two and with it my salary scale, which all came in very handy when, a few months later, I retired and my pension, based on my final salary, kicked in. They reported that BHC Bridgetown was a genuinely regional mission, possibly HMG's first and consequently a good model on which to base others in the future. I have no idea whether this gratifying but nevertheless surprising conclusion was ever acted on, but I rather doubt it.

The military members of my staff, especially the RN captain defence adviser, worked closely with the RN 'West Indies Guardship', a frigate or destroyer on permanent station in the area. This expensive asset, together with its much larger Royal Fleet Auxiliary tender, had once been expected to guard our Caribbean colonies, as its title suggests, but now with no more real colonies and not very much to guard their successor states and territories against, it had morphed into our most visible weapon in the 'war on drugs'. I don't know whether it gave value for money, though every now and again it intercepted a boatload of cocaine en route from Colombia or Venezuela to the USA or to Europe via one of the island mini-states, some of whose governments the drugs cartels had managed to suborn into cooperation as staging posts. Most of the BHC's military were the members of the BMATT, or British military advisory and training team, tasked with helping the island governments build up their own defences against the smugglers.

The ship did, however, play a vital role in humanitarian aid whenever there was a hurricane in the region, which happened most years, sometimes more than once. And as far as I was concerned it proved a godsend once its captain and I had tumbled to the idea that we could boost our representational credentials, while at the same time saving a bit of taxpayers' money, by combining our efforts at showing the flag, making friends and influencing people. As the nominal head of mission in the six states to which I was accredited but in which I was not resident, I was expected to lay on at least one major reception in each of them once or twice a year. Hitherto this had generally been done in a hotel, at steep Caribbean prices. But the Guardship visited the same places, also once or twice a year, and during the visit the captain would generally also hold a reception. We rolled these events together. The captain provided the venue and the waiters, free and far more glamorous than a hotel. The BHC provided the guest lists and the money for the food and drink, which came from RN sources at RN (duty-free) prices. The captain and I then stood at the head of the gangway as joint hosts while the guests were piped aboard, and everyone was happy. The party cost the navy next to nothing and the FCO far less than if it had been held in a hotel. And it was much more fun.

If drugs were one half of my job, bananas were the other. Bananas grown in Caribbean islands with a direct or historic connection with France, Holland and the UK enjoyed privileged access to the EU, which enabled them to undercut those grown in massive Latin American plantations, which were subject to tariff barriers. These factory farming plantations were mainly owned by US companies, whereas the Caribbean bananas were produced by small-scale farmers whose livelihoods the three ex-colonial governments were anxious to protect, for good developmental and political reasons. This protectionist arrangement upset the Americans, their Latin American clients, and consumers in all the other EU countries, particularly Germany, who preferred potentially more plentiful and cheaper bananas to what they regarded as the dearer results of a well-meaning but out-dated paternalism. Battle was waged on the spot, where at times it became quite acrimonious, in capitals and in the World Trade Organisation. The Americans no doubt had international law (the WTO) on their side, but they were wary of pushing too hard for fear of encouraging the development of anti-American governments in their Caribbean back yard. They could do without any more Grenadas, let alone Cubas.

Barbados was a bit of a let-down after Sofia, a lifestyle and career anti-climax, even if eventually it was a grading notch or two up. Drugs and bananas didn't interest me as much as political developments in Eastern Europe, and we missed Bulgaria's cultural infrastructure, climate and surroundings. No more Thracian tombs, or music and opera, or weekends in Turkey or Greece or Macedonia, or skiing, or frescoed monasteries, or massive demonstrations, or indeed a government that sought and sometimes acted on our advice, (which the Eastern Caribbean reckoned they had little need of or inclination to ask for). True, we were living in a 'paradise' island which people paid a great deal of money to spend holidays or even whole winters in, but we found that there was a limit to the amount of our spare time we wanted to pass lounging around on beaches. Now and again we would pull ourselves together and say, "Let's go for a drive, taking in X plantation house and Y beach" and off we'd go. But we were back in Ben Mar in a couple of hours, which is scarcely surprising as Barbados is only the size of the Isle of Wight.

We suffered from islanditis, a condition endemic among our expatriate acquaintances and even some of the locals. Fortunately, my multiple accreditations meant that we enjoyed fairly frequent trips to the other islands, timed to coincide with their national days (attendance obligatory) and the Guardship's visits (for glittery bargain-basement representational entertainment). We would combine tourism with work (calls on ministers, inspections of aid projects, sorting out problems with the RAHCs, and getting in their way). We could never quite decide which was our favourite island. They all had their special points, but maybe St Lucia and Nevis were the joint winners – just.

It dawned on us one year that three of the national days were conveniently consecutive, in Antigua, Dominica and St Lucia, with three or four days between each of them, in that order, which was also their geographic order from north to south on the map. Why didn't we visit each of them for their great day by yacht, combining business with pleasure and, provided we could find two other couples to split the cost, possibly even saving HMG a little money on airfares and hotel rooms? If this putative saving couldn't be achieved, we would stump up the difference.

At first, this idea seemed over-optimistic; could it really work? Would we find two other couples who were also obliged to attend the national days? What if we were becalmed, or wrecked? We could imagine the UK tabloid headlines if things went really wrong, 'Publicly Lotus eating envoys meet their comeuppance' or 'Fatal dip for dippy dips. They deserved to be drowned'.

But we persisted and were happily joined by our own defence adviser and the Australian high commissioner and their wives, all four of them good friends. And as the DA was an RN captain we reckoned the risks of shipwreck might be reduced. We chartered a catamaran in Antigua, owned and skippered by the sort of hardened Scotsman who immediately inspired confidence, and crewed by his wife and a couple of girls, one English and the other Australian, who managed to produce delicious food from a microscopic galley in all weathers, rough or smooth. All four were wonderful company and our week on-board had passed all too quickly when we left the boat in St Lucia.

We called in at Guadeloupe, and our arrival on the morning of Dominica's national day was little short of sensational – at least, that's how it seemed to us. Dominica is a mountainous, steep-sided island, without any natural harbours. Skipper Jim found a sheltered bit of shore half a mile from the jetty where we had arranged to meet our minders the next morning, anchored and then went ashore in the dinghy with mooring ropes which he tied to a couple of palm trees, and there we spent the night, ready to cast off if the wind got up, which luckily it didn't. In the morning we got into our finery – not easy in the cramped cabins of a sailing catamaran. Jim ferried us in the dinghy in dribs and drabs to the jetty, the ladies in their wide festive hats and Iain the DA in his full naval tropical regalia, and all of us barefoot, clutching our shoes in plastic bags, to be greeted by an astonished chief of protocol and an embarrassed-looking BHC second secretary who had gone ahead by more conventional means of transport. When, later in the day, Dame Eugenia heard about our arrival, she gave us full marks for originality and enthusiasm.

So of course life in the Caribbean had its compensations. We had rides in naval helicopters, flew in tiny planes to unlikely looking air-strips, holidayed in ritzy hotels in most of our islands and in the USA and Canada when islanditis threatened to overwhelm us. We even got to the shores of Hudson Bay, by cheap charter flights and Canadian trains that wound their way slowly through wilderness and forest, past moose paddling in a swamp and a black bear getting ready for bed – everyday sights for the regulars in the train's bar, but scarcely believable for us.

And Ben Mar had a lovely garden, populated by hummingbirds, peripatetic monkeys, an enormous tortoise called Fred, even on one wonderful occasion an osprey eating its lunch at the top of one of our mahogany trees, and equipped with the sort of swimming pool you see in the movies, backed by bougainvillaea and ylang-ylang, with a spacious covered loggia in which we did a good deal of lounging around and even some of our official entertaining.

The pool complex was reputedly the creation of Oliver Messel, the famous designer and Princess Margaret's uncle by marriage, who had spent the last years of his life in Barbados. We never established the truth of this provenance, but it was plausible since we had the princess to thank for the pool's existence. Before our time she used to overnight in Ben Mar on her way to her house in Mustique, a practice that, mercifully for us, she had discontinued after a change in the airline schedules made it no longer necessary. She was sorry that Ben Mar didn't at the time have a swimming pool, as she would have liked a refreshing dip after eight hours cooped up in BA First Class and the nearest suitable beach was seven miles away at Sandy Lane, the other side of Bridgetown. The high commissioner saw his chance and deployed her sentiments carefully in his dealings with the overseas estates bit of the FCO, who hastened to remedy the deficiency in time for the princess's next stopover. Mr Messel, who lived only four or five miles away, would have been an obvious choice as adviser, if not actual detailed designer.

We were disappointed to find that Barbados operated in an unofficial, but very real, atmosphere of apartheid. Government, the military, law and the other professions were black, while business, agriculture (mostly sugar) and commerce, including the tourist industry, on which the island's prosperity depended, were white, and the two kept their distance. We did our best to mix things up in our official entertaining and our guests obliged, but always with an edgy wariness. There was far less of this in the other islands, with more, and more unforced, inter-racial harmony.

We were also disconcerted by the colossal wealth of so many of the whites, particularly the winter migrants who either inhabited immodest villas along the west coast or provided much of the clientele of the ritzier hotels. While most of these people came for the whole winter, a significant minority were mere weekenders, who arrived on the Saturday morning Concorde, a couple of local time hours before they'd left London, and returned overnight (First Class, with beds) on the Sunday evening 747, refreshed and ready for their labours in the City on Monday morning. We would occasionally be asked to dinner by people of this sort, perhaps to be inspected as samples of the lower orders living above their station. When the conversation turned to BA's latest iniquities, such as running out of caviar on last Saturday's Concorde, Catherine would take malicious glee in telling them about the people with whom we had recently been consorting in Bulgaria, most of whom had never owned a car, let alone set foot in a plane. This would sometimes induce a short, embarrassed silence, broken by some wag suggesting that it served them right for being commies, having failed to understand that Catherine was telling them about the anti-commies, who had recently ousted the Party fat cats who had for half a century combined oppression with enjoyment of every luxury and privilege known to East Bloc mankind, including cars and plane travel. And on another of these occasions, after we had arrived a few minutes late, having that evening taken delivery of the new car which we were going to take back to England for our retirement, I apologised, offering as an excuse that we had just acquired the car of our dreams.

"What is it? A Beemer? A Jag? Surely not a Roller?"

"No, a Ford Escort," I said and there was general merriment, as no-one believed me until the car had been inspected, after which there was just slightly embarrassed bafflement. These high commissioner johnnies were certainly a rum lot.

Of course, the white plutocracy wasn't all like that. For instance, one couple whom we got to know well, Johnny and Wendy Kidd, were involved in all sorts of things, especially cricket and, curiously, opera, that embraced people of all colours, classes and creeds. They ran an opera festival – a kind of tropical mini Glyndebourne – each March-April in the garden at Holders, their attractive old plantation house up the hill behind Sandy Lane, the grandest of the west coast hotels. We became involved when a Barbadian musicologist friend of theirs suggested that they should put on Inkle and Yarico, a late 18th century opera (by Samuel Arnold) with a Barbadian, anti-slavery theme – ideal material for the Holders festival. The snag was that it existed only in a keyboard version, the original orchestration having been lost, though one or two reconstructions had been written and performed. Johnny asked us whether we knew of anyone who might have a go at writing a new reconstruction, for steel pan and orchestra. We suggested Roxanna Panufnik.

We had got to know the Panufniks when she and our daughter Phoebe had been at school together. And Rox was beginning to forge a reputation in her own right as the composer scion of her composer father, Sir Andrzej. She leapt at the idea – good experience, and in Barbados. She spent a number of weeks on the island, partly at Holders but mainly with us, composing afresh for one song for which the music no longer existed and orchestrating the rest, all on her computer with its magic 'Sibelius' software. She also wrote her 'Oh Puss One' for us, a piece for oboe, cor anglais, euphonium and viola entitled Willy Snoring, to commemorate the splendid racket one of our King Charles spaniels made when taking a nap. I'd asked for sousaphone, but Sibelius wouldn't oblige, so we had to make do with euphonium. We had this magnificent fifteen bar *parvum opus* framed and it hangs to this day among the pictures in our dining room. When Rox played it to us on her laptop it really did sound like Willy, if a bit more mellifluous.

Rox's new version of Inkle and Yarico was a huge success. The pans were played by a local star and the orchestra was the RPO, scaled-down for outdoor tropical duty. There was a children's chorus, recruited from the primary schools where Rox ran a very popular outreach programme. There was a second production later on in London, but since then Rox's version has not been revived. It's time it was.

So we had our opera after all, and what's more we were involved, which made it all the more fun. In our other two years in Barbados, the festival put on The Mikado and Cosi Fan Tutte in modern dress, with the young officers as polo players, a witty acknowledgement of Holders' other main function as the island's polo ground. And Alexander found temporary employment as Johnny's gofer.

In Bulgaria, Catherine had spent a good deal of her time and energy in aid of the disabled children locked away in grim institutions, out of sight and mind and for a while, after our arrival in Barbados, it seemed that there would be no comparable opportunities or need for a contribution by her in so prosperous and relatively enlightened a place. But before long she had become involved with a Leonard Cheshire establishment, the Thelma Vaughan home, where she became the much-loved Aunty Catherine for most of a day twice a week, helping with activities for the children (many of whom were in fact young adults) with learning difficulties who lived there. This voluntary work of hers was the origin of my connection with Leonard Cheshire Disability, whose international chairman I became after retirement. In a fairer and more logical world, this appointment should have been Catherine's, not mine, as my involvement with the home had amounted to little more than the occasional visit or presentation.

On 18 February 1998, I would turn sixty and therefore, under current public service rules, a nobody as far as the FCO – and probably everyone else – was concerned, even if they would from then on be obliged to pay me a pension. I had no wish to celebrate this unaccustomed nugatory status in Barbados, so we left on the 17th and celebrated my birthday first over breakfast in a Miami airport hotel and later at dinner in Crested Butte, a ski resort in Colorado where Alexander was working as the Ski Club of Great Britain's resident rep. There we were joined by our old friend Corinna (Cog) Haward. We spent a few days slithering down Crested Butte's few non-extreme black slopes (Al's preference, but most definitely not ours), before heading for home via Death Valley, Las Vegas, San Francisco, Los Angeles, where we said goodbye to Cog and to our hired car, Christchurch NZ, Sydney and Bathurst NSW, Cairns and Townsville QLD, Singapore and Heathrow, where we were met by an FCO car, our last perk in a career that had lasted a bit over thirty-six years. This odyssey took nearly two months, much of it spent in Australia with Catherine's mother and other members of her family. We paid for most of it by cashing in our heads of mission end of posting first class entitlement in favour of steerage the long way round – far better than the direct route for just eight hours in the front of a BA 747.

Chapter 35
Piano

British ambassadors' and high commissioners' residences are equipped with pianos. Their purpose isn't necessarily or even primarily musical. Pianos, especially grand pianos, are essential platforms on which to display framed photographs, usually signed, of politicians, royalty and above all the Queen. Upright pianos do not afford much space, with room perhaps for only half a dozen photographs, but they have one great advantage over grand pianos with their far more generous space and room for battalions of pictures, which is that they can be played with the photographs in situ. With grands on the other hand, musically inclined guests, or even the odd real musician, may well insist on folding over that big flap behind the keyboard in order to get at the music stand. This entails removing more than half the photographic display, thus reducing its power to demonstrate the brilliance of the incumbent ambassador's career just at the moment when, with impressionable guests present, it is most needed. Why can't these musicians just memorise their pieces and do without the music stand, like those Proms soloists you see on the telly, who never need crib-sheets, instead of causing all this trouble? And as for those real show-offs, who insist on opening up the whole caboodle, well! Don't they realise that it isn't easy to find somewhere else at the drop of a hat to put all those *lares familiares,* somewhere that will not demean them?

When we arrived in Barbados, I was dismayed to find that the residence, Ben Mar, rated only an upright, whereas in Sofia we'd had a grand. Both these instruments were Danemanns, a now-defunct make whose reputation for robustness and durability had no doubt endeared it to the old Min of Works when the latter had been responsible for kitting out the overseas diplomatic estate.

"Don't mess with Bluthners or Bechsteins if you want something that'll support fifty silver-framed photos. Stick with good old Danemann," as no doubt

MoW functionaries had advised each other. And besides, Danemanns were British, even though saddled with a misleadingly Teutonic name. It wasn't that I was inconveniently burdened with too many framed photographs, having served in posts where visiting royalty and cabinet ministers were rare commodities. It was just that my now inflated sense of my own importance should continue to be reflected in piano size and prominence. An upright hidden in my study, as though it was intended merely for playing rather than as a status symbol, wasn't good enough. What was needed was a grand, in the spacious front hall where, I optimistically surmised, we might also hold little musical soirees from time to time.

A few weeks after our arrival, we heard that a musical couple were leaving the island and wished to dispose of their piano, a Yamaha grand. There was enough in the post's local budget kitty to meet the asking price, a very reasonable $US 2,000 and one or two local pundits assured me that the instrument was a good one. We might get $500 for the upright, so for not much more than £1,000, we should be able to bring Ben Mar up to pianistic scratch. I told Catherine that I was off to inspect the Yamaha. If it was as good as people said it was, I would make arrangements to pay for it and have it brought round to Ben Mar.

I was home again an hour or so later, accompanied by two Cavalier King Charles spaniels, called Willie and Edwina, who were apparently closely related to each other – mother and son perhaps, or maybe brother and sister. Either way, they almost immediately made it demonstrably clear that they were not over-concerned about the niceties of the rules and customs surrounding incest, but even so I was sure that we would get to love them dearly and that for their part they were looking forward to moving in with us.

Catherine, it seemed, didn't fully share this optimism.

"Where on earth did you come across them and what possessed you to think that we would want them?" I confessed that on my way to the piano owners' house I had started to have Serious Doubts. What if some unkind journalist got hold of the story and twisted it into a tale about an unscrupulous and greedy diplomat – an envious envoy perhaps – misusing public funds on a needless luxury, which might also be exactly how some unfriendly functionary in personnel at home might see things, enabling him (or even her, though female functionaries tended in my experience to be warmer-hearted – and more musical – than their male counterparts) to bring my career to a sudden and unwelcome conclusion? By the time I reached my destination, these doubts had become

246

overwhelming. But such was the vendors' excitement at the prospect of at long last getting shot of their piano, and for the asking price, and so great their disappointment when they learned that I had merely come to apologise for raising their hopes, only to dash them in the twinkling of an eye, that I had been unable to offer any resistance to their pleas to relieve them instead of their dogs, free and gratis. So here they were, complete with collars, leads, feeding bowls and a couple of tins of Chappie.

Catherine knew when she was beaten. We had had to leave behind our much-loved mongrel Sophie in Sofia, where she had moved in with Veska, our butler and promptly had a litter of dozen or so puppies, so maybe – just maybe – Catherine could begin to love this canine duo. She leant down to give one of them a tentative pat but withdrew sharply when she saw that they were both hopping with fleas and ticks, a state of affairs that we never quite managed to cope with. For this and other reasons Willie and Edwina were given their own apartments in the yard at the back of the house, where they spent the night before being let out every day after breakfast to patrol the garden and terraces. They were decorative – at a distance – and apparently perfectly happy with their new mode of existence, never making any serious attempt to come inside.

And not long afterwards, when our musician friends were on the point of departure with the piano still unsold, I learned that one of Barbados's secondary schools made a point of offering music as a specialisation. The school was the island's closest approach to a conservatoire, but its only half-decent piano was in sore need of replacement and the education ministry's budget for musical instruments, never generous even at the best of times, was completely exhausted. With the help of the Heads of Mission Gift Scheme that school is where the piano went, and everyone was happy.

Chapter 36
Retirement

Now, in 2019, I have been retired for twenty-one years, which is more than half as long as my entire career in the diplomatic service. I am sure that I could have carried on for another five or six years, but in 1998 retirement from the DS was compulsory at 60, as it was in the entire civil service. No doubt this rule – since abolished – made sense in the middle of the nineteenth century, when life expectancy was a good deal shorter than it is now, but as my time came ever nearer I resented it and grew worried. How would we manage on a salary (pension) suddenly cut to less than half, and no more overseas allowances?

Some of my colleagues, when confronted with these same gloomy thoughts, seemed able to segue effortlessly into highly paid consultancies and directorships. Admittedly, most of these people had retired from more exalted positions than mine and had probably ensured along the way that they were in good odour with the right contacts. I had never had the faintest idea of how to network, and when in the last year or two of my career I realised that maybe I should try to rectify this deficiency it was already too late. I let it be known, I hoped, among the holidaying plutocracy of Barbados's west coast, that I would shortly be available, on suitable terms of course, as an indispensable adjunct to whatever it was that they did in the City of London, but the offers of lucrative sinecures that I so confidently expected to ensue failed to materialise. One intriguing and slightly alarming, possibility did however emerge, unprompted, when I was telephoned by Humphrey Maud, who had many years earlier been my boss in financial relations department.

Humphrey had already been retired for three or four years and was serving as assistant secretary general of the Commonwealth, in charge of the economic work of its secretariat in Marlborough House. Did I know that I had been mooted as his successor? I didn't, but naturally was only too delighted to hear this totally unexpected news. The ASG(Econ) slot was apparently traditionally occupied by a retired British DS person and my profile and the timing of my availability fitted well. According to Humphrey and also to Prosper, an outfit in the FCO that helped find employment for retired DS members, my appointment was virtually certain. The secretary general – a distinguished Nigerian – would, of course, have to be consulted, but he was not expected to raise any objections.

Humphrey sent me reams of paperwork as examples of the kind of thing that I would be required to do, some of it alarmingly formidable, but he assured me that, once installed, I would find it easily manageable. I explained that I planned to spend a couple of months travelling home, visiting Catherine's family in Australia, but was told that I wouldn't be expected to start work in the secretariat till three or four months after leaving Bridgetown. All I needed to do was to leave some contact phone numbers and addresses and then to report to the appropriate chap in Prosper as soon as I got back to the UK, who would by then be almost certain to be in a position to confirm my appointment.

It sounded almost too good to be true, and it was. After a wonderful few weeks, spent skiing in Colorado, driving across the western United States, exploring New Zealand and then linking up with Catherine's mother and other family members in Australia, I formed up in the Prosper office, ready and eager, only to learn that the Marlborough House slot had already been filled. Oh dear, hadn't anyone told me? A bit lax. But I'd be glad to know that the person who'd got the job was tremendously well suited and would be sure to make a wonderful success of it. As indeed she was and did.

I didn't have long to nurse my disappointment. My parents, now in their nineties, had become too frail to manage any longer on their own. It was time for me to join my sister Elizabeth in finding them carers before helping them get settled in residential care, a depressing and time-consuming process. And besides, Catherine and I had to make up our minds about where we were going to live.

We had a small flat in Bloomsbury, occupied by Alexander, and a scruffy, isolated cottage in Kent, which we hoped to trade in for something in a town or village equipped with shops and so on that we could get to on foot. But in the end, having failed to find anything that we could afford, we stayed put in the cottage, which we added to a couple of times till it became a sizeable house with two acres of garden – a paradise for a growing posse of grandchildren, but gradually more and more lonely and inconvenient for us. We were midway between Rye and Tenterden, three miles from the nearest shop and virtually neighbourless, which is why we eventually moved just eight miles away to Winchelsea. In the mean-time, we made the flat over to the children, who after the statutory seven years were able to sell it and thus launch themselves a few rungs up the housing ladder.

It was while all this was going on that I was approached by what is now known as Leonard Cheshire Disability. I became a trustee in 1999 and international chairman the following year, a position I held until 2005, working closely with the international director, Rupert Ridge, who had been Catherine's contact while she was involved with the Thelma Vaughan home in Barbados. As a trustee of the parent charity and chairman of its international arm, I was an unpaid volunteer, whereas Rupert was International's full-time, paid professional. I was a part-timer, with a job that took up about twenty hours a week, many of them spent working my way through the reams of paperwork that preceded the monthly meetings of the trustees and multifarious committees and sub-committees of what I soon realised was a large and unwieldy bureaucracy, occupying a biggish chunk of the Millbank Tower complex – more like a government department than my earlier, untutored idea of a charity headquarters. Over the years after I stood down, a succession of chairmen succeeded in paring down and simplifying the committee structure, with greater concentration on delivering services for disabled people and less on bureaucracy.

Leonard Cheshire Disability is one of the UK's leading charities. It works with and for disabled people of all ages and in the broadest spectrum of disability, both in its well-known Cheshire Homes and, nowadays even more important, in the community. During my time it had about 35,000 service users and a budget of around one hundred million pounds, about a third of which were its own charitable funds and the other two thirds public funds, which financed the statutory care which it provided on behalf of the public sector.

LCD is, however, only one of well over fifty autonomous Cheshire organisations spread around the world, in South and South-East Asia, Africa, China, Russia, the Caribbean, USA, Canada and closer to home in a number of European countries. In my time Leonard Cheshire International was a division of the UK charity, with its own chairman, who was subordinate to the chairman of the whole UK organisation. It provided general linkage and information for the world-wide LC family, and training for LCs in developing countries, through a network of regional training and development offices (Rupert's great innovation). It also provided some budgetary support for emergencies and start-ups, but never for running costs, which would have run counter to Leonard's own belief in the importance of self-governance and self-reliance in each national organisation. I managed to visit Cheshire facilities and personnel in Tanzania, Zambia, Botswana, South Africa, Canada, China, Japan, Malaysia, India and Nigeria and was hugely impressed by the work and spirit of both the service users and the service providers, in vastly differing circumstances, and learned a great deal from the experience, though I don't suppose that any of these people derived much if any benefit from my fleeting presence.

In fact what if anything did I achieve during my five years? *Si monumentum requiris...* Maybe two things, both negative, but both, I believe, paradoxically beneficial, and both achieved mainly by inertia. I allowed 'World Week' and 'Friends of Leonard Cheshire Inc' to wither away, largely unnoticed and now, I hope, unmourned – if they are even remembered.

World Week had happened a couple of times before I joined the charity. It consisted of a week-long gathering and jamboree in London of Cheshire folk from all over the world. Its purpose, presumably, was to foster togetherness while garnering favourable publicity which could benefit fund-raising. The previous one had been graced by the Prince of Wales and sundry other luminaries. The participants, as far as I could gather, had indeed come from the ends of the earth, but most of them had been national trustees and committee members, with only a token sample of real, disabled, service users. It had cost a bomb, as would its planned successor, which I was instructed to set in motion – three-quarters of a million pounds or so. When I suggested that three-quarters of International's annual budget spent on a gigantic party to be attended mainly by paternalistic trustees, most of them well-heeled and able-bodied, struck me as poor value for the disabled people around the world whom we were supposed to be trying to help, I was told not to worry; the money wouldn't come out of the budget (heaven forbid!), it would be from sponsorship, which I would conjure up.

It gradually transpired that few, if any, of the previous World Week sponsors were prepared to repeat their generosity. Fearful of admitting defeat to my fellow trustees, I managed to spin things out, at first by getting agreement for a postponement and then, as memories began to fade and enthusiasm to wane, by floating a modified proposal, dreamed up by Rupert. How about holding World Week somewhere else, away from the UK, to show how truly international and non-Anglo-centric we were? And perhaps on a slightly smaller scale than the last one? How about India, where there were dozens of Cheshire homes, or South Africa, the new Rainbow Nation in the throes of desegregating its homes? By transferring the event to another country, with its own autonomous Cheshire organisation, we would be responsible neither for organising the Week nor for conjuring up the necessary funds.

The response from all but one of our sister organisations was underwhelming, not least because, by agreeing to hold a World Week of their own, their nabobs would be missing out on a trip to London. The exception was South Africa. They would be happy to host a 'regional' World Week, to be attended mainly by the other African Cheshire organisations, with only token representation from the rest of the world. My fellow trustees bought this idea, which then in its turn gradually fizzled out – less gradually once the South Africans had become aware of the limited scope of our likely financial contribution.

When I joined LCD, it was intent on expansion, in the UK and, vicariously, abroad, particularly in South America, where the Cheshire family was barely represented. But expansion in South America would be expensive, at least until such time as local, self-financing foundations could be set up, and International's modest budget was already stretched. So why not get the Americans to provide the start-up funds? South America was, after all, in their backyard. And maybe, while they were about it, they could support the Caribbean operation as well? There was a functioning US Cheshire foundation, which ran a few homes, but it would need supplementing if it was to raise additional funds to be spent outside the USA. So the idea of The Friends of Leonard Cheshire Inc was conceived and it was already alive and (faintly) active when I joined LCI, with one of our staff, a retired diplomatic service Latin American specialist, already at work on it. In due course, The Friends Inc acquired legal persona, an office in Washington and a CEO. And by the time it had been wound up, having achieved very little else, it had got through over four hundred thousand pounds. It was still limping along when my time with Leonard Cheshire came to an end. I cannot claim all the credit for killing it off, but I had raised the alarm and had at least got my ex-DS colleague to forego his LCDI salary and manage on expenses and his DS pension (to his credit, entirely willingly). Within a few months, new brooms had swept away the whole ill-conceived operation.

Rupert fell seriously ill and had to take early retirement. He had fallen victim to a mix of inappropriate anti-malarial prophylaxis and managerial hostility, which would nowadays be called workplace bullying, and endured several months of mental illness. I admired him and his achievements and made plain my dislike of the innuendo and sniping directed at and about him by one or two of my fellow trustees and by senior management. As a result, I became their next target. I resisted their efforts to dislodge me long enough to be able to ensure that the charity appointed excellent successors to both Rupert and me, and to witness the foundation chairman's departure some months before my own – a cause for a little schadenfreude, which I hope I managed to keep suitably veiled.

I could have done without the internal politicking, which had come as a distasteful surprise. I had naively assumed that an organisation that did so much good would be run entirely by paragons of selflessness and good behaviour. It had not occurred to me that the personnel of a large charity would be unlikely to differ much in terms of ambition or interactions from those of a company or a civil service division, and as luck would have it a good deal of my six years in LCD coincided with a distressing bout of internecine strife. Nevertheless, I learned a great deal, and left with tremendous respect for the work of the majority of the staff and volunteers and for the dignity and bravery of the disabled people whom they were doing their best to support.

Closer to home, Catherine and I became involved with two local arts festivals. We were committee members of one of them, the Rye Arts Festival (I was its chairman for three years) and remain keen supporters of the other, the Peasmarsh Chamber Music Festival, a magical happening which brings us a few days of perfect music-making each midsummer. We worked as volunteer book conservers for a number of worthwhile and amusing years at Charleston, the Bloomsbury Group's country retreat near Lewes, and we went on free holidays on cruise ships thanks to four stints as a guest speaker, who was permitted to bring along a guest (Catherine). I seemed to be typecast as an Iceland specialist, so all four trips were in the North Atlantic and enabled us to visit for the first time the Norwegian fjords, the Faroes, the Azores and Greenland and to revisit Iceland, Canada and the United States. This episode gave us a taste for cruising, particularly, after experimentation, along rivers.

Our three children graduated, married (and in one case got divorced) and between them produced eight grandchildren, the oldest of whom is now an undergraduate and the youngest in her second year at primary school. One family live in North Yorkshire, one on the Cote d'Azur and one only twenty-five miles away in Kent. We envy some of our neighbours who have ended up with all their children and grandchildren within easy reach, with comings and goings almost every weekend, whereas we get to see the Yorkshire and France families only a couple of times a year. This scattering of the next generation seems, unsurprisingly perhaps, to be the lot of people like us who have spent their working lives in far-flung corners of the world. We can be thankful that our family are at least in Europe and not on the other side of the world, though that is where the whole of Catherine's own family is.

Catherine visited Australia every eighteen months or so while her mother was still alive and once more after her death when the two of us went on a kind of memorial tour of New South Wales, Victoria and South Australia. When the plane took off at the end of that trip Catherine said that she doubted if she would ever be back. I assured her that of course she would, but it has become increasingly clear that she was right. I shall die in the familiar surroundings of the country of my birth and upbringing, whereas she will have only memories of the optimism, the sunshine, the flowers and perhaps above all the birdsong of far-off New South Wales.

The Corona virus pandemic interrupted the final stages of publishing this book. It is now 2021 and we have moved to the Kentish village between Ashford and Canterbury where our son Alexander and his family live. Lockdown notwithstanding, this is a great comfort.

Postscript

I have appended to this account five pieces which I wrote about recently deceased friends. Only one of them is a proper obituary, commissioned by *The Independent*, on Zhelyu Zhelev. Another, on Jeremy Carter, is what I said at his memorial service. The other three can best be described as informal tributes. As all five impinge and in some cases enlarge on, many of the events recounted in the preceding pages, I thought it worth attaching them as a postscript, trimmed and adjusted where necessary, mainly to avoid repetition.

The Zhelev obituary, however, is exactly as it appeared in *The Independent*, to which I am indebted for permission to reprint it. I wish now, with hindsight, that I had gone a little further in emphasising Zhelev's modesty, lack of pomposity, even humility. For instance, I made no mention of his refusal to move into the official presidential residence, preferring to remain in his simple flat in one of the grey prefab tower-blocks that surround Sofia and other towns in the former Soviet bloc. Nor did I point out that he also insisted on taking only half his official presidential salary, while ensuring that the other half was distributed to charities that helped people in need. There were editorial space exigencies. Even so, these omissions were regrettable and I am happy to be able to repair them now.

In Memoriam – George and Andrea Sisson

One morning in the summer of 1957 I pitched up at an elegant Georgian townhouse in Newcastle, straight off the night sleeper from London and ready to start my vacation job as a tutor to two small boys called David and Alexander Sisson. I was at Oxford and in need of gainful employment. I had been hired to help David with his Common Entrance preparations, but I never knew why Alex had been included in my remit, as he was only eight. They turned out to be part of a cheerful Anglo-Scots family who spent every summer holiday in Scotland, and everyone was rushing about getting ready for the long drive north. There were four children altogether. They gave me a cursory once-over and then got on with whatever they had been up to.

"Another of them," I could almost hear them thinking.

"We'll soon sort him out."

Seven people and a dog meant two cars. I was relieved to learn that I had been assigned to Mrs Sisson's, a choice that promised at least a few hours' gentle run-in. I had been a bit alarmed to see that Mr Sisson sported a military-looking moustache, and confidence was not one of my stronger points. (I was nineteen, only five years older than the oldest Sisson boy, John.) And in those more deferential days, it was most definitely Mr and Mrs. It was many years before I was able to say George or Andrea without a slight feeling of *lèse-majesté*.

I need not have worried. Within a few days, George had recruited me as his unofficial ally: two Sassenachs surrounded by a horde of Scots, deep in an Angus glen north of Kirriemuir. Our otherness showed up with startling clarity when, along with masses of other families in the district, the Sissons attended an all-ages ball at Glamis Castle, where George and I were the only two males not clad in tribal gear. But George, of course, knew all the steps, while I, the only real outsider present – I had never been north of Yorkshire before – was pushed and twirled and dragged through a bewildering series of reels and strathspeys and I know not what.

George was nothing if not an active and innovative dad. I still have a photograph of him mountaineering up a massive pine tree. I say 'mountaineering' because that is clearly what is going on in that fifty-two-year-old slide, with George, seen from below, equipped with the whole gamut of rope, belays and pitons. I forget what the purpose of the expedition was; perhaps it was a lesson in climbing techniques for the benefit of his children.

Climbing was one of George's passions and later, encouraged by him, it became one of mine. He and Andrea invited me to join the family for 1963 New Year in the Lakes, where we stayed in a cheerful and well-victualled farmhouse in Borrowdale, called Manesty, for a few days' ice climbing. We were at the start of what turned out to be the longest and coldest winter in living memory, perfect for climbers, if not for most other people. Each morning, we set out in high alpine conditions, for a hard and exhilarating day in the Scafell range, before returning to a huge high tea, with log fires and pikelets and ham and Cumberland butter.

But to return to that first summer in Glen Prosen. George was an engineer and he could perform amazing technical tricks. One of his favourites was to launch a forty-gallon drum hundreds of feet into the air. That year he and his friend the laird, Charles MacLean of Balnaboth, chose a good sound drum, minus its lid, in the bottom of which they drilled a small hole into which they fitted a car sparking plug. They dug a forty-gallon-sized hole in a meadow, well clear of animals and buildings but within reach of a drivable track, where Andrea's Morris Minor was parked, minus one of its sparking plugs. They ran a long thin wire from the distributor to the plug in the base of the drum, measured some carbide into the bottom of the hole, added water, slid the drum rocket into its silo bottom side up, withdrew to the car, counting off the seconds all the while and pressed the starter. There was a faint whoomph from the drum, but nothing much else. There followed a series of adjustments to the timing and the quantities, until at about the fifth attempt there was a mighty bang and the drum rose hundreds of feet into the air before landing the other side of the meadow, more or less undamaged and still equipped with the Morris's missing sparking plug.

This experiment was apparently repeated every year, with enthusiasm and good humour, to mark the arrival of the lily-livered Sassenachs who had taken the shooting. They had come from Bournemouth and Surbiton and other imagined centres of pampered southern living dreamed up in Captain MacLean's craggy mind. I suppose he reasoned that if they could withstand the fright of such a noisy and dangerous welcome they would be good enough to shoot his grouse, and as most of them were regulars who came year after year no doubt they took it all in good part. Even though I did not come from either Bournemouth or Surbiton, or indeed from a town of any kind, I was a dyed-in-the-wool Sassenach and made myself as unobtrusive as possible. George of course, in the laird's eyes, was an honorary Scot. But soon I was forgiven for my origins and treated in Balnaboth to my first taste of single malt whisky, a rarity in those days outside Scotland.

A couple of years later, in the blazing summer of 1959 when the British Isles temporarily joined the tropics, George led his three sons and me, a guest now, no longer an employee, over the mountain to the highland games in the next glen. He set a cracking pace and I thought I would die before I got to the top. But not far short of the ridge we came across a lochan.

"Everyone in!" he ordered. Obediently, we stripped and jumped into the dark, peaty, ice-cold water. Fears of death by heat exhaustion were replaced by an apparent certainty of heart attack. But all was well and we continued on our way cooled and refreshed. Andrea and Julia had wisely gone around by car, with the picnic.

Time passed, and gradually the contacts grew less frequent. I did my national service, much of it spent as Northern Ireland Command HQ's adventure training officer, a job which meant that for weeks on end I was on a climbing holiday at public expense and one for which ultimately I had to thank George and Andrea, who had first stimulated my love of mountains and wild places. And straight after the army, in autumn 1961, I joined the diplomatic service.

Immediately after Catherine and I got married in February 1966 in Ghana, where I was technically persona non grata, we were to be transferred to Paris, after a period of home leave. But it was not home for Catherine, who had never before set foot in Britain, and I whirled my unfortunate new wife all over the place, showing her off to innumerable friends and relations. We were to spend the night with the Sissons on our way to Scotland, in March 1966.

"Come in good time for dinner," wrote Andrea, and come dinner time we were still miles away from Wall in Northumberland where the Sissons lived (called Wall because it is on the Wall – the Roman Wall). We were in a second-hand Mini which was apparently suffering a terminal illness, with dimming lights and no heat. It was very cold, with snow flurries. When we tried using the heater, the lights went out altogether and we dared not stop the engine, or even stop vrooming it for fear that it would never start again. Every few miles we had to pull over to let the battery recover a little by revving the engine with the lights switched off. Mobile phones had yet to be invented and we never saw a single phone box.

I had told Catherine that we were going to a wonderful house on Hadrian's Wall where we would stay with a marvellous family called Sisson. She had visions of a massive stately home, with butlers and footmen and other appurtenances of this strange and distant land that she had married into, a pile curiously named Planet Rees – which is what Planetrees looked like in my address book – and here we were, disgracing ourselves by being hours late. She was not at all looking forward to our arrival, if it ever happened. But when it did, all was sympathy and hospitality. Dinner was almost over, but was hastily reassembled for us, and we were ravenous.

The next morning the Mini was completely dead. George, ever the engineer, reckoned that without the drain on its suspect electricals imposed by the headlights, there was a good chance that it would revive if we tried to bump-start it down the long hill to the valley, and that if this failed there was a garage at the bottom which should be able to sort it out. Four or five Sissons gave us a hefty push out on to the hill and away we went, with the engine phut-phutting every time I let the clutch in. After nearly a mile, suddenly all was well and away we went to Skye where, a couple of days later, I realised that all our travails had been caused by nothing more serious than a slipping fan belt.

My 1957 pupil David and his sister Julia stayed the odd night with us over the next couple of years in Paris and Brussels, but direct contact with any Sisson almost fizzled out, mainly because we were in distant postings or busy bringing up our three children. So it was a case of Christmas cards and the odd letter. But in 1971 George and Andrea met our two moppets (Andrea's word), Phoebe and Alexander, when they took us in on our way south. We had abandoned poor Catherine in a hospital in Inverness, where she was (successfully) trying not to have our third child, who had threatened to arrive two months premature. Years later we stayed again at Planetrees. Corinna, the cause of all the trouble in 1971 and now a senior teenager, was with us. So George and Andrea met all three of our offspring, which pleased me.

In 1975, during a visit to Australia (Catherine's first since she had left it ten years earlier on what she thought would be a two-year posting), we spent a day with David's older brother John, by now a scientist working in Australia's CSIRO, who was living in a kind of superior shack in Kuringai Chase, twenty or so miles out of Sydney. This reunion prompted a summons by George and Andrea to lunch at the Oxford and Cambridge Club, for a debriefing. They had not seen John for some time and were busting for first-hand news. The O and C is now my club and I am reminded of that meeting whenever I see into the special functions room, which in those days of men-only clubs was the guest dining room where visiting ladies were permitted and where the lunch took place.

Over the years, Catherine and I learned about George's work on some of the world's largest new optical telescopes, which he built at his works in Newcastle, Sir Howard Grubb Parsons Ltd. In 1994 we visited the one at Siding Spring Mountain in New South Wales and sent him a postcard to tell him so. This news produced another summons to lunch, this time to Planetrees. George and Andrea seemed as full of energy as ever, but the moustache, which had so alarmed me on that first meeting in 1957, was now snow white. George told us how he had been invited to the opening of Siding Spring, but had been disappointed to be left out of all the arrangements for the opening of the even bigger William Herschel telescope in Grand Canary a few years later, which his firm had also built. This clearly rankled, not surprisingly.

Our last meeting took place in 1999. We had just spent a week with friends in, of all places, Glen Prosen, where they went most years to stay in a cottage a mile or more up Glen Tairrie. We were put in the Old Dairy, in the back yard of Balnaboth, got to know the new generation of MacLeans over another shot of malt, forty-two years after that first, revelatory one, reminisced about the forty-gallon drum experiments, which the new laird Hector had witnessed as a child, went for walks up to Loch Brandy and over the top of Glen Doll to Balmoral (where Catherine, seated in our friends' Land Rover, was mistaken by sightseers for the Queen!) – in short, relived many of the 1957/59 experiences, with another family and another set of children. Everything in Glen Prosen seemed much as I remembered it; with the exception of Glen Tairrie Lodge itself, which was now a souvenir shop, painted bright yellow. This called for a postcard to George and Andrea, and of course we were summoned to lunch, for what was to prove the last time.

Things really had come full circle. We had just come from Glen Prosen, where I had first got to know George and Andrea and their family more than forty years earlier. And Andrea's sister Elspeth was there, she who had in 1957 and 1959 given me my first lessons in fly-fishing, in Glen Tairrie burn. She was amused to hear that her lessons had stood me in good stead over the years in places as far apart as Iceland, Kashmir and Bhutan and communist Czechoslovakia, where a colleague and I had spent an uneasy day fishing the upper reaches of the Vltava, rather too close to the forbidden border zone for the authorities' comfort. We were supervised, from the other (forbidden) side, by an unfriendly looking chap with a Kalashnikov, and we caught nothing.

George was frailer now and there was a housekeeper or carer present. It was a lovely day and conversation flowed as easily as ever. But we sensed that our hosts were tiring, so we did not stay long. As we drove away we wondered whether we would ever see George again and as things turned out that proved to be our last meeting with them both. It was a gentle and peaceful coda to a long friendship.

I am very glad to have known George. He was a man of great energy and talent, but modest and outgoing, always more interested in hearing others' news than in recounting his own. He had a great gift of friendship, from which I was lucky enough to benefit. And the same goes for Andrea. They were a solid team, whom I thought of always as "George and Andrea", never just the one or the other.

In Memoriam – Rupert Ridge

Rupert came into our lives one day in 1995 in Barbados when he was visiting the local Cheshire home in his capacity as the director of Leonard Cheshire International. Catherine had been deeply involved in efforts to improve the care of disabled children in post-communist Bulgaria and had been looking for something interesting and worthwhile to do in our new post, if possible in the same general field. Rupert helped her get accepted at the home as a regular volunteer, where she became Auntie Catherine two mornings a week for the ensuing three years. Without his intervention, this might never have happened, as the home's director had until then made it plain that she discouraged volunteers.

Rupert very quickly won us over with his friendliness and charm. He was witty and unstuffy, with an ability to get along with everyone he encountered. He was a good listener and he laughed at our jokes, even the feeble ones. He was the best sort of person to have to lunch and we enjoyed that first visit, wishing that it could have lasted longer. From then on Catherine had a contact at Cheshire HQ whom she could rely on for wise and sympathetic advice.

By the time our East Caribbean posting had come to an end, in February 1998, and with it our time in the diplomatic service, we reckoned that Rupert had become more of a friend than an official contact, though we probably both realised that we were unlikely to remain in touch with him for long. Perhaps Christmas cards for a couple of years, and that would be that. We had become inured to the evanescence of friendships formed in the course of a peripatetic life.

But, happily, that was not to be. A year or so later, Rupert asked us to lunch at his London club where he and his other guest, Sir Patrick Walker, asked me if I'd like to become involved with Leonard Cheshire International, with a view maybe to succeeding Patrick in due course as its chairman. I was hesitant. Chairing the international wing of an important charity, the workings of which I knew next to nothing, was a daunting prospect. And besides, it was Catherine who had been involved with a part of it and with disabled children, not me. But she said, there and then, that I would be a fool to dismiss the idea, and a few weeks later I reported for duty at the Cheshire HQ in Millbank Tower.

From then on I saw a good deal of Rupert, usually in his office, which was a cheerful, slightly shambolic room in which anyone who cared to pop in was always welcome, greeted with easy conversation and a mug of tea. As well as Rupert's own desk it contained a couple of tables, one of which was always available for use as a spare desk, on which Patrick and I could spread out all the paperwork to be covered at the next meeting of the international committee or its ad hoc offshoots, or of the trustees of the main charity.

By shadowing Patrick, I gradually learned the ropes of what turned out to be a large and surprisingly bureaucratic organisation, awash with committees, trustees, advisers and paid staff. After a few months, it was arranged that I would accompany Rupert on a tour of Cheshire facilities in Tanzania and South Africa. I suspected – rightly as it later transpired – that this trip had been devised as a kind of trial run during which Rupert would be able to see whether I was made of sufficiently chairman stuff. But he never let it seem that way; he treated it as a standard liaison visit which would enable me to see how things were run in other countries. It also, of course, enabled me to see Rupert in action and to experience his magic touch.

We flew to Dar es Salaam, from where we went by bus to Dodoma, the Tanzanian capital, three hundred miles to the west. This took all day, and we shared our seats every now and again with an assortment of chickens, babies and the occasional adult who had nowhere else to sit. Rupert became firm friends with everyone within shouting distance, including the poor chap immediately behind him who had a hacking cough, spraying sinister tropical germs in all directions. When at last we reached Dodoma I was ready for bed, but Rupert bucked me up, as we were expected at a welcome dinner with the local LC committee, municipal and political worthies without whose support the local home could not exist. Ten minutes into the meal, Rupert had them wrapped around his little finger.

The next day, after we had visited the home, we were fetched by a comfortable minibus belonging to an Italian mission hospital, a hundred miles back towards Dar, which was part of the Tanzanian Cheshire network. Rupert had been there before and assured me that I would be charmed not only by the priests and brothers who both ran the place and formed most of the medical staff, but also and above all by the nurses, who were all nuns.

"I love nuns," he said and he meant it. And they evidently loved him, not only at that mission hospital, but wherever we went where there were nuns, with whom he always and almost instantaneously formed a cheerful and empathetic friendship. Later, when I was travelling on my own in other countries and encountering the nuns who formed the staffing backbone of so many Cheshire establishments in the developing world, they would enquire after him, even if they'd never met him. His reputation, as an encouraging and sympathetic soul, had spread to the ends of the Cheshire earth.

From Tanzania, we went on to Johannesburg, via an apprehensive four hours spent in an airport transit lounge in Harare, where the Zimbabwean government had started to make things difficult for the local LC organisation and our own resident LCI representative. We had not been granted visas to enter the country, so we hoped that our presence at the airport would pass uneventfully, which fortunately it did. Rupert was cheerfully unconcerned. I did my best to emulate him.

We visited three Cheshire facilities in Johannesburg. One of them, situated in a prosperous and until recently exclusively white neighbourhood, was a residential home for old people, some of them with dementia. It was still largely white, but the South African Cheshire foundation had started to implement racial integration, as the law required, so there were also a few black and Asian residents. I sensed, I hope wrongly, that they felt slightly uncomfortable and that some of their white fellow residents were giving them the cold shoulder. I don't know whether Rupert shared this uneasy feeling, but, if he did, he didn't let it show. Instead, he spread his usual aura of friendly interest and concern, which in some way magically reduced the edginess which I had felt when we arrived.

The other two homes were in townships, in Daveyton and Soweto. I don't remember much about the former, except that it was well run and problem-free and still exclusively black, as integration seemed to be a one-way process in South Africa's Cheshire world. The one in Soweto, also all black, had governance problems, which were holding up its development and even threatening its continued existence. For reasons which now elude me its management committee (formed of local movers and shakers) had stopped functioning. The home was running out of funds and had no voice through which to deal with the municipal authorities or even the South African Cheshire foundation. So, there and then, Rupert convened a meeting of the home's leading lights, who struck us as capable and articulate people, the result of which was that they declared unilateral independence, with a management committee formed entirely from among the residents, which would deal directly with the municipality and the foundation. Some of the new committee members were afraid that their self-declared authority would not be recognised, particularly by the lofty and distant foundation, but Rupert said that he would see to that. And he did, to everyone's satisfaction. It was not long before that self-governing Soweto home was recognised as a South African Cheshire paragon.

I must have passed muster, as I succeeded Patrick as international chairman when he retired in 2000. And, more tiresomely and unpleasantly, Rupert must have been in the firing line of the man doing all the coughing and sneezing behind him in the bus, as he succumbed to a nasty feverish illness which took him several weeks to shake off.

Having become international chairman, I was automatically a trustee of the LC foundation, which meant a lot more meetings to attend, some of them of a tediosity that still defies description, by me anyway. But there was a silver lining; I saw a good deal more of Rupert and of his friends and colleagues in the international department. And it was not long before Catherine and I met Blanche and other members of his family, at Brockley Elm House near Backwell, in North Somerset.

We were enchanted by the family, the house and the garden, and were made very welcome, with abundant hospitality. Blanche presided over a ménage that seemed to ebb and flow, with beautiful Pre-Raphaelitish daughters and prospective daughter-in-law, and the odd dog or two, coming and going, sometimes needing feeding and sometimes not. Homegrown vegetables and meat – there were sheep grazing in the further reaches of the garden and deer bred for the table by one of Rupert's brothers a couple of fields away – were turned by Blanche with the help of an Aga into huge and delicious meals, washed down by the excellent claret that Rupert had discovered could be procured from the local branch of Lidl.

The house looked as though it had started life, probably in the eighteenth century, as a solid country gentry dwelling, stone-built, with three storeys of Georgian sash windows. At some stage it had been divided, so that it had effectively become a pair of generously proportioned semis. The second brother and his Dutch wife lived in one, Blanche and Rupert in the other. Their part was

L-shaped, with a bewildering number of rooms, nooks and crannies. We were accommodated in a comfy spare bedroom approached up a secret staircase all of its own. And, luxuriously, we had our own bathroom, fashioned out of what had once been the estate's main water reservoir, perched at the end of the former domestic offices' wing, above a glory hole of a room containing gumboots, gardening tools, miscellaneous stores and the very latest top of the range Miele dishwasher, which rumbled comfortingly beneath us as we drifted off to sleep. The bathroom, an enormous cast-iron erstwhile water tank, clanged and echoed when we used its facilities. Our staircase dropped directly into the centre of activities, a room full of books, squashy chairs and sofas and family life.

The garden, or rather those parts of it within easy reach of the house, was divided by high hedges into a series of outdoor rooms, a selection of lawns, one of which could usually be relied on to provide shelter from the current prevailing wind. There was even a ground elder border, a novel feature that we hadn't come across before. After all, it's quite a pretty plant and almost impossible to get rid of. So why not just enjoy it?

Across the yard lay the Brockley Academy, a long-defunct schoolhouse that now housed Motivation, David Constantine's remarkable charity that was revolutionising the design and affordable manufacture of wheelchairs all over the developing world. I had already met David in international committee meetings in Millbank Tower and been mightily impressed by him. Rupert and Blanche had rescued his then embryo organisation, squeezed into inadequate and uneconomic accommodation in London, and had provided it with the attractive and relatively spacious premises in their outbuildings that it occupied till very recently, more or less rent-free. This was typical of the generosity and enthusiasm with which they engaged in activities and organisations dedicated to helping others less fortunate than themselves, such as Leonard Cheshire and ABCD (Action around Bethlehem Children with Disabilities).

Rupert and I travelled together on Cheshire business on two further occasions. The first was when we attended its far eastern regional conference in Wuhan in China, where we were treated like visiting heads of state in a flurry of speeches, red banners and banquets that struck us as having less to do with the welfare of disabled people than with demonstrating the might and ideological correctness of the Chinese government organisation under whose auspices Leonard Cheshire China was permitted to operate. But things were more human and genuinely Cheshirish in the Wuhan facility, an impressive day centre where some hundreds of disabled people were cared for and given training that would enable them to live independent lives. There Rupert soon found himself surrounded by kindred spirits who were drawn to him and encouraged by his friendliness and enthusiasm.

The second occasion was when we toured some of the facilities for disabled children in Bulgaria. One of the reasons that had encouraged me to become involved with LC International was the thought that I might be able to encourage it to help foster good practice in Bulgaria, then still in very short supply in the aftermath of an overwhelmingly inhumane approach to the welfare of the 35,000 institutionalised so-called 'orphans' (or even 'idiots') locked away in remote children's homes during forty-five years of a communist dictatorship. Fifteen years had passed since the collapse of the communist regime and much had been achieved, notably by Johnny Stancioff's Karin Dom day centre in Varna and half a dozen other centres of excellence that had learned from it, but there was still a very long way to go, and the thought that these institutions might become affiliated to LC, to their great and possibly regionally incremental advantage, had become a bee in my bonnet.

I am not sure that Rupert was quite as starry-eyed about the prospect of a Bulgarian LCI programme as I was, but he was certainly greatly taken by the country and by the determination and friendliness of so many of the people we met there who were working to improve the lot of disabled children, especially at Karin Dom, which had by then already become a world-class institution in that field. But there was to be no real chance for him to take this any further, as his health broke down soon after our return and by the end of that year, 2004, he had had to retire.

Rupert was convinced, or so he told me, that the main reason for his breakdown was the anti-malarial drug Lariam, then already suspected of inducing harmful side-effects and now banned or strictly restricted world-wide. But I am sure that Lariam's effects were compounded by his unhappiness at work, where relations between him and the foundation's chairman and, though to a lesser extent, the director general, had soured. The chairman had taken against him, for reasons that I could never really fathom, and was constantly undermining his authority. He tried to recruit me, with hints and snide remarks made lightly but insidiously during meetings at which Rupert wasn't present, and when he realised that I found this distasteful and, goaded, sometimes said so, he took against me too. Rupert had been gone barely a month before the chairman had me to lunch, to discuss 'future plans', which turned out to consist of asking me to tender my resignation as international chairman. When I baulked and asked why, he said that my time would soon, in any case, be up and that it was important for the future strength of LC that I should create an immediate vacancy which he could fill, as his time was also almost up, so that he could continue to play a directing role, as international chairman. This would enable him to keep up his international travel programme, which was of such benefit to the charity and the people it supported. (In an earlier, fatuous, exercise he had directed all the trustees to devise straplines for themselves. His own was: *Travels the world in support of disabled people*. He certainly did a great deal of travelling, but I'm not convinced that the world's disabled people derived much benefit from it.)

Most of my fellow trustees encouraged me to stand my ground, so I said that I was unwilling to go before we had found a new international director and given him or her time to get settled in, and in the end I departed a few months after the chairman, who from then on took no further part in the charity's affairs. I was hoping that the deputy director Mark O'Kelly, who had been doing an excellent job as acting director throughout Rupert's illness, would agree to stay on as his substantive successor, but Mark was not enthusiastic and a new director, Tanya Barron, was recruited through an open competition.

I still cannot understand what the chairman had against Rupert. Maybe he was subconsciously jealous of his easy way with people and innate leadership qualities. He should have been grateful to him for the great reforms that had taken place on his watch, whereby well-intentioned but ad hoc and amateurish efforts to develop the charity's reach around the world, and to instigate training programmes, had been replaced by regional structures, each headed by a professional regional training and development officer who reported to the assistant director (training and development) in London. (This was Sarah Dyer, someone with an impressive track record in this field.) But instead of gratitude and support, he provided a whispering campaign and subversion. Nowadays this would be called workplace bullying, but for Rupert, it was just plain obstructive hostility, and I am sure it contributed to his breakdown.

Fortunately there were happier interludes, such as the away days when Rupert, Mark, Sarah and another member of the LCI team, Roger Brown, came down to Whole Farm Cottage, our house between Rye and Tenterden, for brainstorming and 'cow pie' lunch, provided by Catherine. And the atmosphere in the international department remained in general optimistic, with new liaisons with other disability organisations being created, especially in Latin America, and a gradual easing of tension between the crusty old army generals in Delhi who headed LC India and our newly appointed regional director (T&D) in Bangalore.

But the best bit for us was that the Ridges and the Thomases were getting to know each other better. We were invited to stay at Brockley Elm House both before and after Rupert's illness and they came to stay with us at Whole Farm Cottage a couple of times. We enjoyed each other's company, in expeditions to local gardens, churches and cathedrals, on picnics and walks. Rupert was surprised by Winchelsea, where we now live, with all its humps and bumps covering the remains of long-lost mediaeval buildings, and we were all enchanted by the Romney Marsh churches and by Camber Castle's unrestored and isolated presence, surrounded by sheep and – a joyous discovery – a showy and well-named plant, Stinking Shepherd. Catherine and I were treated to a terrific performance of Hamlet at the Tobacco Factory in Bristol and were deeply impressed by Rupert's enormous, manicured and highly productive kitchen garden, which he created more or less from scratch while he was recovering from his breakdown. We were honoured to be invited to a family wedding, where Lucie Špičková, the young opera singer to whom Rupert had been such a comfort in a bumpy episode during her time as his secretary at LCI, sang gloriously.

We also enjoyed a wonderfully happy holiday together on neutral ground, in a rented cottage at Achiltibuie near Ullapool in the far north west of Scotland. Catherine and I went ahead by car and met Rupert and Blanche off the plane at Inverness. They had promised to bring a few supplies, revealed as a considerable understatement as we watched them claim enormous, shapeless sacks and packages off the baggage carousel. These turned out to contain generous quantities of vegetables and meat, all homegrown at Brockley Elm House. We were barely able to cram them all into the car.

We explored lochs and brochs and rocky coves, where we saw otters and deer and all manner of birds. Later, during an exploration of Assynt, with its weird mountains, we noticed that its tangled landscape was peppered in the Ordnance Survey map with places and features called Drum This and Drum That. In an improbably located book-cum-teashop, miles from anywhere, we bought a Gaelic dictionary. 'Drum' meant 'ridge'. From then on Rupert and Blanche were Mr and Mrs Drum.

We last met nearly seven years ago. I think we would have teamed up to do something together again, but illness intervened. Rupert and I were keeping in touch now and again in an exchange of emails, in one of which we learned of the Ridge-Drums' new and unlikely amenity, a campervan, in which they were making forays up hill and down dale, visiting aunts and cousins all over the country. We thought we too might soon catch a glimpse of this most un-Ridgelike conveyance, but then the initial, misleading blow fell. In one of his emails, Rupert complained of a tiresomely painful chest, which was making gardening difficult. Soon it was worse than that. A condition of the bones of the ribcage had been diagnosed for which nothing much could be done, though the pain could possibly be made more manageable by heeding the advice of a pain clinic. And then, a year later, in 2014, came the hammer blow of the late, but this time correct, diagnosis of lung cancer.

Rupert, normally the most even-tempered of men, was justifiably angry. That wasted year could cost him dear. But he was determined to fight the disease in every way available, conventional and experimental. And fight it he did. Some of the treatments for which he was a willing guinea pig proved harder to bear than the disease itself and twice he nearly succumbed to pneumonitis. But, through all this horror, he maintained an astonishing detachment, reporting on each latest stage of his illness almost as though he was an oncologist describing the progress of one of his patients. He was, I'm sure, sustained throughout by his strong religious faith and by the constant love and support of Blanche and his four children, and of his many friends. He and Blanche summoned up the strength to go away from time to time, once even as far as Padua. And he also kept up a steady correspondence, with me still lucky enough to be one of his email partners. We discussed all sorts of things: Brexit, Trump and other forms of political madness, the books we were reading or planning to read, our families and their doings and antecedents, our dogs, even that old staple, the weather.

A month ago, he sent me an email clarifying something he'd written in one a couple of days earlier. He apologised for its brevity, as he was going through a 'bad patch'. He died the next day, two months short of his seventieth birthday.

What a marvellous man. I am so lucky to have known him.

Richard Thomas, 29 March 2017.

In Memoriam – Cog

Every few months over the last ten or fifteen years, Catherine and I have been in the habit of meeting Cog for lunch and a catch-up, usually in a pub or restaurant. Now and again during the last few weeks, one of us has thought, momentarily, that it's about time for Cog to ring to arrange the next occasion, only to remember that there will never be another one. For Cog died a few months ago, only three or four weeks after our last lunch together.

Cog was one of our oldest friends. We had enjoyed each other's company and laughed so much and done so many things together over the past half-century, that she had become a kind of constant in our lives and it is still hard to accept that that is all now firmly in the past, just memories.

Cog was really Corinna, named we believe after the girlfriend of the seventeenth-century poet Herrick, one of her parents' favourites, rather than after Sappho's acolyte. One of her brothers couldn't get his tongue round this pretty name, so he hit on Cog instead. And Cog she remained, to her family and to her closest friends. We named one of our children Corinna after her and she cheerfully agreed to become her secular godmother. We couldn't quite cope with the idea of full, godly godparents, as we were neither of us of that way of thinking. This didn't worry Cog, and an excellent secular godmother she proved, eventually spreading the scope of her generosity to include Corinna's three children, who were the lucky recipients of a steady supply of books and toys and even an iPad.

Catherine first met Cog a few days after we arrived in London in 1966, fresh from our wedding in Ghana, but I had already known her for three or four years. She was part of a gang of young people just embarking on their adult careers, to which I had become attached soon after I emerged from national service and started work in the Commonwealth Relations Office. In the autumn of 1963, I was due to leave on posting to Accra, and part of my preparations during the summer was the acquisition of a car, a brand-new Ford Cortina – a model deemed by higher authority appropriate for a second secretary and therefore, fully funded by the CRO's car loan scheme. The car would undoubtedly have to be run in – they had to be in those days – and I had been granted a month's leave before departure. Where better to do the running in than France and Italy and maybe Switzerland?

So, Cog and I set off, with a rather hazy plan to meet up in Milan with another member of the gang, Sally Wilson, under the station clock. We assumed that Milan would have a station and a station clock, assumptions that fortunately proved justified. Sally, Cog's firmest friend from college days, had set off ahead of us with Martha, an American girl intent on cramming in as much European culture as could reasonably be fitted into a summer vacation. Once in Milan, Cog planned to head off on her own, leaving the rest of us a couple of weeks to 'do' Italy before all meeting up again, once more under the same clock.

Astonishingly, this sketchiest of plans worked perfectly, though it nearly came unstuck almost before it began. Milan proved an awfully long way from Calais, much further than we had allowed for. This was before the days of much in the way of motorways and we had probably confused miles with kilometres in our calculations. So we had to get a move on, skirting Paris and then down the N7 to the Cote d'Azur before heading east to Italy and Milan. We camped in someone's front garden the first night. That someone evidently took us for a honeymoon couple, cooked us a delicious supper, and charged us next to nothing the next morning.

We agreed to share the driving from then on, so after my early morning three-hour stint I handed over to Cog, helpfully suggesting that she should try to keep up a steady seventy (mph, not kph) if we were to have much hope of reaching our next night-stop at a reasonable hour. I thought she seemed a bit startled, but she soon built up speed and I was just beginning to relax when she chicaned, still at seventy, through a z-bend level crossing over the main railway line, which ran parallel to the road. Somehow the car remained upright, on the right side of the road and we agreed that perhaps we needn't go quite so fast after all.

'Keeping up a steady seventy' entered Cog's vocabulary and remained there for the rest of her life.

Having returned from Accra, newly married, Catherine and I were sent to Paris, a real honeymoon posting, where I was a member of the UK delegation to NATO. During our time there, Cog took up residence somewhere on the Left

Bank. One day she appeared at our flat in a state of some agitation, bearing a matchbox containing a yellowish bug about the size of a large ladybird.

"Richard, is this a bedbug?"

I wondered why she thought I would know, though in fact I did, and confirmed that it was. Cog said that it had lots of friends and relations in her no doubt picturesque but evidently rather sordid digs, and decided there and then that she would have to find somewhere else to live. And in next to no time she had moved into an empty *chambre de bonne* in our block, so for a few months, we were close neighbours.

One evening, she appeared at our front door to announce that she had been stabbed, something she seemed to have quite taken in her stride – momentous rather than alarming or dangerous.

"My dears, I've been *stabbed!*" as though this was the kind of excitement that merely needed reporting, in sensationalist tones perhaps, rather than medical treatment. Fortunately, the wound, to her chest, proved fairly superficial and she continued to make light of what most of us would have regarded as a terrifying event.

We were never too sure exactly what Cog did in Paris to keep body and soul together. All we knew was that it was vaguely financial, rather beyond our ken, and possibly a little glamorous, involving film-making and the odd pop-star. Whatever it was, it seemed to keep her busy and cheerful and ever ready for adventure. Once, while we were holidaying in Provence, she joined us for a few days, evidently to take refuge from a rich, importunate suitor, impressively named Plunket-Greene and equipped with a Rolls-Royce, in which he had been parading her up and down the Promenade des Anglais in Nice. Cog's adventures with P-G, recounted at length and with many an elegant embellishment, kept our house-party in stitches for hours at a time.

For a number of years, we saw Cog only intermittently, during spells of home duty or leave, but she never failed to perk us up, with tales of extraordinary goings-on and sometimes, even better, astonishing scandal. We wondered about her private life – whether she enjoyed any lasting attachments – but were never any the wiser. For her private life was precisely that – private. But at last came the good news that she was hooked, to a romantic-sounding sea-dog called Peter Haward. Peter and Cog had met and fallen for each other while waiting for a delayed flight at Athens airport. Peter, who delivered yachts across oceans and sailed replica galleons around the world for a living – and then wrote books about his adventures – had no doubt just handed a yacht over to its Greek owner, little expecting to acquire a wife on the return trip.

Peter and Cog set up shop in a flat in the middle of London, in Lloyd-Baker Street, before moving to the Sussex coast, where they bought a house in St Leonards, from where Cog could, in theory, see Peter as he sailed past in the *Golden Hind* or some other commission. Every now and again, she would fly out to join him for a while at some agreeable port of call, and they were blissfully happy together. Our teenage children declared them classy, their highest accolade, rarely conferred on adults.

But all too soon this idyll came to a distressing end. Peter fell seriously ill, with motor neurone disease, and died in January 1993. Cog nursed him to the end. They had been married barely eleven years. We were living in Sofia and had not heard from them for some time, unaware that Peter was ill till, only shortly before he died, Cog wrote to explain the awful reason for her silence. Her letter was a model of dignity and restraint, totally devoid of self-pity, but eloquent in its expression of her love for her by a now helpless husband.

A year later, she spent a week with us in Bulgaria. We took her skiing and sight-seeing. The whole stay must have been something of an ordeal for her, coming comparatively soon after Peter's death, but she remained resolutely cheerful and good company and we hoped we had helped a bit.

Another three years went by before our next holiday together, this time in the Caribbean, where we were enjoying our final diplomatic posting, Barbados. Cog and another member of the original gang, Sally Wilson's brother Alex, joined us for a few days on a chartered yacht, which took us slowly round a few of the islands near St Martin, where it was based. Cog and Catherine enjoyed a morning exploring the absurdly pretty – and astonishingly expensive – boutiques in St Bart's, while Alex and I sampled a *pression* or two in a handy bar. But that evening our host and skipper served up his *pièce de résistance,* an unappetising looking blue cocktail. Cog had great difficulty containing her mirth and for years afterwards her chief memory of our Caribbean charter was this unpleasing drink – a memory which always reduced her to happy giggles.

"My dears, will you ever forget that ghastly *blue* drink?"

When I retired – compulsorily on my sixtieth birthday in February 1998 – Cog joined us for part of our long, wrong-way-round-the-world trip home from Barbados. We met up in a ski resort in Colorado called Crested Butte, where our son Alexander was doing a stint as the Ski Club of Great Britain rep. Cog arrived,

274

fresh as a daisy after a journey of thousands of miles, promptly in time for the birthday dinner. We spent the next few days in Crested Butte, slithering down the only route graded below black and visiting the resort's other attractions, including the Oxygen Bar where in theory one could be revived if suffering from the effects of high altitude (it was always shut), while Alexander did his alarming stuff on extreme routes. Our guesthouse was strictly non-smoking, so Cog, who was an enthusiastic smoker, felt obliged to lean out of her bathroom window in order to enjoy a few illicit puffs. But the smoke from her cigarette managed to find its way in through an adjacent window, where it set off the smoke alarm and she was severely chastised by the management.

After a few days, we rented a car and set off. Soon we were inching our way over an alarming, icy Rockies pass. This took several hours, during which we saw barely another vehicle. Luckily, the weather was fine and the rental people had insisted on upgrading us, free of charge, to a four-wheel-drive car, as in their rather worrying opinion no ordinary car would make it in one piece over the pass. But once over, the going was easy enough and during the next day or two Cog was in her element, interviewing ancient, rugged characters artistically arranged in rocking chairs on porches in a string of Hicksville towns, in one of which she insisted on having her hair done (always the best way of getting the local low-down).

We headed for Monument Valley, competing for space on the highway with clumps of tumbleweed bowling along in the wind and admiring the cactuses seemingly dotted about by Central Casting for the use of John Wayne and the baddies, against a background of the mesas and buttes we had seen in a thousand B movies. There was not a cowboy or Indian to be seen. But neither were there more than a handful of tourists. Judging from the number of empty stalls along the roadside, the place would have been a seething mass of them in summer. At the visitor centre, Cog was able to restock on the Jerkies and other snacks that she regularly munched, along with her breakfast leftovers, curled up on the back seat, longing for a cigarette.

I had carefully researched a scenic route that would avoid Las Vegas, which I assumed none of us had any desire to visit. But I had assumed wrongly. Cog had set her heart on an evening or two at the tables and had packed a glamorous outfit for the occasion. So we made an advance booking at the Imperial Hotel, which our Fodor's Guide assured us would be suitable and certainly big enough, with over a thousand rooms ("suites").

By the time we had reached the improbably and as far as we could see inaccurately named Tuba City, we were well into the Navajo reservation and the weather had closed in, to gale-driven sleet. We were aiming for Second Mesa, in the Hopi reservation, where we had booked ourselves for a night in an establishment claiming to be the only Hopi owned and run motel in the world. All we could see of Tuba City through the storm consisted of a charmless collection of shacks, redeemed by one shiny, clean, brightly lit and very tempting branch of Macdonalds, into which we fell, hungrily and gratefully. It proved full of earnest young Hopis, chomping on Big Macs while doing their homework or playing chess, while waiting for the bus home. Catherine and I installed ourselves at the only empty table, while Cog ventured out into the tempest in search of a phone box, as she had promised to contact the people in Los Angeles with whom she had arranged to stay at the end of our trip. When she reappeared we too had Big Macs, before setting off into Hopi Land, which suddenly revealed itself, as the storm cleared away, as a surreal semi-desert landscape of buttes and mesas.

Second Mesa turned out to be a largish hilltop village, which would not have looked out of place in a poor third world country in South America or Africa. It certainly didn't look much like the America of the movies or even of our recent travels. It contained a handful of solid, modern, dreary-looking buildings – the reservation's regional offices, the post office, a clinic, a bank, a supermarket, a church or two, a museum, the motel – but consisted otherwise of small, presumably traditional, dwellings clustered alongside narrow lanes, plastered over in adobe the colour of the surrounding sandstone. The motel was comfortable enough in a functional sort of way and well provided with admonitory notices and leaflets warning non-Native Americans of Hopi sensitivities. No photography. No loud music. No inappropriate conversation (which we took to mean no patronising comments or questions).

Dinner featured certain Hopi specialities, chief of which were blue potatoes, and at breakfast we were offered blue cornflakes and blue waffles, made from blue Hopi corn. There was not much in the way of explanation of all this blueness, just bald assertions that the potatoes and the corn grew blue in Hopi Land. Cog was enchanted, though rather less so by the Hopi people's strong facial features. For the rest of her life she maintained – a trifle unjustly, we felt – that they were the ugliest people she had ever seen, hilariously so.

The museum was a bonus, for it contained much of genuine interest, laid out and explained in a way that pulled no punches about the monstrous treatment that the Native Americans had endured at the hands of the white settlers, often uprooted from their traditional homelands and plonked down in inaccessible and semi-desert reservations where they were expected to feel grateful to the authorities for their munificent grants of land, as often as not next to useless. Once again photography was forbidden. And so even were note-taking and sketching. Fortunately, there were ample stocks of postcards for sale, many of them photographs of alarming looking people taken more than a hundred years earlier. Catherine bought a good many and used them over the years as thank-you notes and birthday cards, reserved exclusively for Cog, who was always amused by them. The last one went to thank her for that final lunch together, three or four weeks before she died. The supply had lasted just long enough.

Before leaving this rather sad part of the world, we visited one of its main tourist attractions, an ancient cliff village the name of which escaped me. I could have looked it up in Fodor's guide had it not been for Cog's custom of tearing out the pages of places we had visited and throwing them away. We protested in vain that just maybe we might wish to refer to them again, to refresh our memories, but to no avail. She tore off the pages of paperback novels in a like manner once she had read them, pointing out, reasonably enough, that she was reducing the weight of her luggage.

Then we doubled back, to spend two nights in a lodge overlooking the Grand Canyon, which we were lucky enough to see in bright sun and under a full moon, lightly dusted with snow and not too overrun by fellow tourists. We even saw it from the air, for we hired a little plane (with a pilot) to give us a bird's eye view.

Over the years we had come to recognise, and therefore expect, one of Cog's occasional traits, which was to be dissatisfied with whichever room she was allocated on arrival at a hotel. We have tended timidly to accept whatever we are given (once, in Cassis in the south of France, we had a room without a window, and once in Quebec City, one with a loo in the middle of the room but also, fortunately, with a window, though one which opened into the hotel garage and its car exhaust fumes rather than the open air), but Cog was made of sterner stuff. She did not disappoint in the Grand Canyon lodge and was immediately granted another room, following a quick dispute with the check-in clerk, identified by his lapel badge as Wayne, from Wyoming. We looked the other way when we heard her insisting on using the poor chap's biro, starting, "There don't seem to be any pens for guests, Mr Wayne from Wyoming…" From then on, the hapless Wayne from Wyoming loomed large in Cog's inventory of useless idiots, recalled whenever she encountered someone approaching his level of perceived crassness.

And so, after crossing the dizzying Hoover Dam, we drove into Las Vegas, Cog's putative nirvana. We found the Imperial Hotel easily enough, a colossal but disappointingly sober-looking building, parked the car in its immense multi-story car park and headed for the reception desk queues, past banks of slot machines being fed endless supplies of coins by unhappy-looking, goggle-eyed punters dressed, Cog sadly noted, in shell suits or even shorts and T-shirts. The coins were sold by the thousand from trolleys pushed by young ladies clothed in kitsch approximations of imperial Chinese dress, and it was only then that we understood the identity of the empire after which the hotel was named.

We joined a long queue which snaked, airport-style, to the reception counters, where, half an hour later, we were allocated our rooms, on the twenty-second floor. It was clear that Cog was beginning to compare the Imperial unfavourably with wherever it was that she had stayed in Monte with Plunket-Greene. But she perked up when we were joined in the lift by a bride, in full regalia, flustered and late for her nuptials in the Holy Spirit Luxury Rooftop Imperial Wedding Facility a few floors further up.

The rooms were more spartan than imperial, but adequate enough and decorated with a number of surprising notices warning us of dire consequences if we were caught stealing the telly (difficult, as it was bolted to the wall) or the bathtub (even harder). Furthermore, so we were advised by another notice, we would have to ring for Security to come and vouch for our good behaviour in this regard before attempting to check out.

Later in the afternoon, we went for a walk around central Vegas. It became clearer, as we picked our way through the Roman Forum, past Pompeii and the Grand Canal (strangely juxtaposed), that we had chosen a comparatively downmarket lodging place, unable to compete with the likes of Caesar's Palace (the glorious origin, we learned that evening, of Caesar Salad). But it would have to do, and after one of Vesuvius's regular, hourly eruptions we went back to the Imperial, dodging the spray from the Niagara Falls, to get ready for the evening.

Over dinner, Cog, who had changed into her casino rig, assured us that she was determined to try her luck at the tables. We meanly left her to it and slunk off to early bed.

Next morning we met in the Ming Dynasty Breakfast Bar which, besides the usual waffles, maple syrup, crispy bacon and watery coffee, offered champagne on tap; "Help yourself. All you can drink." And they meant it. For, sticking out of one end of the self-service counter, was a soda fountain which, at the touch of a button, dispensed sweet, fizzy white wine. One sip persuaded us that we could manage without.

Cog reported that she had spent about an hour playing roulette, by which time she had managed to lose a couple of hundred dollars, and so had decided to pack it in. The other punters had proved unremarkable, with no sign of Gregory Peck or John Wayne, or anyone remotely like them. This disappointing evening had left her in a bit of a gloom. But she was amused by the champagne dispenser.

In Death Valley, we were surprised to find our way west barred by a range of high mountains. There was not a hint of their existence in our road atlas, which marked a number of roads heading straight for California, one of which we followed for a few miles till we came to a barrier and a notice advising us that the road would be closed till mid-April, six weeks hence. So we retraced our steps to the nearest Best Western, where the manager assured us that the Sierra Nevada had long been a feature of the local landscape, whether we liked it or not, and that the only way west would mean a northward diversion of some hundreds of miles via Lake Tahoe. So we drove the whole length of Death Valley, which was carpeted with flowers, the result apparently of an unusually active El Nino which had caused the desert to bloom, an unexpected and totally delightful bonus.

After a stay in San Francisco and a final drive south along the Carmel Valley to Los Angeles, we went our separate ways, Cog to her friends and us to New Zealand.

In May the next year, we were once again on holiday together, this time in France. We drove down from Paris to stay with Alex Wilson in his house high on a hill near Conques in the Aveyron. On the way we passed through Montmorillon, home of the world's first macaroon, a detail that pleased Cog, heading for Bourg-Archambault, where I had spent part of my rite-of-passage French exchange when I was sixteen. I assured Cog and Catherine that the building in which I had stayed had wow factor, and as we rounded a corner the château came in view.

"Wow," said Cog, loyally and politely and maybe sincerely, because I had indeed stayed in a pretty impressive pile.

One January evening a year or two later, Cog rang us in a state of high excitement. We could fly to Venice for £14 return, provided she confirmed the booking before midnight. This was in the early days of budget airlines and internet bookings and Catherine and I, not long returned from our innocent expatriate existence and unused to such innovations, were astonished. We readily agreed and so, on a snowy evening in January 2002, found ourselves checking in at the Hotel Flora, a couple of streets away from St Mark's Square. Having done her usual party trick of finding fault with her room and changing to another, more to her liking, and having also pointed out that the Flora wasn't a patch on the Gritti (we wouldn't have known and wondered how she did), Cog declared herself fully satisfied, and we enjoyed a wonderful three-day break in a magically misty, winter-time Venice, almost empty of tourists apart from ourselves.

Cog was ill the next year and had to have a major operation. But she was determined to join us in July on the cruise liner *Discovery,* on which I was a guest speaker, on a trip to Greenland and Iceland, and she completed her post-operative treatment in the nick of time. She was still pretty wobbly, but she summoned up enough energy to have her usual confrontation with the management about her accommodation and got herself switched to a better cabin. One of the other speakers – in fact, the celebrity speaker for that cruise – was Michael Shea, our old friend and diplomatic service colleague who had later become the Queen's press secretary, who was accompanied by his effervescent wife Mona. So, Cog was willy-nilly part of a social gang, which must have been pretty draining for someone not long out of t hospital. But, being Cog, she joined in with gusto.

That trip turned out to be the last of our joint holidays, but we continued to see each other quite often for lunch, sometimes in a pub or restaurant, sometimes at home, or even the occasional picnic on the beach or at her beloved beach hut. We were consulted about her new London flat and Cog gave us valuable gardening advice. We exchanged family news; she was justifiably proud of the achievements of various nieces and great-nieces and she always asked about our clutch of grandchildren. She got to the weddings of all three of our children, respectively in Nancy, Exmoor and the Athenaeum ("How wonderful! I've always wanted to see inside.") and she gave them generous presents.

Cog was never one to let her own troubles and problems impinge on her relations with her friends. When there was a problem with one of her letting properties, or even with the hideous and potentially disastrous business of a hugely valuable consignment of rubies, in which she was wrongly and unjustly implicated for several very worrying months in the 1990s, she made light of it, turning it all into some improbable and very funny nonsense. It seemed that her whole existence was governed by a determination to give pleasure to others, which meant that she was always careful not to draw them into her own difficulties or to crave sympathy over matters with which she reckoned they had no need to be concerned.

Cog always looked stylish and elegant, even when she was gardening or mooching about on holiday. She enjoyed and was very good at making, conversation, provided she was with friends or at any rate with people with whom she reckoned she could easily make friends. But she did not suffer fools over gladly and just clammed up when in the presence of bores or the self-important. She was witty and had an abundance of sparkle, as one of her nieces so accurately put it at her memorial service. She wrote as she spoke. Catherine kept the letter she sent when we asked her, in July 1971, if she would be a secular parent (a godless godparent) to our newly born third child, whom we had named Corinna. This is what she wrote:

My dear Catherine,

Richard has just phoned to tell me the news that you have produced a new and beautiful daughter. I'm so v. pleased that after such a very wretched pregnancy you didn't have too bad a time over the actual production, and send warmest congratulations. I must also congratulate you on what I consider to be a <u>singularly</u> felicitous choice of name. Couldn't have chosen better, in my opinion.

I should be delighted to be a secular parent to her, though I must warn you that my memory for the dates of birth of my other protégés is pretty weak. I'm terribly good at remembering Christmas, however.

I'm so glad that you've got a proper, cheerful, pleasant-to-have-around nanny. I didn't have time to check with Richard whether you had had time to find out about latent alcoholism, nymphomania, drug addiction etc., (one would after all expect you to have at least one of these faults to cope with if the sterling tradition of Thomas employees is to be kept up!) but look forward to a report when I next see you.

I know it's very poor form to send this typewritten missive. Alas, handwritten Cog-missives are now collectors' items, and even typewritten ones have a distressing rarity.

Not sure how up to date your information on my movements is? Probably last time I told Richard about it I was likely to move to Milan. [She was in London at the time.] Since then it has been, in order, (each move absolutely definite, for a period of 1–7 days, till cancelled by latest projects) Lugano, Annecy, and now Milan again. When my boss comes back from his latest trip to furrin parts, I expect to hear of new manoeuvres. Not sure I shall go, in the end, but I do find it rather tempting. The TOP SECURITY job that Richard suggested in Paris sounded so tempting too – so sad that they just wanted a typist (and as you see from this typing, that's just what I'm not good at).

Much love & many congratulations, Cog.

PS (after lunch)

I have just got a striped Jiffikin* for my secular daughter, and do hope that you don't already have dozens of these garments – if you have, please send it back (I'll wrap it tonight and send it separately) and say what else you would rather have. (This one is for an up-to-eighteen pounder. Sounds like cannon fodder!)

*Have no doubt that your experience in these matters has forced you to learn these rather nauseating technical terms!

Do hope that you are feeling completely revived. Until now this must have been the most grim year for Thomases. I have kept thinking of you and hoping that this phase would soon be over – and I'm sure that with Corinna's arrival (said with all due modesty: I refer to my namesake only) a new era of health and flourishingness will begin.

Reading this one can almost hear Cog speaking – her wit, her warmth and her empathy.

We had one last lunch together, only a few weeks before she died, at St Clement's, her favourite restaurant, half a mile from her house in St Leonards. Half the tables had been pushed together to form one long table, ready to seat a party of twenty or thirty people. Cog looked pretty frail, but assured us that she was fine, if a bit worried about arrangements for a guest she was expecting, and we chatted quietly about this and that. Then the big party arrived *en masse* and settled cheerfully and rather noisily at the long table. We wondered who they might be – mostly men, not at all smartly dressed, but clearly enjoying themselves. A film crew perhaps? After all, *Foyle's War* was set in Hastings. Perhaps they were shooting a new series? We asked the waiter if he knew who they were, but he didn't. Cog couldn't contain her curiosity, so she got up and asked one of the party.

"Oh, we're German sausage makers from London, on a works outing."

This intelligence creased Cog up. She practically split her sides. She had another glass of wine on the strength of it. "German sausage makers! How wonderful!"

We took her back to her house, still chortling. That was the last time we saw her, full of Coggish giggles.

Richard Thomas
12 September 2015
(Corinna Haward, 27 December 1935 – 22 March 2015)

In Memoriam – Jeremy Carter
Address at his memorial service,
11 November 2017

Catherine and I first met Jeremy and Mary in Prague in the summer of 1981 where he was our new defence attaché. In the weeks leading up to their arrival we had heard a bit about him, most but not quite all of it reassuring. Chief of our concerns was that he was apparently determined to bring his horse. He was preparing to live in a Cold War Iron Curtain capital, where livery arrangements were unheard of and accommodation for western diplomats, let alone their horses, perfunctory, allocated at the whim of the local authorities once they had ensured that the bugging systems in the designated house or flat were in good working order. The Carters were to have a large, once splendid, first floor flat overlooking the river. It had a balcony, which we had to assume was where Jeremy expected to stable his horse.

But when they eventually arrived, fortunately sans horse, we – the rest of us in the embassy – all fell for them. They were full of fun and enthusiasm and hospitality. Our new DA was a man of charm and wit and multi-talented. He could draw; soon his irreverent cartoons were enlivening tedious chancery meetings. And he was musical. He played the piano and was a knowledgeable and keen listener.

That Christmas the embassy carol party was held chez Carter. Hitherto the only Czech flavoured item at this annual event had been Good King Wenceslas – with words by a Victorian English clergyman and a melody derived from a mediaeval Finnish choir book – but Jeremy taught us real Czech carols, with their dancy, catchy tunes, to add to our repertoire. Even so, the Good King wasn't banished; he couldn't be, for not only was he an old favourite, but he had a special connection with Jeremy's bit of the embassy, as the carol's St Agnes'

Fountain was still there, a tap in a wall in Prague, right by the air attaché's garden gate, next to the no 33 bus stop.

Jeremy mixed a cheerful insouciance with derring-do and real bravery. His job involved a good deal of tourism, meaning that he, often with Mary, would drive around the countryside where (quite by chance of course!) they would come across interesting military installations, many of them very close to no-go areas, or even inside them. This activity displeased the Czech authorities and their Warsaw Pact allies, and once Jeremy and his American colleague were arrested and detained for going too near a SCUD missile installation, at a time of heightened tension when it looked as though the Russians and some of their allies were about to invade Poland, to silence Solidarność.

And on another occasion, when he had taken me up to the headwaters of the River Vltava, for a spot of fly-fishing on a stretch of water that just happened to mark the edge of the forbidden border zone with Austria, he struck up a cheerful conversation with our Kalashnikov-toting tail who was patrolling the opposite bank. Jeremy's Czech was much better than mine and I caught only the odd word.

"What was it that was so *strašný*?" (Czech for 'terrible'), I asked.

"Oh, just your casting!"

The defence section – the colonel and the wing commander and their wives – were frequently subjected to a testing and alarming form of trial by ordeal, from which the rest of us, mercifully, were largely spared. This was dinner-with-the-other-side – the Russians, the Chinese, the East Germans, the Bulgars, all of them in turn, at which the object of the exercise was for the east bloc hosts to render their western guests insensate with bonhomie and alcohol. How Jeremy (and Mary) put up with this I shall never know, but they did, with fortitude and good humour (and monstrous hangovers).

Jeremy was good company with people in all walks of life and of all ages. Our teenage children adored him and he knew the way to their hearts. One Christmas he gave our thirteen-year-old son a book entitled *Everything You Need to Know About Sex*, with an accompanying card urging Alexander to pay special attention to the advice on page 25. Agog, but anxious not be thought too eager, Alex took the book into a discreet corner and opened it. The pages were blank, including page 25. He is now 48, but he's still got the book.

Jeremy was a keen sportsman. He rode, he fished, he shot, he sailed, he skied, he played tennis. The embassy tennis court in Prague was in our garden and many were the weekend mornings when Catherine and I, hoping for a bit of a lie-in, were awakened by the joyful cries of the Carters and their opponents just below our bedroom window. But we didn't complain (well, not too much), as grumpiness was impossible anywhere near Jeremy, with his infectious good humour. Even his car had a zany, if inexplicable, name. It was called the Green Slug.

There were good opportunities for skiing near Prague, enthusiastically investigated and enjoyed by Mary and Jeremy. I was a pretty hopeless skier – too timid, said Jeremy. But he took me in hand and tempted me down the slopes with promises of snorts and tinctures at the bottom. I improved rapidly. Luckily those tinctures didn't run to his delicious but near lethal Foxes' Tails.

Jeremy had a great gift for friendship. He and Mary cherished and nourished the friendships they had formed in Prague and over the years kept them fresh, with visits to friends in Germany, Denmark and the States, to us in Bulgaria and Barbados, and back to Prague once that became possible again after the Velvet Revolution.

In the years immediately following his retirement from the army, Jeremy worked long and hard for the resettlement and welfare of a Czech family – a newly widowed mother with two children – who had been driven to seek asylum in Britain. That act of dedication and kindness, which of course he shared equally with Mary, was a shining example of his other great quality: his self-effacing, no-nonsense, straightforward, humanity. Members of that family, the Frodls, are with us today and I know that they would wish me to say how much they loved him.

Jeremy was a renaissance man – soldier, diplomat, artist, musician, sportsman, compassionate humanitarian. I am fortunate and proud to have known him and to have been counted among his friends.

In Memoriam – Zhelyu Zhelev
Zhelyu Zhelev Philosopher and Political Dissident President of Bulgaria 1992–1997

Zhelyu Zhelev, who died in his sleep in Sofia on 30 January 2015, aged 79, was Bulgaria's first democratically elected head of state, after the years, first of monarchy and then of communist dictatorship which had succeeded centuries of Ottoman hegemony. He was elected president in June 1990 by the newly constituted National Assembly, after the fall of communism at the end of 1989. A year and a half later, under a new constitution which had come into force the previous year, he was re-elected, this time by universal suffrage. He lost his party's nomination for the 1996 presidential election and was therefore unable to stand for a second term.

Zhelev was an intellectual and academic, nobody's idea of a typical politician. He was born in 1935 into a modest village family in Veselinovo, near Shumen in north-eastern Bulgaria. He studied philosophy at Sofia University, graduating in 1958 and gaining a PhD in 1974, a remarkable achievement given that he was under a cloud as an acknowledged dissident, having been expelled from the Communist Party in 1965. After his expulsion he endured years of 'parasitism', or unemployment in communist terminology, which he spent in virtual internal exile in his wife's village, scraping a living with odd jobs on farms.

In 1982, Zhelev published *Fascism*, the book on which his political reputation was based. In it, he drew parallels between communism and fascism and the book was promptly banned.

As he wrote, "Being a rabid anti-communist does not mean that one is a democrat; nor is frenzied anti-fascism a hallmark of democracy. To a democrat, both communism and fascism are abhorrent. Indeed, there has been no greater anti-communist than Hitler and no greater anti-fascist than Stalin, but neither of them is known to have been a democrat. Moreover, the 20th century has seen no greater butchers of democracy than the two moustachioed comrades."

In 1988, when the sort of events that were to topple communist regimes all over Eastern Europe the following year were still unthinkable, Zhelev founded the Committee for the Defence of Russe, a dissident organisation which operated under a conformist cloak of environmental activism, in that its ostensible purpose was to protect the city of Russe from industrial pollution emanating from Romanian factories the other side of the Danube. Early in 1989, still months before the dictator Zhivkov was toppled, Zhelev founded the more openly anti-regime, but cunningly named, Club for the Support of Glasnost and Perestroika and in due course became chairman of the Coordinating Committee of the Union of Democratic Forces.

The new constitution provided for a head of state with few if any executive powers. Nevertheless, Zhelev quickly established himself on the Eastern European and international scene as the leader of a newly democratised nation that was at first eager for change, but which later became disillusioned as its politics sank into an all too familiar pattern of corruption and internecine strife. This dispiriting process had already begun by 1996 and Zhelev's reputation suffered by unjust association with it, which probably accounted for his failure to achieve a second term.

Two incidents can serve as examples of Zhelev's honesty, incorruptibility and high-mindedness. Both happened during his five-day official visit to the UK in 1991, which took place at a time of great personal hardship for ordinary Bulgarians. As a result of a perhaps overhasty switch from a command to a market economy, there was suddenly massive hoarding and almost total scarcity of food and goods in the shops and markets, accompanied by power outages, during a particularly hard winter. Maria, Zhelev's documentary filmmaker wife, could not conceal her astonishment at the abundance of goods in the shops in London which, as she explained to her British hosts, contrasted so markedly with the situation in Sofia. During luncheon at Buckingham Palace kindly members of the Royal Household arranged with the management of one of the main supermarkets for Mrs Zheleva to fill a large trolley with food that she could take back for distribution to the desperate clients of a Bulgarian charity with which she was associated. Maria, of course, checked this offer with her husband, who vetoed it on the spot, as in his view it smacked too much of the old-style corruption which he had set his face against. The shopping expedition took place, but the Zhelevs paid for it themselves.

The other event was quite different, but it illustrated Zhelev's almost romantic high-mindedness. When he became president he made it known that he was determined to get to the bottom of the notorious 'umbrella murder' on the streets of London of the Bulgarian writer and dissident Georgi Markov and to bring those responsible to justice. He asked if he could visit Markov's grave, in a village churchyard in Dorset. As time would be short, the programme provided for a trip to Dorset by helicopter. But the appointed day dawned too wet and cloudy for helicopters, so the pilgrimage had to be by road, which led to a good deal of last-minute programme adjustment. But as Zhelev later explained, a few minutes by Markov's grave meant more to him than almost anything else in the programme and their omission would have been a sad blow.

Zhelev was gentle and not remotely charismatic. His nature could only accurately be described as sweet and kindly, though backed by the steely determination of a true dissident. Off-duty he and his wife, to whom he was devoted, were warm and hospitable and very good cooks. Their marriage was, however, marked by personal tragedy, with the deaths of their only son in infancy and, much later, of their younger daughter. And then Maria died, a year before his own death. They are survived by their older daughter and two grand-daughters.

Acknowledgements

I am very grateful to Sir Mark Tully for his generous foreword. And very many thanks also to Sir Chris Ball for his bespoke translations from the Icelandic sagas. I am grateful to The Independent for permission to reproduce the text of my obituary of Zhelyu Zhelev, and to Ilyana Saraouleva and Aglika Markova for their help with it.

I am indebted to Nigel Hensman and his late sister Celia for the astonishing story of their return to wartime Britain as child crew members of a five-bob freighter, and more generally to the late Jessica Mann and Alistair Horne for all that I learned from their books about the WWII evacuation of children overseas, particularly to Canada and the United States. Much of what I know about the history of the Sagas I owe to the writings of the late Magnus Magnusson, whose daughter Sally kindly authorised my use of excerpts from his translations should the need arise, which in this event it didn't, thanks to Chris Ball.

Every now and again I would write an article or blog, or put together a talk, about some event or person that I had encountered, amusing maybe, or exceptional, or just plain interesting and therefore, to my mind, worth recording. Sir Michael Holroyd encouraged me to keep this up and eventually to consider melding these gobbets as the bones of a book, which is what I did. Dame Margaret Drabble read the completed manuscript and was positive enough for me to hope that it could be published, and I am grateful to them both.

Victoria Glendinning put me right on my grandmother's equivocal links with the John Lewis Partnership, and I am very grateful to her.

Sarah Lampert filled a number of gaps in my memory of the Bulgarian 'changes' during and after the collapse of the communist regime, and then cast a usefully critical eye over the whole Bulgarian section. I am grateful to her for enabling me to correct inaccuracies, and for her overall encouragement.

I am relieved that Philip and Elena Dimitrov were amused by my account of my illusory 'affair' with Philip, which was as much news to both of them as it had been to me. And I am happy that the family survivors of the deceased friends whom I had earlier commemorated have not objected to the inclusion of those recollections in the book's postscript.

I am indebted to Richard Plumb for his clever idea for the cover's design, and to my daughter Phoebe for all her hard work in checking the proofreading.
Thanks are due to the team at Austin Macaulay who saw the book through to publication.

I have picked my sister Elizabeth's brains to correct some of my earlier memories, and I am grateful for her forbearance.

And finally, I am lucky to have a family, and above all my wife, Catherine, with whom I have shared so many of these experiences. They encouraged me to commit them to paper.

– Richard Thomas